GPS MADE EASY

USING GLOBAL POSITIONING SYSTEMS IN THE OUTDOORS

SECOND EDITION

LAWRENCE LETHAM

For Tanya
The only thing left to map is life
and that only in retrospect

Front Cover: Using a GPS receiver to mark the position of a camp in Ellesmere Island, Nunavut, Canada. Photo: Tony Daffern.

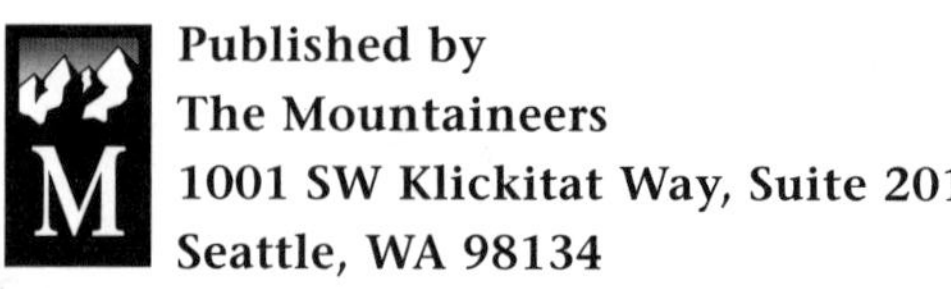

Published by
The Mountaineers
1001 SW Klickitat Way, Suite 201
Seattle, WA 98134

Second edition, 1998

Published simultaneously in Canada by Rocky Mountain Books, Calgary
Distributed in Europe by Cordee, 3A De Montfort St.,
Leicester LE1 7HD, Great Britain

Manufactured in Canada

Library of Congress Cataloging-in-Publication Data

Letham, Lawrence,
GPS made easy: using global positioning systems in the outdoors / Lawrence Letham.-- 2nd ed.
p. cm.
Includes index.
ISBN 0-89886-592-1
1. Outdoor recreation--Equipment and supplies. 2. Global Positioning System. 3. Orienteering--Equipment and supplies. I. Title.
GV191.623.L48 1998 98-38724
796.58'028--dc20 CIP

Table of Contents

Acknowledgements

Thank you to Natural Resources Canada for permission to use the Canadian maps on pages 78, 102 and 111. These maps are based on information taken from the National Topographic System map sheet numbers 83 E/3 Mount Robson Copyright 1980 and 83 C/3 Columbia Icefields, edition 02 Copyright 1984. Her Majesty the Queen in Right of Canada with permission of Natural Resources Canada.

The maps shown on pages 30, 35, 37, 73, 92, 94, 114, 116, 119, 120, 122, 149, 151 and 153 were produced by the U.S. Geological Survey.

The marine charts on pages 128, 130 and 132 are from the U.S. National Ocean Service.

Thank you to DeLorme, for permission to use maps from the Arizona Atlas & Gazetteer on pages 139, 141, 144 and 146. The maps from the Arizona Atlas & Gazetteer are copyrighted material of DeLorme, Yarmouth, Maine and are used with permission. DeLorme also provided the screen shots of the Street Atlas USA 5.0 on pages 159, 165, 166 and 167, which are also reproduced with their permission.

Thank you to MapTech and Wildflower Productions for loaning me their topographical map databases TopoScout and TOPO! respectively. Screen shots from these programs appear in Chapter 12.

Thank you to the several retired colonels from different branches of the U.S. Armed Services who wrote with their critiques of the first edition. Their suggestions have been incorporated wherever possible.

Thanks to Steve Featherstone of Garmin, Margaret Goodall and Conny Cheng of Magellan, Suzanne Coatney of Eagle Electronics and Dan Burton of Nexis-Brunton for the use of their respective companies' receivers (and the Navimap) and technical information.

Thank you to John Hammer and Leigh Longenette for information on the Yeoman XP1 Mouse for Maps.

Thank you to Rick Hood for technical information on the XL1000, USGS map databases and GPS in Search and Rescue.

Thanks to Spence Wilhelm for loaning me his Tripmate receiver and Street Atlas USA 5.0 and for his support.

Trademark List

1 Introduction to the Global Positioning System (GPS)

The Global Positioning System (GPS) is a satellite system used in navigation that allows you to determine your position 24 hours a day, any place on the globe and in any kind of weather.

Times have changed dramatically since the first days of exploration when precise celestial knowledge was required to locate your position in the outdoors. Today, the answer to the modern adventurer's question of "where am I?" is accurately provided 24 hours a day by the most advanced navigational equipment to ever exist. For the price of a small handheld GPS receiver and the knowledge provided in this book, you will be able to navigate with greater confidence and understanding.

The Global Positioning System is a group of 24 satellites that circle the globe and beam radio signals to the earth's surface. A GPS receiver is a small, electronic device used by earthbound travellers or planes to pick up the signals from the satellites. The receiver uses the radio signals to calculate its position, which is reported as a group of numbers and letters that correspond to a point on a map. A GPS receiver, used in conjunction with a map and compass, will help you find that great new fishing hole again or to record the unmarked entrance to a newly discovered cave.

The advantage of using a GPS receiver, for navigation, is that you know your location with certainty. Under most conditions, when navigating with a map, compass and altimeter, you only know your approximate position, but a GPS receiver eliminates the guesswork because it will show your position on a map with an error of between 15 to 100 m (49.2 to 328 ft.). One hundred meter accuracy is great! Even the most experienced outdoor navigators, who do not use GPS receivers, do not achieve such a high degree of precision. In addition to the ben-

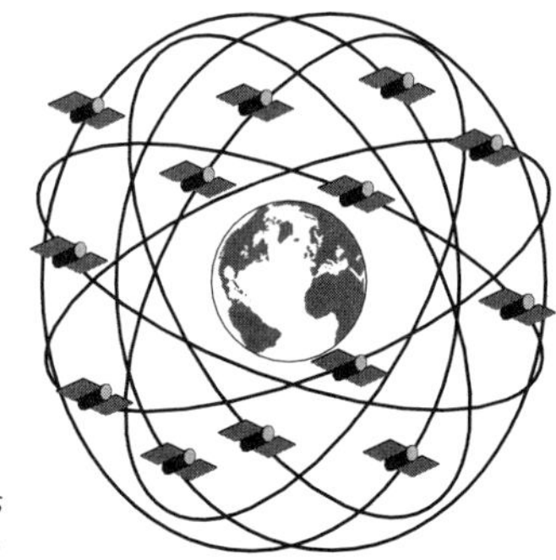

GPS technology is based on a group of 24 satellites that beam radio signals back to earth.

efit of accuracy, GPS receivers work in any weather and at night. It is possible that other forms of navigation, like landform recognition and walking a bearing, also work in bad weather or in the dark, but it is a rare situation where such methods are more accurate than GPS technology. Fortunately, using a GPS receiver is easy once you know how to find coordinates on a map and understand how the coordinates relate to your movements on the ground. Work through the example trips to learn about grids and how to apply map knowledge and GPS receiver readings to GPS navigation.

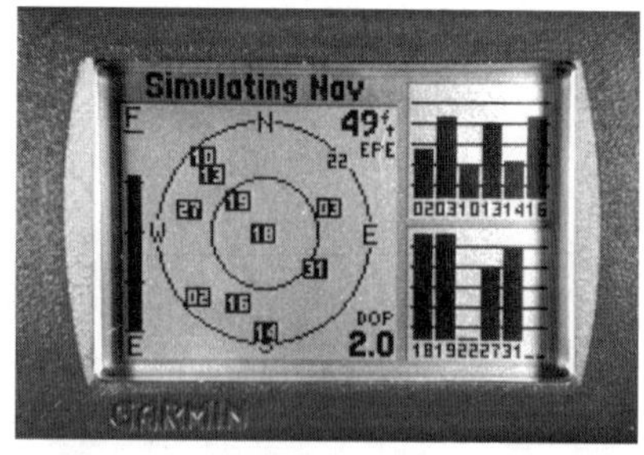

A GPS receiver shows the position of each satellite, signal strength bars and a battery level indicator to the left of the satellites' display.

GPS navigation sounds and is wonderful, but there are limitations you should thoroughly understand. The radio signals from the satellites cannot penetrate dense vegetation, rocks, buildings or landforms, so a GPS receiver will not work in dense jungles or forests, in narrow valleys or among skyscrapers. Furthermore, although the Global Positioning System is designed to provide global coverage, remote areas at any time of the day may be covered by the minimum number of satellites (4) needed to get a position reading and if your GPS receiver's antenna is not sensitive enough to pick up the signals from all the available satellites, you will not be able to get a position fix. It is impossible to predict when the terrain or your receiver's sensitivity will limit GPS reception. The best use of a GPS receiver is to complement your present skills, so do not abandon the navigation techniques you have already acquired. For the beginning navigator, a receiver can help you improve your present skills because it can verify the measurements you make using manual techniques.

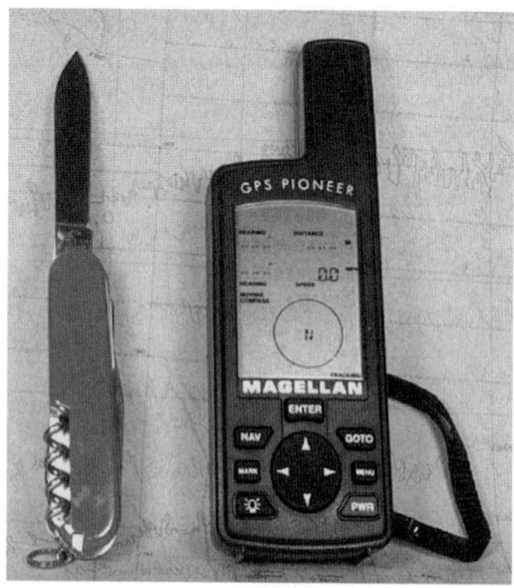

Modern GPS receivers are lightweight and small.

How GPS Works

This section discusses the development of GPS and explains the underlying technology so you understand how it works when you use it in the outdoors. A short section on navigation history provides a background to help you understand the complexity of the GPS, which is by far the most advanced navigation system ever put into operation. At the same time, do not be worried that GPS is difficult to use because, as later chapters show, the GPS receiver transforms a highly technical system into a user friendly, reliable method to help you navigate in the outdoors. Some of the technical terms of GPS are explained and a Glossary is also provided on page 194.

Early Navigation

In ancient times, most travelers ascertained their location by landscape features, some rudimentary observation of the stars and by a detailed knowledge of a relatively small territory passed down from generation to generation. The compass was an important discovery because it oriented the traveler, but it alone could not fix a person's position. The astrolabe, the quadrant and the sextant opened new vistas in travel because they enabled navigators to easily determine their latitude. However, longitude calculations required knowledge of the stars combined with astronomical tables that detailed the exact positions of the planets at exact times. Before the chronometer, few people had the knowledge, training and skill to measure time and longitude from the stars, but an amazing exception was the 15th century voyager Amerigo Vespucci, who taught himself how to measure longitude and made an important discovery.

Vespucci sailed from the Old World in 1499 to the lands that Columbus had recently discovered and claimed were India. He read Columbus' report and wanted to believe he was in the Indies, but he had also read reports of the cities and people of India and the sights he saw as he sailed along the coast were different from what he expected. He carried with him an astronomical book called an almanac, which listed the exact times and positions of various planets. The book was made in Italy, so the times of the celestial events were based on time as measured in Ferrara, Italy. At midnight on August 23, 1499, the moon would cross Mars in Ferrara, so Vespucci put ashore on what we know today as the Brazilian coast. He first measured the stars to determine his exact local time, then he watched the conjunction and noted it occurred 6.5 hours after it was seen in Ferrara. Using the difference in time and Ptolemy's value of the circumference of the earth, he calculated his distance (longitude) from Ferrara. The result proved he was not in the Indies, but on a new continent. Vespucci was the first person to know the truth about Columbus' discovery and only because he could determine his exact position.

The development of accurate chronometers in 1735 was an important event because it made celestial navigation accessible to people with less training and specialized education. Mathematical and nautical tables developed by Nathaniel Bowditch enabled seamen of all classes to translate simple celestial observations into their position on the globe. Although celestial navigation was becoming easier to perform, it still took a lot of practice and it was accurate to about 1 mi. only when the skies were clear. All the hard work and dependence on weather were eliminated by radio.

Radio Navigation

The use of radio signals to determine position was the next major advance in navigation. Equipment for radio navigation appeared in 1912, but it was not very accurate. The next milestone was pulse radar, developed during World War Two, which made it possible to measure the short time differences between transmitted and received radio waves. Radar used by police demonstrates how the equipment sends out a radio pulse and measures the time it takes for the pulse to travel to a vehicle, bounce off of it, and arrive back at the radar gun. The time difference tells the radar's computer the car's distance from the gun. The radar measures the car's distance from the police car at two different times t1 and t2. At time t1, as shown in the figure, the car was the distance d1 away from the police car and at time t2 it was d2 away. Velocity is simply

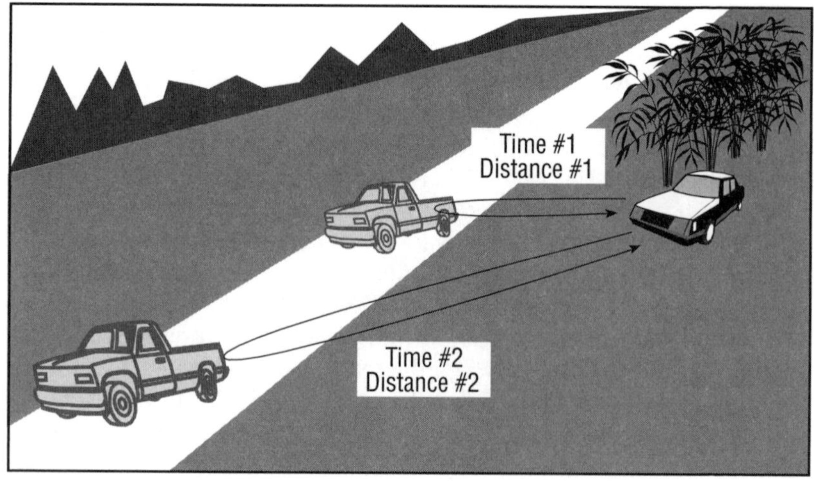

the distance traveled divided by the time it took, so the radar's computer calculates the car's speed as velocity = (d2 - d1)/(t2 - t1).

Early radio navigation systems used the same principle of sending radio waves and measuring time differences. Radio signals are sent from the two towers, shown in the figure, at exactly the same time and travel the same speed. The navigator's receiver detects which signal arrives first and the amount of time until the arrival of the second signal. The navigator knows the towers' exact positions, the speed of the radio waves and the time difference between them when they arrived at his position. If the radio waves had both reached the navigator at exactly the same time, $\Delta t = 0$, his position would lie exactly between the two towers, but in this example the west signal arrived two time units before the east signal, so the navigator's receiver knows its position is closer to the west tower than to the east and calculates its one-dimensional position accordingly.

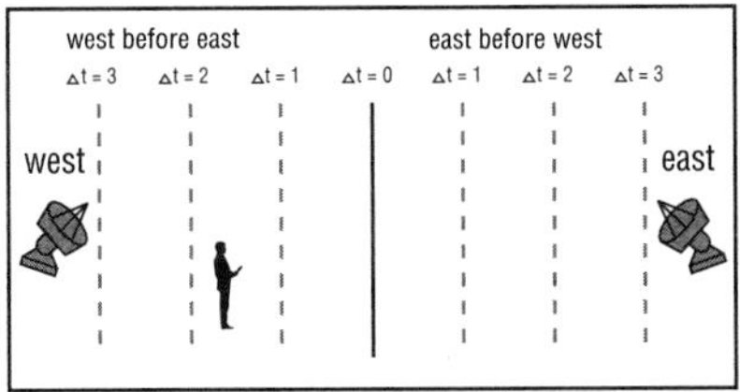

Two signals give the position of the receiver on a line between the two sources.

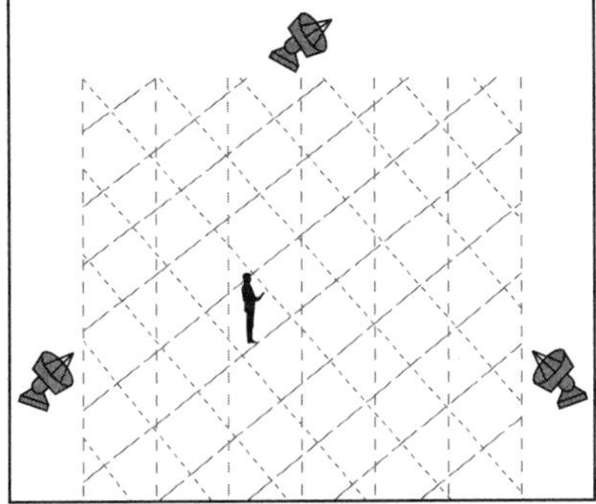

Adding a third source allows a two-dimensional position to be calculated.

A one-dimensional position is not very useful, but if three radio towers are used, a two-dimensional position can be calculated. Once again the navigator's receiver records which signal arrives first and the time differences between it and the others. Using knowledge of the towers' positions, the speed of the radio signals and the difference in arrival times, the receiver calculates a two-dimensional position.

The Global Positioning System also uses radio waves, but with a new twist. First of all, the land-based radio towers are replaced by satellites orbiting 20,200 km (12,552 mi.) above the earth and instead of broadcasting radio pulses, the GPS satellites send a sequence of numbers that enable a GPS receiver to measure its distance from each satellite instead of its relative position between the satellites.

Starting at a known time, t0 in this case, the satellite broadcasts a number sequence. In this simple example, the satellite sends the number 10 at t0, 23 at t1, etc., and continues sending a different number each time segment without repeating itself for a millisecond. The receiver already has the same number sequence stored in its memory and knows the exact time when the satellite started broadcasting its numbers. At time t0, the receiver starts at the beginning of the number list in its memory and advances one number for each time segment. The table below shows the sequence of events:

	t0	t1	t2	t3	t4	t5	t6	t7	t8	t9	t10
Satellite sends	10	23	16	19	48	79	35	42	63	75	91
Receiver's list	10	23	16	19	48	79	35	42	63	75	91
Receiver detects	—	—	—	—	—	—	—	10	23	16	19

When the receiver detects the number 10 from the satellite, it notes it is at number 42 in its own list, which means it took seven time segments for the radio wave carrying the numbers to get from the satellite to the receiver. If the radio wave travels 3219 km (2000 mi.) per time unit, the receiver knows the satellite is 22,531 km (14,000 mi.) away. This technique is known as ranging and requires exact time synchronization between the receiver and the satellites in addition to a known number sequence.

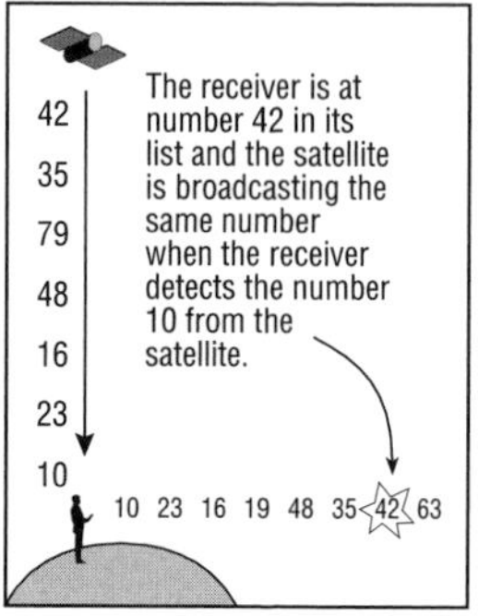

Satellite sending and receiver detecting a number sequence.

Finding your position using GPS signals is done by triangulation, which means if you know your distance from three fixed locations, you can calculate your own position. The figure shows in two dimensions how a navigator finds his position using a GPS receiver. The receiver measures its distance from satellite #1, which means the navigator is somewhere on the circle that surrounds satellite #1. Next, the receiver measures its distance to satellite #2. The receiver lies somewhere on the circles that surround satellites #1 and #2. There are only two positions where the receiver can be and that is where the two circles intersect. Next the receiver measures its distance from satellite #3 and just as before, it knows its position is where the circles intersect. There is only one place where all three circles intersect, so the receiver has calculated the navigator's position.

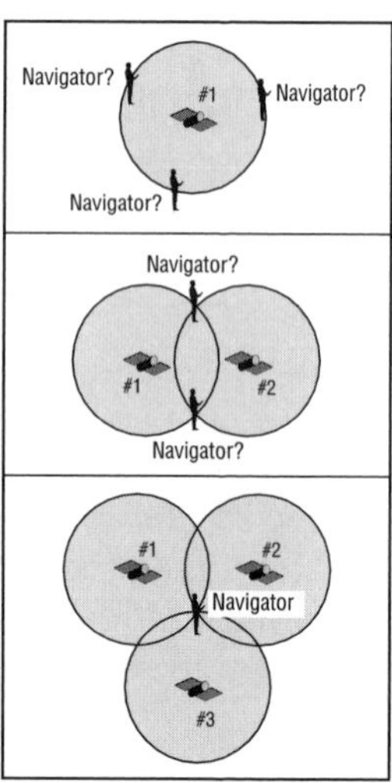

Triangulation to find position from GPS satellites.

The GPS system is even better than described above because it uses intersecting spheres to determine a three-dimensional position: latitude, longitude and altitude. The above example also clarifies the importance of precise time synchronization between the receiver and the satellites, and exact knowledge of the satellites' positions. If there is a time difference between the satellite and the receiver, the receiver will not be able to accurately measure its distance from the satellites. Signals from only three satellites are enough for a GPS receiver to calculate its three-dimensional position, but a signal from a fourth satellite is used to synchronize the time between the satellites' highly accurate atomic clocks and the receiver's less accurate quartz timepiece. If signals from only three satellites are available, one must be used to synchronize time, leaving only two signals to calculate a two-dimensional position.

The other vital aspect of positioning with GPS signals is knowledge of the satellites' exact positions. Even if a receiver could precisely measure its distance to the satellites, it would not be able to calculate its own position if it did not know the satellites' positions. Each satellite knows its own position and the positions of all the other satellites and sends the orbital information to the receiver.

The important nature of time synchronization and the satellites' exact positions are stressed here to help you understand the concept of Selective Availability, which is described later. For now, just remember that if the receiver is not exactly synchronized to the satellites or if it does not know the satellites' precise positions, the position the receiver calculates will be inaccurate.

GPS navigation sounds complex because it is, but fortunately the GPS receiver does all the work and hides the nasty math it takes to solve for position.

The Global Positioning System

The Global Positioning System was conceived in 1960 and was the consolidation of other navigation projects. It started development under the auspices of the U.S. Air Force, but in 1974 the other branches of the U.S. military joined the effort and renamed the project Navstar Global Positioning System. Nevertheless the name GPS persisted. The system cost $10 billion to develop and was declared fully operational in April 1995. Twenty-four satellites circle the globe once every 12 hours to provide worldwide position, time and velocity information. The system is presently monitored and administrated by the U.S. Department of Defense.

System tests in 1972 showed the worse case accuracy to be 15 m (49.2 ft.) and the best case accuracy of 1 m (3.3 ft.). A concern arose that enemies of the United States would use GPS against U.S. installations, so two tiers of accuracy were implemented: the most accurate for authorized (military) users and the least accurate for unauthorized users (civilians). Military GPS receivers are specified to be accurate to 16 m (52.5 ft.), but generally provide accuracy to 1 m (3.3 ft.). The accuracy of civilian receivers varies randomly between 15 m (49.2 ft.) and 100 m (328 ft.) because they are subject to Selective Availability, which is the technique employed by the U.S. Department of Defense to limit the accuracy of all receivers but their own. In March of 1997, a Presidential Decision Directive was issued stating that within a decade, the U.S. Pentagon will review its Selective Availability policy and remove it if it is no longer needed. Selective Availability is discussed in more detail below. Removing Selective Availability would allow civilian receivers to be accurate to 15 m (49.2 ft.).

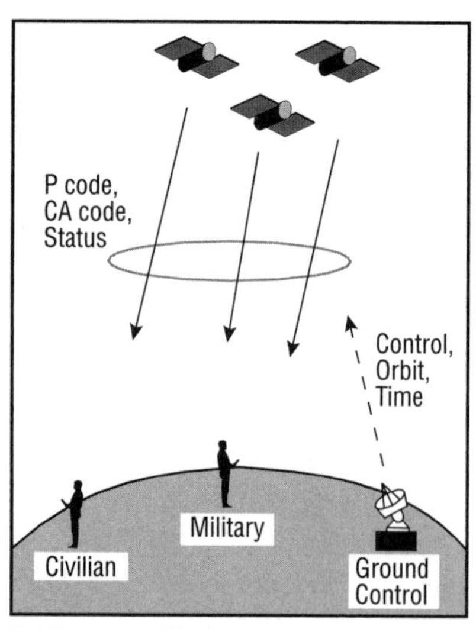

The three parts of the GPS: ground, space and user.

The complete GPS setup has three parts as shown in the figure: the ground control segment, the space segment and the user segment. The ground stations track the satellites to monitor their exact orbits and send all the orbital information to each satellite so it can be broadcast to receivers on the ground. Ground control also synchronizes the atomic clocks carried by each satellite. The time is called GPS time, but it can easily be converted to Universal Time Coordinated (UTC).

The satellites broadcast the signals used by GPS receivers to calculate position. As described earlier in the section on radio navigation, each satellite beams toward earth a radio wave that carries sequences of numbers that are called codes. GPS satellites send not one but two number sequences: Precision (P) and Coarse Acquisition (CA) codes. Each satellite has a unique P and CA code so the receiver can tell the difference between signals sent by the various satellites. The P code is a sequence of numbers so long that it repeats itself only once every seven days while the much shorter CA code repeats every one millisecond. The longer P code with its higher modulation rate is what provides greater accuracy to the military receivers, and civilian receivers are incapable of understanding or using it. The satellites also broadcast on two frequencies: 1227.6 MHz (called L2) and 1575.42 MHz (called L1). The P code is carried on both frequencies for reasons described below; whereas the CA code appears only on the L1 frequency. The satellites also broadcast information on satellite heath, position and formulas to correct for atmospheric distortion of the radio signal. Each satellite also carries precise atomic clocks because exact synchronization is vital to radio navigation.

GPS receivers comprise the user segment of the system. A receiver only listens to the satellite transmission and does not interact or provide any feedback, so the number of simultaneous users is limitless. A military receiver uses the P code for increased accuracy, but stores both the P and CA codes in its memory because it first locks on to the CA code, then waits for the right time to switch over to the P code. Civilian receivers can access only the CA code, which limits their best case accuracy to about 15 m (49.2 ft.), however, the situation is made much worse by Selective Availability. Selective Availability is the policy implemented by the U.S. Department of Defense that randomly degrades the accuracy provided by the CA code. As mentioned earlier, exact time and satellite position information is vital for accuracy. Selective Availability changes the time the CA code is broadcast, so it is not synchronized between satellites and limits the accuracy of the satellite position information sent to the receivers. The result is the civilian receiver's accuracy randomly varies between 15 and 100 m (49.2 and 328 ft.) and the user never knows how much error has been introduced or in what direction. A technique, called Differential GPS (DGPS), can be used by civilians to eliminate the effects of Selective Availability, making them as accurate or even more accurate than military receivers. DGPS is discussed in Chapter 15. The P codes, and hence military receivers, are not affected by Selective Availability.

When a GPS receiver is turned on, the first thing it does is download the orbit information (almanac) of all the satellites. Each satellite has the complete almanac for the entire system, so a specific satellite does not have to be in sight for the receiver to know its position. The time it takes for a receiver to download the almanac and lock on to the satellites is called Time to First Fix (TTFF). Loading all the satellite orbit information takes 12.5 minutes, so getting the first fix can take at least that long. However, most receivers, after they are used for the first time, store the almanac in their memory thereby reducing the time to lock on for subsequent uses. If a receiver is not used for over six months or is moved over 300 mi. from the last place it got a fix, the almanac stored in the receiver's memory is outdated and locking on may take more time than usual.

As mentioned earlier, the P codes are broadcast on two different radio frequencies, which allows military receivers to measure and eliminate ionospheric interference. When radio waves travel through the clouds of electrons in the ionosphere, they slow down a little bit, causing the receiver to think the satellites are farther away than reality. There are two ways to correct for the delay through the ionosphere: assume a reasonable delay and use it to compensate, or measure the exact delay and accurately eliminate the error it causes. The delay through the ionosphere can be measured only if two different radio frequencies are used. Radio waves of different frequencies slow down by different amounts as they travel through the ionosphere. The P code is sent on two frequencies at the same time and should arrive at the same time, but the ionosphere makes the P code on one frequency arrive after the other. The receiver measures the difference and can accurately compensate for ionospheric delay. Civilian receivers work on only one frequency and cannot measure ionospheric delay, so they compensate for it by using an atmospheric model that predicts the delay. The atmospheric information is sent to the receiver by the satellites, so it is always up to date and fairly accurate.

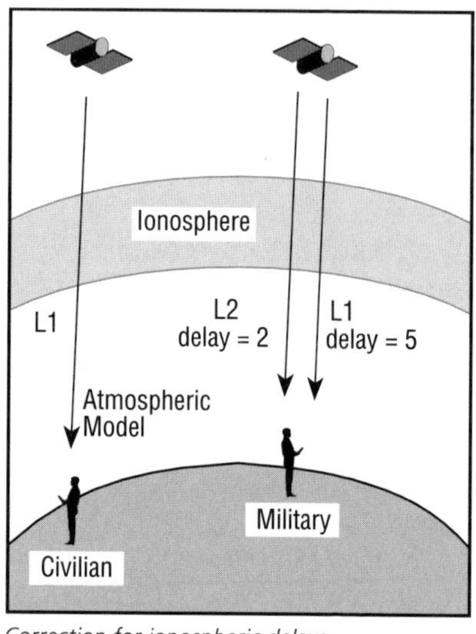

Correction for ionospheric delays.

There is a class of receivers, known as codeless receivers, that use neither the P nor CA codes—at least not directly. A codeless receiver first locks onto the satellite signals using the CA code, then it monitors the L1 and L2 carrier frequencies and does not use either code. Using complex signal processing and a technique called interferometry, a codeless receiver provides position computations down to 10 mm (0.39 in.). Their accuracy is incredible, unfortunately, it takes several days to make a single measurement.

2 Why Buy a GPS Receiver?

Owing to advances in electronics, the prices of GPS receivers are dropping. It is no longer a question of "why should I buy a receiver?" but "why shouldn't I buy one?" Before you head out to get a receiver, you need to understand what it will do for you.

A GPS receiver excels at three basic tasks:

- it will lead you to a destination you choose from a map
- it will calculate your present position so you can locate it on a map
- it will store your present position in memory to help you return at a later date.

Whether on marked trails, in the desert, on the water or on polar ice, a GPS receiver can be an indispensable part of your navigation plan. The examples listed below will give you an idea of how GPS makes your favorite outdoor activity more fun.

Hiking

A hiker on established trails with a reasonable map has little fear of getting lost, but a GPS receiver does so much more than keeping you found. Have you ever wondered how close you are to the next turn-off or if you will reach your favorite camping area before dark? A GPS receiver will calculate your present position with accuracy you have never before enjoyed. It will show you how far you are from the next intersection and even tell you what time the sun will set. Adventurers who travel poorly marked trails, bushwhack through the great unknown, wander trackless deserts or traverse the Arctic regions will find a GPS receiver indispensable because it will not only show you where you are on a map, but it also records your route and tells you how far you have traveled.

A GPS receiver's true value becomes apparent in poor weather when vital landmarks are obscured by mist, rain or snow. Instead of waiting for the weather to improve, the receiver can pick up the satellite signals through the clouds so you can continue your trip.

Hikers use only a small fraction of a GPS receiver's capabilities. Most units can provide numerous navigational statistics like speed, azimuth, CrossTrack Error, estimated time of arrival, etc., but the information is available only if it is on continuously. Your arm quickly tires of holding the unit out in front and the batteries needed to keep it going all the time weigh a lot. The best use of a GPS receiver on a hike is for an occasional position fix. Most of the time the unit will be turned off and in the backpack. The GPS receiver features most important to hikers are light weight and low power consumption.

Ski Mountaineering

Have you ever tried to cross a large icefield in a whiteout? It is not easy groping through the mist with a companion walking behind to keep you on the right bearing all the while hoping you will find the little bamboo wands you set out as destination markers. It is not a very fun way to get back to the base camp. A GPS receiver will overcome some of the difficulties by allowing you to record the locations of important features on the trip out, then use the receiver's Goto and steering functions to guide you through the fog on the trip back. The receiver's accuracy with Selective Availability will definitely get you close to each marked position, but for absolute surety in the worst of conditions, still place a few wands at critical junctures like passages over crevasses and the base camp. The use of a GPS receiver to locate your camp when the cloud is down is described in Chapter 7.

Car Travel by Road

Some rental cars are equipped with GPS receivers and a computer that provides written instructions on a small video screen or audibly tells you how to get where you want to go. Advances in GPS receivers and computers are making more sophisticated systems available to everyone. If you already have a portable computer, software is available to guide you in any city of the United States on every road. The receiver sends your position to the PC, which displays where you are on a screen along with a map of all surrounding roads. As the vehicle moves, the map on the computer screen moves to constantly track your position. An automated map is perfect for night travel, strange cities, back roads or travel with a companion who does not want to be a navigator.

For those who do not have portable computers, recent advances make it possible to provide maps of major roads and highways in a handheld GPS receiver. Of course, the PC provides much better maps, but if you are on a budget or if you want a receiver you can use both on the road and in the field, a handheld receiver with built-in maps or plug-in modules is perfect. Even if you have an older receiver without maps, you can use it to mark important intersections so you do not miss them. A receiver can also give estimated time of arrival, time en route, speed and distance traveled.

Purchase the power adapter that plugs into the cigarette lighter, so you can leave the receiver on all the time and buy the mounting hardware to put the receiver on the dash. Also, an external antenna placed on the car's roof makes it easy for the receiver to pick up the satellites. It is possible to place the receiver on the dash to let its internal antenna see the satellites through the windshield, but it is difficult to see the receiver's screen when it is up there and some windshields have a transparent layer of metal inside the glass that blocks the signals.

The use of a receiver in a vehicle on roads is demonstrated in Chapter 10 while computer map software and a receiver with a built-in map are explored in Chapter 12.

Road Rally

Today's powerful receivers have nearly ruined road rallies because many of them come with maps stored in their memory. The first rule of a GPS road rally is that all maps are forbidden. A map combined with a receiver, whether it is a paper map or part of the receiver, makes the rally too easy. Fortunately, all receivers still come with compass navigation screens that provide only the bearing and a direction arrow to the next point. Rallies can be as much fun as they were in the past, but you have to have some way to make sure no one cheats by using any form of map.

Fishing

If you fish in remote locations with or without a guide or on a large body of water where every shore looks the same, a GPS receiver can get you there and back every time. One thing you need to keep in mind is the receiver's accuracy is only 100 m (328 ft.), so if you want to mark the exact position where the fish were biting or the narrow trench in the middle of the lake where the biggest trophies hide, you need to use DGPS equipment that can give you accuracy from 1 to 15 m (3.3 to 49.2 ft.). DGPS is described in Chapter 15.

Hang Gliding

Serious hang gliders use a radio and a GPS receiver to inform the ground crew of their whereabouts. Some competitive events are long flights of 400 km (248 mi.) over remote areas that make it difficult for the ground crew to follow without GPS position information.

If you are also interested in plotting your flight path on a map, a GPS receiver can track the glider's movements and once you have landed produce an overlay. Most GPS receivers already automatically record their position at regular intervals, so it is an easy matter to use a computer to transfer the data from the receiver to a plotting program.

It may be difficult to fly and hold a receiver at the same time, so either buy a receiver designed as part of the flight deck or find a way to mount it. Remember, the antenna needs to see the sky and part of the hang glider should not get in the way. It may be worth the money to purchase a remote antenna. The accuracy of the receiver's altitude measurement is only ±150 m (492 ft.), so you may need to buy a separate, more accurate altimeter.

Professional Outdoor Uses

Anyone whose work requires high resolution surveying or accurate position recording should consider using GPS technology. Forestry personnel, prospectors, oil and gas exploration crews, geologists, archaeologists, biologists, etc., can all benefit from using a GPS receiver. An example of how a receiver can assist the outdoor professional is given in Chapter 6. Also take a close look at Chapter 15, which explains Differential GPS, because most professionals need more accuracy than ordinary handheld receivers can efficiently provide. A Differential GPS receiver can dynamically provide accuracy from 1 to 15 m (3.3 to 49.2 ft.) depending on the amount of money you are able to spend.

Outdoor recreational agencies need not forgo providing accurate maps just because their budgets cannot afford high-end DGPS equipment.

Many economical, handheld receivers now provide an averaging function that pinpoints a location to within 25 m (82 ft.). Although the receiver must stay at each point for a few hours to average out the effects of Selective Availability, the averaging function makes accurate recreational maps possible. Guidebook authors should also take note that it is now affordable to accurately put useful information not provided by most agencies on your book's maps. Correctly marking the rapids on a river or showing geological or historical locations is now easy. No guidebook author should be without one.

Amateur map makers will revel in what GPS can do for them. Making extensive maps using the averaging feature may take more time than the weekend allows, so consider investing, individually or as a group, big money into a powerful DGPS receiver capable of quick, highly accurate measurements or consider leasing one for the day you want to get the work done. GPS technology will make your maps more accurate in far less time than it has ever taken before.

Kayaking and Canoeing

A GPS receiver is useful on any trip that involves finding a certain point on a river or lake. If you have to portage your boat on an unfamiliar route, a receiver saves a lot of extra work by locating the correct take-out position. It also saves physical effort on a lake because it guides you on the most direct route. On a large lake with few distinct landmarks, a GPS receiver keeps you from getting lost while sea kayakers also benefit by not getting lost along strange shorelines. It is impossible to paddle and hold a receiver in your hand simultaneously, so steering and continuous navigation statistics are available only if the receiver is mounted on the craft.

Receivers are either water-resistant or waterproof. Water-resistant means you can use it in a moist environment, but it should not be submerged, whereas waterproof receivers can be completely submerged with no damage. Receivers can still detect the satellite signals through a plastic bag, so it is possible to protect a water-resistant receiver from accidental submersion. Waterproof receivers are usually designed to float, making them retrievable if they slip from your grasp. However, water-resistant receivers may or may not float, so keep the lanyard secured to the boat or it may sink to the depths. Mounting the receiver to the boat exposes it to potential damage if the boat overturns and scrapes bottom or the receiver is raked by low hanging branches. The best use of a receiver will depend on the conditions, but at a bare minimum a GPS receiver will give you the occasional position fix needed for confident navigation.

A waterproof or highly protected water-resistant receiver should be used for expeditions in sea water because the salt in the spray is highly corrosive and will ruin any electronic components it touches. The receiver must be completely sealed against the intrusion of water or it will not survive.

Navigation using latitude/longitude is described in Chapter 8 in a kayak trip across an Alaskan inlet and in Chapter 9 with a trip in a sailboat.

Search and Rescue

GPS receivers are invaluable in search and rescue because they keep the searchers from getting lost, they enable easy coordination of several groups, and they allow accurate documentation of which areas were searched. Receivers are useful on land, sea or air and make it easy to coordinate between the three if necessary. Each group needs radio contact with the central command post, which coordinates and documents the search. Periodic reports from each group allows the search coordinator to monitor progress and know where to send replacement or additional searchers. Once the person is found, the coordinate of his or her location allows evacuation teams to proceed directly to the spot. If the search is conducted in heavy forests or other terrain that blocks the satellite signals, a receiver is valuable even if it only provides occasional position fixes because some data helps the effort more than no data. Receivers cannot be used for searches in caves.

Documentation can be facilitated by requiring each searcher to record their position at regular intervals. At the end of each shift, the recorded locations are transferred from each receiver to a computer that combines, stores and even displays the areas searched. Accurate, indisputable documentation is important in today's litigious society.

Caving

Sorry! Cavers are out of luck, at least while in the cave, because rock blocks the satellite signals rendering receivers useless. However, GPS receivers are excellent for marking cave entrances, so next time you discover a never-before-explored cave, do not leave physical signs that may be discovered by others—simply mark the location as a waypoint in your receiver and you will easily find it again.

3 Backing up Your GPS Receiver

Advertisements for GPS receivers can create a false sense of security if the buyer is led to believe that a receiver is the only navigational tool required and that with it they will never get lost. GPS receivers are fantastic! They will help you navigate better than you have ever navigated before, but they are only one of the navigational tools you need to assure you will get back every time. Regardless of what anybody says, maps, compasses, altimeters, pedometers, watches and field notebooks are all important to staying found and in most cases are not optional. A backup plan with appropriate backup skills is vital. Even the ICBMs that GPS was designed to guide have maps burned into their electronic memories and have a backup inertial guidance system.

When taking a trip it is possible to use a map in advance to store all the important points into the receiver's memory, then once in the field the receiver can guide you to each point along the way. There are even handheld receivers that have entire maps stored in their memories, so when you look at the screen it is like looking at a map. In theory, it would seem that maps, compasses and all the other gear we have previously used for navigation are no longer necessary. However, Murphy's Law predicts: when you need it the most, the receiver may not be able to perform its job. Whether terrain blocks the signals, the signals are too weak to be picked up by the receiver's antenna, the batteries are dead or the receiver is broken, something can go wrong to ruin the theory of map-free navigation. There will be trips where everything goes perfectly and the GPS receiver is the only navigational tool used, but never stake you life on a single method of navigation—always have a backup plan.

If you are a beginner navigator, do not let the fear of an inoperable receiver keep you home. The skills you need to find your way back depend on where you are going, but for most travelers a map, watch, compass and a notebook are the only equipment you will need to find your way back. Learning to use a map and compass is easy and your receiver can help teach you. Those who wander far from the beaten path or in featureless areas should always carry a map and may need to learn celestial navigation skills. The use of a notebook and map for backup navigation are discussed below.

A Travel Notebook for Backup Navigation

A small notebook, pencil and watch are invaluable tools to the navigator. They can help you get back just in case your receiver malfunctions. Use the notebook to make any notes that will help you remember the course you traveled. Make a quick sketch of the intersections and show which fork you took, record the number of tributaries you passed in your canoe and note the kilometer or mile marker numbers closest to where you turned off the main highway. Keep track of your position relative to any prominent landmarks. It is important to record the time as you make notes, so you can estimate the distance you have traveled. The farther you travel from the established trail, the more descriptive and important your notes become, but as a bare minimum on any trip over a new trail, regardless of how easy you think it may be, keep track of the time between intersections to help you more closely estimate how long it will take to return. Also record from your receiver some navigation information such as the bearing traveled, but be sure you have the receiver set to magnetic bearings so you can use them with your compass if necessary.

If your receiver stops working, there is no reason to panic because the information in your notebook will guide you back to your starting point. All you need to do is traverse the route in reverse and watch for the landmarks you noted. If your notes include direction of travel, calculate the reverse direction and use your compass to walk it. Refer to Chapter 16 to understand math with bearings and how to calculate the opposite direction of a bearing. Continue making notes on the return trip to be able to verify that you are on the right course and how long you have been en route. Use your compass to take bearings, and make note of the surrounding landmarks to ensure that they are the same ones you saw on the way in. A notebook is vital in the field because it helps you accurately remember even in stressful moments.

1. 6:00 am	*Break camp. Rough road to here.*
	Followed faint trail.
2. 6:42 am	*At Smith Ravine Spring.*
	Spring is damp, but not running.
	Continue down dry wash.
	Ridge on left.
3. 7:50 am	*Pass between two small peaks.*
	Road on map visible, very rough.
4. 8:05 am	*Followed visible valley.*
	Not very steep. Peak rises ahead.
5. 8:35 am	*Easy ascent. Good View.*

Sample fieldbook entry.

A notebook is important even when your receiver is working just fine. A receiver stores the coordinates of a location and some receivers allow you to store a descriptive message, but it is not long enough to describe why you marked the spot. You could record a camping location and even type in the message "GREAT CAMPING SPOT," but three days later you will not remember why it was so great. If you make an entry in your notebook, you will remember the wood close by for fires and the overhanging rock that provided shelter from the rain. Your notes do not have to be extensive, but if you record what you see and feel, your notebook will bring back enjoyable memories for years to come.

Using a Map for Backup Navigation

Unless you are in an area you know really well, your navigation gear should include a map. While the receiver is working, the map is used to track your position and the notebook records time and information about significant waypoints as explained above. You can also write down bearings between waypoints if you want to, but that information is available from the map. If you do put bearings in the notebook, be sure to indicate if they reference magnetic or true north. Maps are not always up-to-date, so add any important features directly to the map because they may be important if you have to return without the aid of your receiver. The map becomes the visual record of your journey while the notebook provides any memory jogging information that will help you recognize your location. Once again, the notebook is a valuable aid in recognizing the return route.

If your receiver stops working, you will use the map, notebook, compass and watch to get back to your starting point. The direction of the return route is measured from the map and sighted with the compass. Do not forget to account for declination, which is discussed in Chapter 4. Using a map and compass to track your journey is much better than the notebook alone because the map provides more information than could ever be written in a notebook. Refer to Chapter 11 for an example of how to deal with poor reception or a broken receiver.

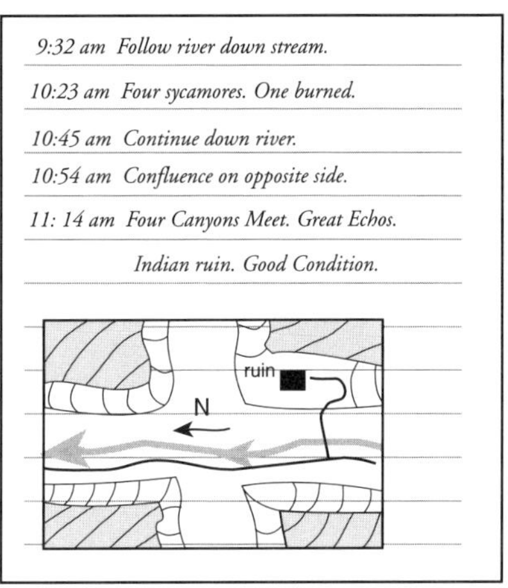

9:32 am Follow river down stream.
10:23 am Four sycamores. One burned.
10:45 am Continue down river.
10:54 am Confluence on opposite side.
11: 14 am Four Canyons Meet. Great Echos.
Indian ruin. Good Condition.
ruin
N

If a picture helps you remember your route, draw it in your field notebook.

Why GPS Receivers Stop Working

One thing you do not need to worry about is the elimination of the satellite signals broadcast from space. The U.S. Department of Defense controls the GPS satellites and although they could turn off the CA codes, so that civilian receivers are useless, the chances of them restricting civilians is almost nil. Even in times of war, civilians will not be denied access because many military units use civilian receivers. In fact, not only was the system left entirely functional during the Gulf War, the satellites' positions were changed to provide increased coverage for civilian receivers in the Middle East. Another reason the civilian signals will never be cut off is because too many industries like airlines, shipping, trucking, etc., depend on GPS positioning. Denying civilian access would cause an enormous international uproar.

It is the everyday occurrences that will leave you without your receiver: dead batteries, low performance antenna that cannot pick up the satellite signals, getting it wet or dropping it. Whatever the cause, one minute you know where you are and the next you are wondering if you will ever find your way back again—that is if you are unprepared.

It is also unlikely your receiver will just stop working under normal conditions. Today's receivers use integrated circuits and advanced assembly techniques, so they are as reliable as your computer, television or stereo. Most are designed to sustain the rigors of outdoor use, which means you probably will not be left stranded. If you are careful and have enough batteries, your receiver will be fine.

4 About GPS Receivers

There are a lot of GPS receivers on the market and new units are introduced annually. Their sizes range from big units weighing several pounds that are designed for boats or some other type of vehicle, to small, handheld ones. Advances in integrated circuits and production methods have brought even more features to affordable handheld receivers. There are important elements common to all receivers such as antenna sensitivity, accuracy, map datum and grids that are discussed first. The importance of other features depends on how you use the receiver, so each feature is described to help you decide if your application requires that capability. Fortunately, affordable GPS receivers have lots of power and features, so you may not have to make a choice between a feature and your pocketbook.

Important GPS terms are defined in this section, but if you happen to forget one or two, check the Glossary for a quick review. Near the end of the book, on page 202, a table shows the specifications of receivers available on the market. It is not comprehensive, but it represents most of the currently available handheld receivers. Phone numbers of GPS receiver manufacturers are listed on page 200.

Some handheld receivers.

Antennas

The antenna picks up the signals sent from the satellites. It is the most important part of a receiver. It does not matter how little your receiver weighs, how long the batteries last, how many channels it has or any other feature because if the antenna cannot detect the satellite signals, there is no way the receiver can even begin to calculate your position. The saying "you get what you pay for" is especially true when it comes to antennas. Better performing, more sensitive antennas cost more to manufacture, but do not think you cannot get a high performance antenna for a reasonable price. The cost of receivers is falling rapidly thanks to manufacturing efficiencies and improved technology. Most users will find that the antenna in any unit available on the market, even the least expensive, will meet their needs and the receiver will perform correctly. However, if you plan to travel in remote areas where the satellite coverage can be limited to the four satellites guaranteed by the system's design, you may want to purchase a receiver that can accept an external antenna and use it in the field because they usually perform better than the receiver's built-in antenna.

Handheld receivers are equipped with one of two types of antennas:

Quadrifilar Helix

- Rectangular in shape, usually external to receiver.
- May swivel, to point to the sky for best reception.
- Can detect satellites on the horizon.
- Cannot detect satellites directly overhead, unless very good.

Patch (microstrip)

- Smaller than quadrifilar helix.
- Usually internal to the receiver.
- Held parallel to the sky for best reception.
- Can detect satellites directly overhead.
- Satellites must be above the horizon.

Garmin GPS 3 with external helix antenna and Garmin GPS 12 with internal antenna.

The satellite geometry for best reception and accuracy is one satellite overhead with the others evenly spread out around the horizon. Quadrifilar helix antennas can detect satellites closer to the horizon than patch antennas, but not directly overhead. Patch antennas easily see a satellite directly overhead, but not as close to the horizon as a quadrifilar antenna. Each have their limitations, but both will perform properly and sufficiently in the field. There is one advantage of a quadrifilar over a microstrip antenna: Many quadrifilar antennas can easily become a remote antenna by removing it from the receiver and connecting a coaxial cable between the receiver and antenna. This simple and inexpensive adaptation allows the antenna to be placed on the outside of a vehicle for better reception, while the receiver is inside directing the driver. The cable cannot be made too long or the signal that reaches the receiver is seriously attenuated and rendered useless. The microstrip's internal construction protects it from harm. If you do not exercise care, a quadrifilar antenna can be damaged from passing branches or objects.

External Antennas

External antennas are a must if the receiver is used inside an enclosure like a boat's cabin, the interior of a plane or vehicle. The receiver's antenna must have an unimpeded view of the sky to pick up the satellites' signals. Although it is possible for a receiver on a car's dash to detect the signals through the windshield, it is hard for the driver to see the receiver's screen at the same time. It is far better to place an external antenna on the roof of the vehicle and mount the receiver, so it is accessible and usable to the driver. External antennas are designed to be waterproof for use in any type of weather. They mount magnetically to a vehicle's roof or with suction cups to the inside of the windshield and a wire carries the signals to the receiver. Using an antenna through a windshield may not work on all vehicles because some have transparent metal sandwiched between layers of glass that block the satellite signals.

Garmin external antenna.

A vehicle is not the only place you may want to use an external antenna. As mentioned above, antenna sensitivity is important when using a receiver in areas where only four satellites may be present at any given time. The GPS constellation guarantees at least four satellites in all places of the world at all times. External antennas are usually more sensitive than internal antennas and make it possible to lock onto the satellite signals in situations when the internal antenna alone may not work.

Not all receivers are designed for external antennas, so if you think you may want to use one in the future, be sure to buy a model that accepts one. Usually the manufacturer is the only source of an external antenna for a given receiver. An "active" remote antenna amplifies the signal before sending it to the receiver to compensate for attenuation or signal loss through the cable. It is best to have an "active" antenna if you have the choice.

What is a "Good" Antenna?

There is only one way to know if an antenna is good: use it in the field. It does not matter what the receiver's antenna specification says, at least for consumer grade receivers. The amount of gain, the minimum signal strength detectable or any other laboratory measurement is not as important as the way it performs in your hand in the middle of nowhere. If you are in an open area where the terrain does not block the satellite signals and the receiver has been properly initialized, a good antenna will allow the receiver to lock. If the receiver shows which satellites should be in the sky, but shows their signal strength to be low or zero, you know you have a poor antenna. Move around to see if the signal strength improves from different vantage points and wait a while for the satellite geometry to change before giving up. If the receiver never locks and you plan on using it in the same area again, it is time to get a new receiver. Before buying a receiver, talk to your friends and acquaintances, especially those who range far and wide, to see how their receiver's antenna performs.

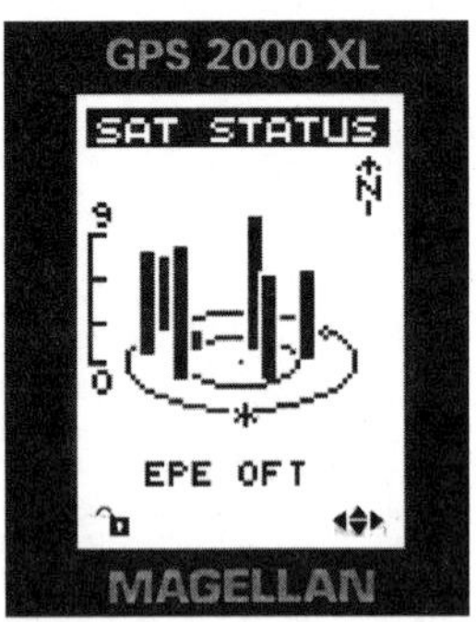

Strong signal bars indicate that the receiver can pick up the satellites' signals.

Testing the receiver's antenna in the field is another excellent example of why you need backup navigation skills that do not require a GPS receiver. A receiver with a mediocre antenna will work fine in an area with good satellite coverage, but when you need it the most, to find your way through a distant wilderness, you may discover the antenna is not good enough. Backup skills will save the day.

Accuracy

The first question everybody asks is: "How accurate is my receiver?" The answer is 100 m (328 ft.), but you need to understand more. The first thing you need to understand is there are two classes of receivers: military and civilian. Military receivers are not affected by Selective Availability (described in Chapter 1), so their accuracy is constant. Selective Availability was introduced by the U.S. Department of Defense to deliberately make civilian receivers less accurate. There is a possibility that it will be eliminated some time, so information on accuracy with and without Selective Availability is given below.

Military Receivers

- Accurate to 1 m (3.3 ft.)
- Not available to non-military people

Civilian Receivers—with Selective Availability

- Horizontal accuracy varies between 15 and 100 m (49.2 and 328 ft.)
- Vertical accuracy (altitude) varies between 100 and 156 m (328 to 512 ft.)
- U.S. Department of Defense controls the accuracy of the civilian receiver signals sent out by the satellites

Civilian Receivers—without Selective Availability

- Horizontal accuracy to 15 m (49.2 ft.)
- Vertical accuracy (altitude) to 100 m (328 ft.)

In the field, a military receiver will take you to exactly the same place every time; a civilian receiver will not. Selective Availability changes randomly, so the receiver's accuracy varies between 15 and 100 m. The receiver never knows how much error Selective Availability introduces or in what direction. Error also depends on a coordinate's original accuracy. Selective Availability results in up to 100 m error when navigating to an accurately measured coordinate. Coordinates recorded in the field can be off by up to 100 m when stored. Another 100 m error can occur later when navigating to the location resulting in an error of up to 200 m. Be sure stored coordinates are accurate—use a map or the receiver's averaging function (see page 34).

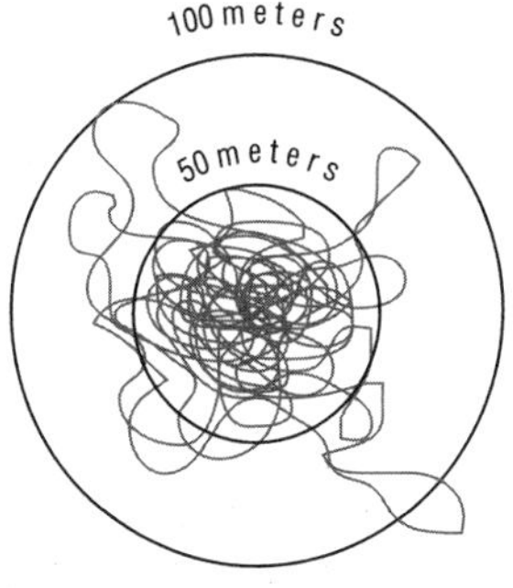

The random lines represent position calculations over a period of time. Selective Availability causes a stationary receiver to provide inaccurate positions.

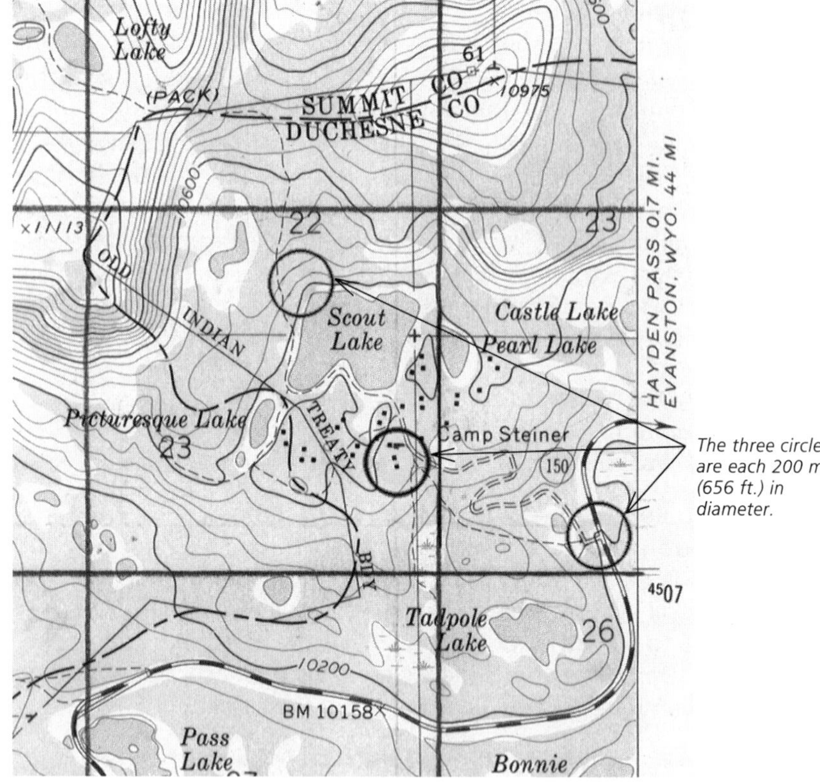

The three circles are each 200 m (656 ft.) in diameter.

A geographical representation of civilian accuracy is shown in the figure above. The map is the U.S. Geological Survey map of Mirror Lake, Utah (scale 1:24,000) with grid lines 1000 m (3281 ft.) apart. Three circles, one near Scout Lake, a second southwest of Camp Steiner and the third on the road, are each 200 m (656 ft.) in diameter, which means the edge of the circle is 100 m from the center point. If you want to go to one of these locations, the receiver would get you somewhere within the circle. With or without Selective Availability, a GPS receiver will get you within sight of the destination every time.

For most people traveling in areas of optimal satellite coverage, all you need to remember is that a receiver is accurate to 100 m. If you travel in remote areas or simply want to understand more about receiver accuracy you need to understand all the factors that reduce a receiver's accuracy. The main sources of receiver error are:

- Selective Availability
- Ionospheric Interference
- Satellite Geometry
- Reflected or Multipath Signals

Selective Availability

Selective Availability was discussed above and also in Chapter 1. Presently it is the predominate source of error and at times it can be more than 100 m (328 ft.). It is implemented so that 95% of the time a receiver's accuracy lies somewhere between 15 and 100 m. The remaining 5% of the time, the error caused by Selective Availability can be as much as 300 m (984 ft.). Most of the time, your receiver will be accurate to better than 100 m, but if there is an occasional occurrence of much worse accuracy, it may be owing to the 5% of the time that the error is more than 100 m. When Selective Availability is removed, the other sources of error described below will determine a receiver's accuracy.

Ionospheric Interference

Ionospheric interference was also described in Chapter 1. Military receivers use dual frequency transmission to completely eliminate error from ionospheric distortion. Civilian receivers do not have access to both frequencies and must rely on mathematical models of how free electrons distort the satellite signals. Ionospheric delays account for 5 to 10 m (16.4 to 32.8 ft.) of the 15 m generally quoted for receiver accuracy without Selective Availability. Unless the atmospheric models improve, this error will always exist and there is nothing you can do about it.

Satellite Geometry

Satellite geometry, or constellation, refers to the satellites' positions in the sky relative to your position. The amount of error introduced by satellite geometry is called Dilution of Precision (DOP). There are several components of the DOP: vertical, horizontal, time, position and geometric. The receiver calculates each component for each combination of four satellites it has in view and uses the signals from the four satellites that provide the lowest Position DOP (PDOP) number. Poor geometry increases the receiver's position error by hundreds of meters in addition to the error introduced by Selective Availability. When Selective Availability is terminated, error owing to the constellation will still exist. Normal PDOP values of between 1 and 3 will provide 15 m accuracy. PDOP values between 4 and 6 can cause inaccuracies ranging from tens of meters to hundreds of meters. If the PDOP value is greater than 6, the receiver will not lock, resulting in what is known as an outage. An outage can also occur if terrain blocks the satellites that would provide the lowest PDOP. There is not much you can do when there is large geometric error or outage except to wait for the constellation to change. The satellites are constantly moving, so an outage that is not caused by terrain will last only a few minutes. There are, however, two factors in selecting a receiver that can help minimize outages. The first is the receiver's mask angle and the second is antenna sensitivity. If you plan to use your receiver in remote areas where satellite coverage is not as great as over-populated areas, you want a receiver that has a low mask angle and a very sensitive antenna.

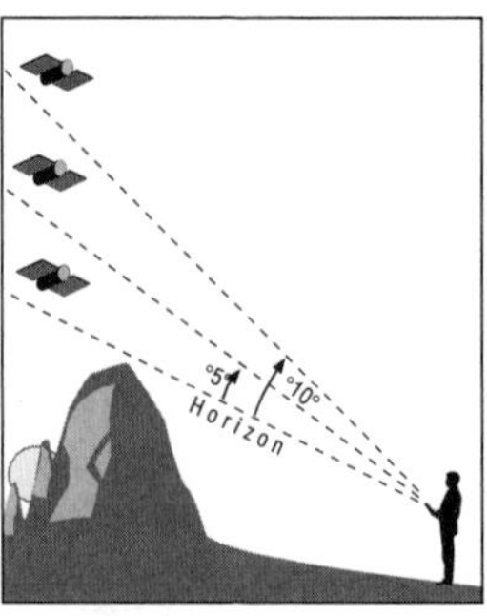

Mask angle.

Each receiver is designed to improve accuracy by ignoring satellites that are too close to the horizon. The mask angle refers to the number of degrees above the horizon a satellite must be before it is used to calculate a position. The usual numbers are between 5° and 10°. The larger the mask angle, the more a receiver is affected by outages because it stops using satellites near the horizon sooner than a receiver with a lower mask angle. The constellation that provides the lowest PDOP is when one satellite is directly overhead while the others are evenly spread across the horizon. If a receiver has a high mask angle, it will prematurely ignore the satellites providing the best constellation.

The GPS constellation is designed to provide coverage from at least four satellites at all times every place in the world. The U.S. Department of Defense controls which areas of the world get coverage from more satellites simultaneously. As a side note, during the Gulf War, the U.S. reconfigured the constellation to provide increased coverage in the Middle East. The change left people in California wondering why their receivers were not working as well as they use to work. If you travel in areas of minimum satellite coverage, you need to have a receiver with the best antenna money can buy. The system guarantees four satellites wherever you go, but if your receiver cannot pick them up because the antenna is not good enough quality, it is useless.

Most receivers do not display DOP values, but they do provide an Estimated Position Error (EPE) that is an indication of the PDOP. The amount of error contributed by Selective Availability is not part of the EPE measurement because the receiver cannot know how much error Selective Availability is contributing. EPE shows only the amount of error owing to the satellite geometry. As you navigate, occasionally look at the EPE to see if you need to cope with more error than might be present with a better constellation.

A sure way to decrease error caused by poor satellite geometry is to increase the number of satellites circling the globe. More satellites means there are more choices when trying to find that perfect geometry. The U.S. government probably will not increase the number of satellites in the constellation. However, the Russians launched a GPS system called Global Navigation Satellite System (GLONASS). This provides the same accuracy as the civilian part of the U.S. system except there is no Selective Availability. GLONASS sends radio waves to earth, but the Russian frequencies are different from the U.S. frequencies. Current civilian receivers cannot read the GLONASS signals. However, one equipment company has developed a receiver that understands the signals from both systems, which in essence doubles the size of the satellite constellation, making it much easier to find a good geometry regardless of your position on earth. Presently the cost of the dual capability receiver is several thousand dollars and it is not known if it will ever reach the commercial outdoor market.

Reflected or Multipath Signals

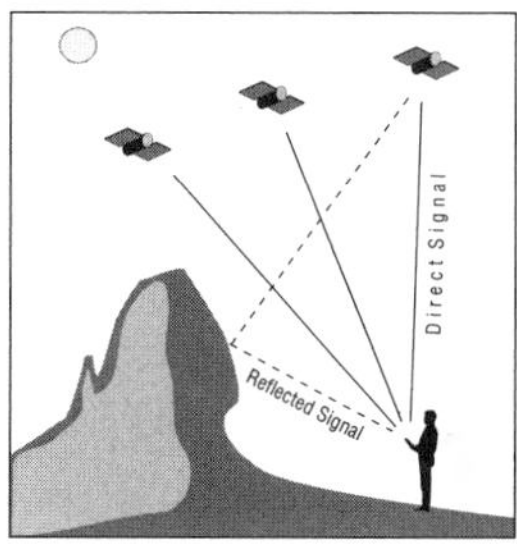

In ideal conditions the GPS satellite signals have only one path: directly from the satellite to the receiver. If the signal is reflected by something in the terrain, it can have more than one path to the receiver's antenna and it is called multipath. In the figure, the signal arrives both from the satellite and as a reflected signal from a nearby cliff. Presently, only survey grade (which means very expensive and usually heavy) receivers can detect and eliminate the reflected signal. A consumer grade receiver cannot tell the difference between the direct and reflected signal, and if it uses the reflected signal to make a position calculation, it will be wrong. As you use your receiver, be conscious of your surroundings and avoid terrain that may result in a multipath error.

Altitude Accuracy

The altitude provided by a GPS receiver is not as accurate as the horizontal position even without Selective Availability. If you travel in situations where knowledge of altitude is important to navigation, purchase a good altimeter.

In addition to an altimeter and thermometer, the Casio Triple Sensor has an electronic compass.

Do not rely on your GPS receiver in situations where an accurate altitude is important.

Accuracy in the 2D Mode

Position readings in the two-dimensional (2D) mode are less accurate than readings in the three-dimensional mode (3D). A receiver needs to lock onto four satellites to be able to get a 3D position fix. It uses the four satellites as follows:

- One satellite's signal: synchronize receiver with satellites' atomic clocks
- Three satellites' signals: find 3D position

If the receiver locks onto only three satellites, it still has to use the signal from one of them to synchronize the time, so only two are left to calculate the position. The altitude is dropped and the horizontal position accuracy ranges from 150 to 1524 m (492 to 5,000 ft.). A receiver working in the 2D mode may not even get you to within sight of your destination. You may have to lean a little more heavily on your manual navigation skills in such a situation. Yet another reason to keep your manual skills practiced.

Position Averaging

Position averaging increases the accuracy of coordinates marked in the field. When you press a receiver's button to mark a location, many ask if you want to average the position. In averaging mode, the receiver assumes it is standing still and takes a lot of position readings. Because the receiver is not moving, it knows that any change in position is because of Selective Availability. It averages all the position readings to find the one that is right in the middle. If a receiver performs averaging for tens of minutes, it can resolve a position to within 21 to 25 m (69 to 82 ft.).

Differential GPS (DGPS)

The principals of Differential GPS (DGPS) are explained in Chapter 15. DGPS makes an ordinary civilian receiver as accurate or more accurate than military receivers. When Selective Availability is removed and civilian receivers are accurate to 15 m (49.2 ft.), most people will not need DGPS. However, if you need accuracy better than 15 m now or in the future, read the chapter on DGPS before buying a receiver.

The phrase "DGPS Ready" does not mean a receiver already makes differential corrections. All it means is that a receiver is capable of understanding and applying the correction information if you purchase the extra beacon to pick up the correction signals.

Map Datum

Selecting the NAD 27 datum.

Maps are drawn so every point is a known distance and height from a standard reference point called a datum. A grid is a series of lines on a map that helps you describe a location in reference to the datum point. A map can have several grids, but only one datum. Before you buy a receiver, make sure it supports the datum for the maps you want to use.

Most receivers support the two most common datum for North America: North American Datum 1927 (NAD 27) and World Geodetic System 1984 (WGS 84). If you travel or live internationally, you may need different datum, so know which datum you need before you buy.

Before entering any coordinate into your receiver, be absolutely sure you set the receiver to the correct datum or there will be an error in the coordinate. Before GPS, each country independently chose their own datum, then made their maps, so the same location can have different coordinates on different countries' maps. Imagine you want to fly over Humphreys Peak, which is the highest point in the state of Arizona, USA. From a USGS topographical map you measure the coordinate:

Humphreys Peak N 35° 20' 48", W 111° 40' 41"

When you enter the coordinate into the receiver, you do not notice that the Reunion datum is selected instead of NAD 27. When you get in your

Mapped by the U. S. Forest Service

Edited and published by the Geological Survey

Control by USGS, USC&GS, and U. S. Forest Service

Topography by photogrammetric methods from aerial photographs taken 1967. Field checked 1972

Projection: Utah coordinate system north zone (Lambert conformal conic)

10,000-foot grid ticks based on Utah coordinate system, north and central zones

1000-meter Universal Transverse Mercator grid ticks, zone 12, shown in blue. 1927 North American datum

Most maps contain a reference to UTM zone number and datum.

plane, the receiver directs you to the point you stored, but it is not even close to the peak. When you check the receiver and change the datum to NAD 27, the coordinate you stored changes to:

Humphreys Peak N 35° 19' 55.8", W 111° 40' 21"

Entering the coordinate with the wrong datum resulted in a position error of 1.7 km (1.05 mi.). The Reunion datum is an extreme example because the differences between some datum is small, but all the same, it is something you do not want to have happen. Be sure to set the datum correctly before you enter any coordinates.

There are hundreds of map datum. Some examples are:

WGS 84: World Geodetic System 1984
A datum for the whole world as defined by GPS.

NAD 27: North American Datum 1927 Continental
Used at present by Canadian and U.S. maps.

NAD 83: North American Datum 1983
To be used by U.S. maps in the future.

OSGB: Ordnance Survey Great Britain
Great Britain, Scotland, Isle of Man....
Note there is also a grid by the same name—do not get confused.

Geodetic Datum 1949
New Zealand

Built-in Maps

Some receivers actually have road maps stored in memory, so when you use the map screen on the highway, the road is actually displayed on the screen. Maps of all types, including those stored in receivers, are discussed in Chapter 12.

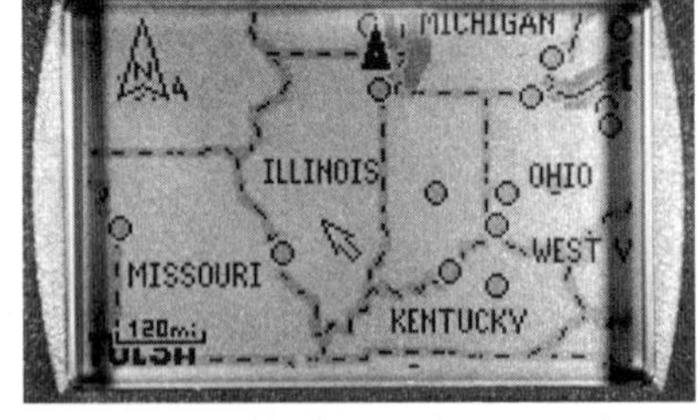

The maps stored in the Garmin III cover the entire U.S.

Coordinate Grids

A coordinate grid is a pattern of lines drawn on a map to uniquely identify every point. The grid describes a place on a map with a combination of letters and numbers called coordinates. Different locations cannot have the same coordinate. GPS receivers display coordinates, so once a receiver locks onto the satellite signals, the letters and numbers it displays are your position on the map. It is important to buy a receiver that supports the grid used by the maps you have available.

Do not buy a receiver that does not support the Universal Transverse Mercator (UTM) and latitude/longitude grids because together they cover the world. You will always be able to find a map that has one or the other. Some receivers only support UTM and latitude/longitude, which is enough for most users. However, there are grids that pertain only to specific countries, such as the Ordnance Survey

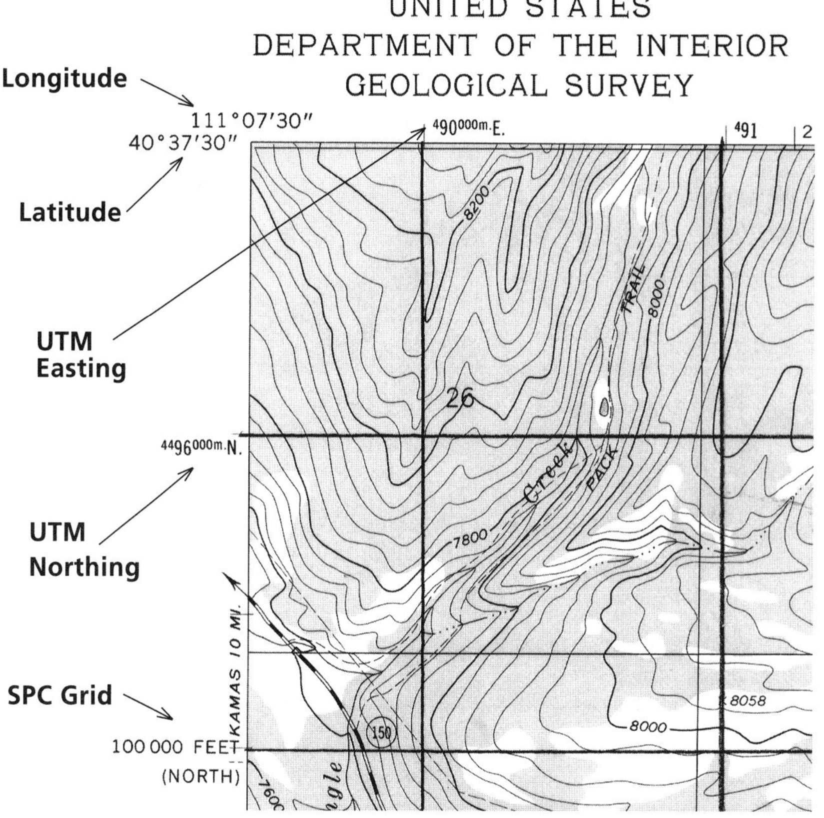

grid of Great Britain. If you plan to use your receiver in that country, it is better if your receiver supports that grid because you will be able to find a much wider variety of maps.

Some popular grids

- Universal Transverse Mercator (UTM)
- Latitude/Longitude
- Ordnance Survey of Great Britain (OSGB)
- Universal Polar Stereographic (UPS)
- Thomas Brother's Page and Grid
- Military Grid Reference System (MGRS)
- Maidenhead

Typical setup screen showing the UTM grid selected.

The most common grids, UTM and latitude/longitude, are thoroughly explained and demonstrated in Chapters 5 through 10. The other grids are briefly described here with more information found in Chapter 14.

OSGB
Used by the excellent Ordinance Survey maps of Great Britain.

UPS
Developed to cover the Arctic and Antarctic regions. Similar to the UTM grid.

Page and Grid™
A grid used by road maps for motorists, although few receivers support this grid.

MGRS
The grid used by the U.S. military. It is based on the UTM grid, but replaces some numbers with letters. Until the advent of electronic map databases, the MGRS was not readily accessible to civilians. Now anyone can custom print maps with the MGRS grid. See Chapter 12 for more information.

Maidenhead
A grid system used by amateur radio operators.

In the United States, there is another system known as the State Plane Coordinate (SPC) grid. The U.S. is split up into different zones with one or more zones per state. The grid is a lot like the UTM grid, but it uses feet as its basic unit instead of meters. An example of an SPC tick mark and coordinate number is identified in the figure on page 37. The SPC is not available on most receivers, but can be programed if the receiver has a "user grid."

All receivers can switch from one grid to another, but some make it really easy. If you know you will need to use coordinates in two different grids, buy a receiver that allows conversion between the two to be done by pressing as few buttons as possible.

Here are some examples of the coordinates of three places using different grids. Note the OSGB grid is valid only in Great Britain.

Calgary, Alberta, Canada	
11 U 7**03**421m.E. 56**62**738m.N.	UTM
N 51° 4' 55.2", W 114° 5' 44.6"	lat/long
11 U QG 03421 62738	MGRS
DO21WB	Maidenhead

New York, New York, USA	
18 T 4**53**924m.E. 45**06**327m.N.	UTM
N 40° 42' 30.5", W 75° 32' 43.6"	lat/long
18 T VA 53924 06327	MGRS
FN20FR	Maidenhead

Harrogate, England	
SE 31000 55000	OSGB
30 U 5**96**556m.E. 59**82**957m.N.	UTM
N 53° 59' 23.7", W 1° 31' 37.7"	lat/long
18 T WE 96556 83957	MGRS
IO93FX	Maidenhead

Subsequent chapters explain more about the grids and will help you decide which one is best for your navigation needs.

Computer Interface

The day is coming when a computer will be the heart of your navigation strategy. Either you will use a portable computer as a moving map or you will use digitized maps on CD-ROMs to plan your trip and load waypoints into the receiver. For some, the associated expense of a computer and software may make that day later rather than sooner, but all the same it will come because even the price of computers is dropping drastically. Until then, your receiver alone will help you navigate just fine. A computer is an extremely friendly, powerful interface to a receiver. It removes all the drudgery of finding coordinates from maps and typing them into the receiver, but by no means is a computer a must-have item.

For those who have access to a computer and the necessary software, do not buy a receiver that cannot communicate with a computer. You do not need to worry about the computer not talking the receiver's language because there are standards set by the National Maritime Electronics Association (NMEA) that are adhered to by both software and hardware manufacturers. The thing you must look for is a receiver that has an input/output (I/O) port—not all do.

Computer serial cable connected to an I/O port on a receiver.

To take full advantage of the available software, you want a receiver capable of both input and output. It should speak and understand (i.e. output and accept) at least one of the following NMEA protocols:

183 version 1.5

183 version 2.0

Selecting RTCM (DGPS corrections) protocol for input and NMEA 183 version 2.0 protocol for output.

In addition to the uses described in Chapter 12, a receiver with an I/O port or an output only port can be used with the equipment listed below. In these cases the communication is one way because data flows only from the receiver to the equipment and never back.

Moving Map
A computer tracks and displays your position on a map. See Chapter 12.

Position Plotters
Also known as chart plotters, a position plotter is much like a moving map. The receiver reports your position and it is displayed on the plotter. The surrounding terrain, whether it be land or water, is also shown.

Automatic Pilots
An automatic pilot needs to know its position to be able to steer aircraft. The receiver provides position information and the automatic pilot does the rest.

Mapping
The receiver sends all the information stored in its track memory or all the waypoints you marked to a computer that overlays your path onto a map. This capability is important to search and rescue teams, guidebook writers or other professionals because it electronically documents the areas traveled.

Post Processing Software
The receiver stores time and satellite information in addition to position and transfers everything to a computer after returning from the field. The computer uses orbital data and other corrections to make the waypoints recorded more accurate.

Most other uses that require communication with the receiver need both input and output traffic. Look at the moving map and the map database applications described in Chapter 12.

Channels

When trying to decide how many channels your receiver needs, simply buy the receiver you can afford, understand the performance differences between single and multiple channels as described below and use your receiver appropriately.

A receiver with more channels helps to:

- **Lock onto the satellites in less time**
- **Provide more accurate position readings if you are moving**
- **Maintain lock in heavy foliage**

The bottom line on channels is this: if two receivers have equally good antennas, the multiple channel receiver will perform better than a single channel receiver. Better performance does not mean greater accuracy. It means that multiple channel receivers will maintain lock better when you or your surroundings are moving. If you use a receiver in a vehicle, plane or in woods and forests, it is better to have more channels than less. Today's best receivers have 12 channels, which is the maximum you will ever need because rarely does an area get coverage from more than 10 satellites. The figure illustrates why more channels help.

In both cases, the satellite signals enter through the antenna, then go to the channels. A channel locks on to the signal from a specific satellite and tracks it as long as it is in view. A multichannel receiver monitors the satellites simultaneously. If you are walking past a big tree in the woods that suddenly blocks a satellite signal, the navigation processor immediately grabs the information from a different satellite to do its position calculations.

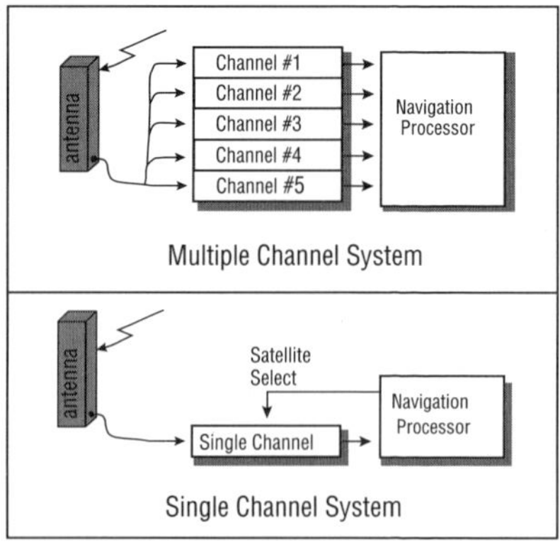

Multiple channels means the receiver always has up-to-date information to calculate your position, so it stays locked when a single channel receiver loses lock. A single channel receiver monitors one satellite's signal for a few milliseconds and stores its information. It then looks at the signal from the next satellite and stores it. It serially processes all the satellite signals before the information is passed off to the navigation processor. A single channel receiver has a more difficult time staying locked than a multiple channel receiver in situations where the terrain randomly blocks the satellite signals. Such a situation could occur simply walking through the woods. As you move, the trees block the signal from one satellite, then another. During the short time a single channel receiver looks at a satellite, its signal may be momentarily blocked. If several satellites are blocked exactly when the receiver is supposed to be reading them, there may not be enough information to stay locked.

If you are standing still, there is no difference between single and multiple channel receivers. Even in a situation where everything is moving around you, if you stay in the same position long enough, the single channel receiver will get all the information it needs for a position calculation. More channels does not mean more accuracy except in high velocity situations. However, the term "high" velocity is relative because some single channel receivers function properly up to 161 km/hour (100 mph) while others work fine at 1609 km/hour (1000 mph).

Weight

Your use of a receiver determines if weight is an important or an unimportant issue. If you plan to use your receiver only in a vehicle or a boat, the size of the screen is far more important than its weight. In a vehicle, you want the largest screen size available and the brightest backlight possible to illuminate it at night. A large screen allows you to easily see details from the driver's or pilot's seat.

If you travel on foot, kayak or pack animal, weight is a concern, but fortunately technological advances are making receivers lighter every year. You will easily find a receiver that meets all your needs including weight. If you travel in a vehicle most of the time, but occasionally need to use the receiver in the field, you should address the concerns of using a receiver on foot first and get a lightweight version. When you use a receiver with a smaller screen in your vehicle, you need to mount it closer to the driver than if you had a unit with a larger display.

The size and weight of handheld receivers approaches that of a compass or watch.

Waypoints or Landmarks

The coordinates of a location are called either a waypoint or a landmark. Receivers require not only the letters and numbers of a coordinate, but also a name.

Navigation with a GPS receiver starts when you enter the waypoint of where you want to go into the receiver's memory. The receiver determines your present position, calculates the distance and direction to the destination and directs you to it. Because waypoints are the foundation of GPS navigation, you want your receiver to store as many as possible. As an indication of how many you may need, it takes 10 to 15 waypoints to adequately describe a 16 km (9.9 mi.) trail. A receiver with lots of memory can either store waypoints for one very long trip or many shorter ones. Most receivers have capacity for at least 100 waypoints.

An example of a waypoint displayed on a receiver's screen. The coordinate of waypoint HJFALL is displayed using latitude/longitude.

Each waypoint must be named, but unfortunately the length allowed is limited for most receivers to six characters. You want the name to remind you of the location, so you may have to be creative. Some receivers also provide enough memory to store a short descriptive line or a symbol to help remind you of the location.

Because the number of characters available to fully describe a waypoint is so limited, you should carry a small notebook to record more detailed information. Your notebook will soon become invaluable as comments are combined with position and navigation data.

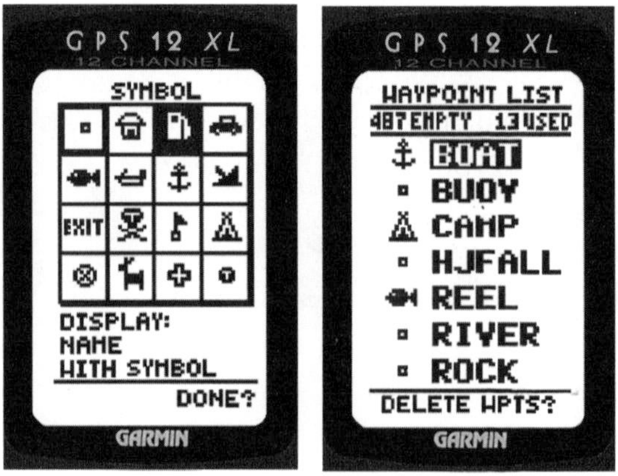

Some receivers allow you to select a symbol for a waypoint, which is displayed next to the name on an alphabetical list.

If you do not want to type in a name, most receivers will automatically generate one for you. For example, the first name would be 001 or LMK001, the next 002 or LMK002 and so forth. If you are on a trip and need to enter a lot of waypoints quickly, let the receiver name them and you can go back later and change them to something that is a better mnemonic.

LMK006 is an automatically generated name.

The coordinates of a waypoint can either be the coordinate of your present location or of any point in the world you want to type in. The power of a GPS receiver lies in the fact that you can get the coordinate from a map of a location you have never visited and the receiver can calculate your distance to it and show you how to get there.

All waypoint information—the name, the coordinate and the comment—are stored in the receiver's memory. The memory is not lost when the receiver is turned off and the batteries are not dead. Some receivers have small backup batteries inside that preserve the memory even when the AA batteries are completely removed.

Waypoint or Landmark Manipulation

Because waypoints and landmarks are fundamental to GPS navigation, your receiver must make it convenient and easy to enter, retrieve and modify them. If the receiver makes you press a lot of buttons to do something, you will not enjoy using it and it will collect dust on the shelf. You do not want a receiver that requires you to type in every letter of a waypoint's name before it is displayed on the screen. Below are listed the convenient ways many receivers allow the user to access the waypoints stored in memory:

- Single waypoint access with prompting of stored names.
- Alphabetized list of waypoint names.
- Waypoints listed by proximity to present position.

Imagine you have the following waypoint names stored in your receiver: BOAT, BUOY, CAMP, REEL, RIVER and ROCK. Here is how a typical receiver will access these waypoints using the methods listed above.

Single Waypoint

If you know the name of the waypoint you want to review, the fastest way may be to simply access the receiver's waypoint screen and type in its name. Once you have entered the name, the waypoint's coordinate and other information appears on the screen. Typing in an entire name can be time consuming (see the section on Data Entry, page 71), but a feature called prompting makes it go faster. Prompting enables the receiver to jump to the appropriate waypoint by typing only the first few letters of the name. Good receivers use prompting whenever you need to specify a waypoint's name, like when selecting waypoints to form a route. Receivers are not like a typewriter where you can randomly select any letter of the alphabet. To select a letter, you start at the beginning of the alphabet and cycle sequentially through the letters until it displays the correct one. For example, you press a button and the receiver displays the letter "A." You press it again to increment the letter to "B," then again to go to "C," etc., until you reach the letter you want. Cycling through the letters is slow, so the receiver speeds up the search for waypoints by prompting with the names of waypoints already stored in memory.

For example, if you want to see the waypoint ROCK, you cycle through the alphabet for the first letter. When you press the button the letter displayed on the screen changes from "A" to "B" and the receiver displays the name BOAT. It is prompting you to select the first waypoint stored in its memory that starts with a "B." If you want to see the BOAT waypoint, you would press enter, but as you are looking for ROCK you press the button again, the letter changes to "C" and the receiver prompts you with the waypoint named CAMP. When you press the button again, only the letter "D" appears on the screen because there are no waypoints in memory that start with "D." Once you get to the letter "R," the receiver prompts you with the name REEL. It is not the name you want, so you start searching for the second letter. When you reach the letter "I" for the second letter, the receiver prompts you with RIVER. You continue cycling on the second letter until the name ROCK appears, then your search is complete.

Alphabetized List

Usually the fastest way to access a waypoint is to select its name from an alphabetized list. The list of alphabetized waypoints for this example would be:

BOAT, BUOY, CAMP, HJFALL, REEL, RIVER, ROCK, TOWER, TUCMAC, TZEGI, VORTEX, WSRC AND XTREE

When the receiver displays the list, you can use the buttons to scan through it in either direction. If there are a lot of waypoints, the receiver displays them one screen at a time. If you wanted to see the information for the BOAT waypoint, you would push a button, usually the one with an up or down arrow on it, until the word BOAT is highlighted. Then you press another button, usually ENTER, and the waypoint's information is displayed. An alphabetized list provides fast, convenient access to waypoints.

Nearest Waypoint List

If you have a receiver with lots of memory to store waypoints, a list sorted by nearness to your present position helps separate the waypoints of totally different areas. If you are in a certain location, you are probably only interested in the waypoints local to your position. A nearest waypoint list is great for those receivers capable of storing several hundred waypoints and saves you the time of hunting through a large alphabetized list because if a waypoint is close, it appears at the top of the list. Selecting a waypoint from the nearest waypoint list is fast and simple because all you have to do is use the buttons, usually the up and down ones, to highlight the waypoint you want.

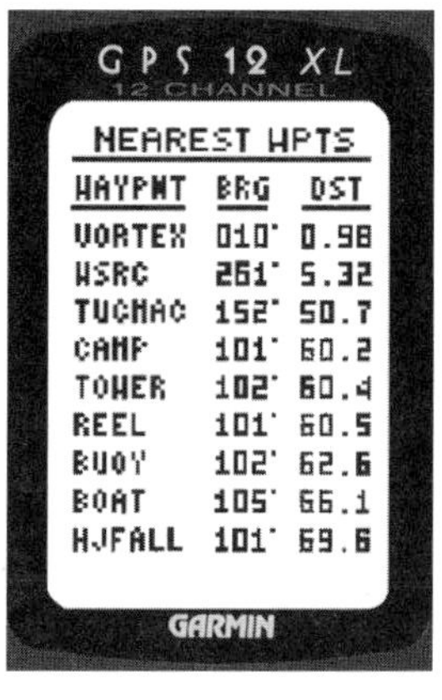

Proximity or Dangerous Waypoint List

Some receivers provide a proximity list to warn you when you approach hazardous locations. The proximity list can be used to keep your boat out of shallow waters or you out of a sinkhole. The coordinate of the dangerous area must be entered as a waypoint, then placed on the proximity list. The list allows you to specify how close you can get to the object before the receiver sounds a warning. If the receiver's units were set to statute miles, the list shown would keep you 0.5 mi. (0.81 km) from MINE, 1.4 mi. (2.3 km) from PIT and 2.0 mi. (3.2 km) from SINK-H.

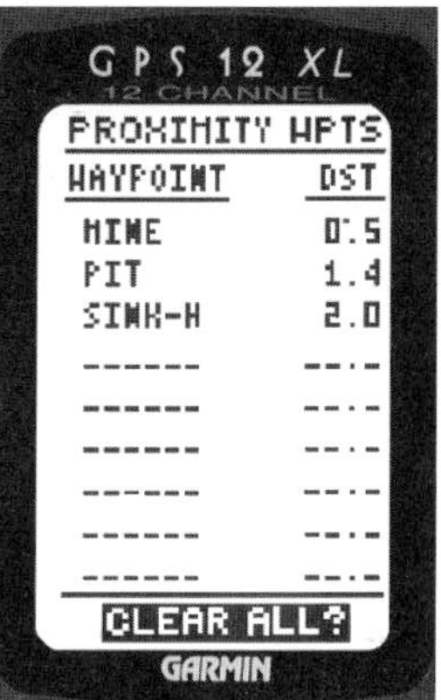

Goto Function

The true power and utility of a GPS receiver is summed up in the word Goto. All receivers are capable of leading you to any place you have specified using either a Goto or route capability. You simply find the coordinate of your desired destination by measuring it from a map, you enter it into your receiver as a waypoint, then you tell the receiver to guide you there. The power to Goto any place is fundamental to GPS navigation.

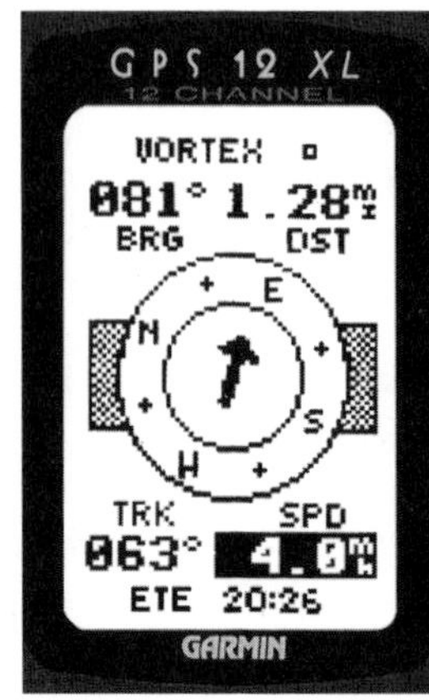

The compass screen shows how to Goto the VORTEX waypoint.

The receiver guides you to your destination using a steering screen. There are several different versions of a steering screen, many of which are described below, but they all fundamentally do the same thing: They point the direction you need to go to get from your present position to the waypoint you selected. The receiver not only points the way, but it tells you if you are off course, how far you are off course, your speed, when you should arrive and a host of other useful information that is described in the section titled Navigational Statistics.

Most receivers have a separate Goto button. When it is pressed, the receiver prompts you with the names of all stored waypoints. You select the destination of your choice and follow the receiver's directions displayed on the steering screen. The Goto function leads you in a straight line directly to the waypoint. If the best route is not direct or if the direct route has obstacles, you may be better off using the route function. The route function allows you to specify several intermediate points between you and the final destination, which can be used to steer around difficult or dangerous terrain.

Most receivers have a dedicated Goto button for ease of use.

Routes

A route is a list of waypoints that describe the path you will travel. It is like the Goto function, but it leads you to many points sequentially instead of just one. The Route function is important because it enables the receiver to guide you from the first point in the route to each successive waypoint until you reach your final destination. It is similar to the Goto function because it allows you to specify where you want to go, but it is more powerful because you can also choose the path you take. The Route function is also more automatic than Goto. When you reach one waypoint on a route, the receiver automatically switches to guide you to the next waypoint without touching a single button. With the Goto function, you have to manually select the next point before you start out again. It is difficult to find a receiver that does not have at least one route and most have several.

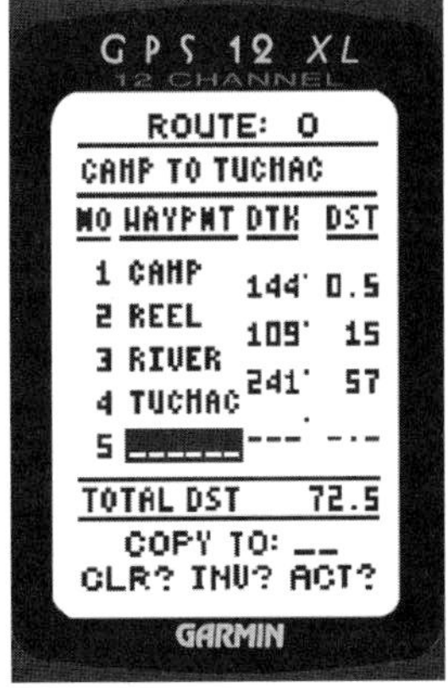

This screen shows the route from CAMP to TUCMAC. It gives the bearing and distance of each leg of the route and also the total distance.

The route function should also have the following capabilities:

- At least 10 waypoints per route
- Automatic route reversal
- Display navigation information between points

All of the waypoints of a route must already be in the receiver's memory before a route can be organized, so find their coordinates from a map and enter them into the receiver. Then you must place the waypoints on the route list in the order they are to be traveled. Forming a route is easy because the receiver prompts you with the names already stored in memory.

Once the route is developed, you activate it and the receiver points the way you should go to get from the first point in the route to the second. It uses the same steering displays as the Goto function. When you arrive at the second waypoint, the receiver informs you and immediately points the way to the third waypoint. The process continues from one waypoint to the next until you reach the last one.

Automatic route reversal means the receiver makes the destination the starting point, the starting point the destination, and puts all the intervening waypoints in the correct reverse order. Automatic reversal means you do not have to manually form another route when you want to return. Once the route is reversed and activated, the receiver once again points the way from one waypoint to the next until you arrive at your original starting point.

All receivers calculate and display the bearing and distance between the waypoints that form the route. It gives you a rough idea of the trip's total length.

The route function is best used when there are obstacles between the start and finish or when you have to follow a trail in a forest or the streets of a city. The receiver points the straight line course between each waypoint in the route. It is up to the user to ensure that the direct course between each waypoint is the best and most passable. Routes are explored in detail in Chapters 5 through 10.

Compass

Do not throw your compass away. It still provides information your receiver cannot. All receivers report the direction of your travel as a bearing and some even draw a circle that looks much like a compass, but most receivers are not equivalent to a compass. A compass uses the earth's magnetic field to measure your bearing relative to the magnetic pole. If you are standing still, a compass still knows which way is magnetic north—not so with a receiver. A receiver can only measure direction of movement. If you are standing still, do not expect the receiver to tell you which way is north. Stand in a fixed location holding your receiver and slowly turn around. The compass and bearings shown by the receiver will not change because it calculates bearing by finding the difference between your present position and the last position. The second you stop, all it knows is the direction you last headed. If you hold a compass in your hand while turning slowly around, the needle will always point to the magnetic pole. Even while standing still, you can orient yourself with a compass.

There is one receiver on the market that does include an electronic compass capable of detecting the magnetic field. It can be used exactly like your manual compass. An electronic compass burns very little power, so you can use the receiver occasionally to determine the bearing to the next point and the electronic compass to keep yourself on course.

Bearing (Azimuth)

The term bearing as it is used in this book is really an azimuth. Look for both terms in the Glossary if you want a deeper explanation, but for most people the word bearing is simply the compass direction between your present position and your destination. The bearings of the cardinal compass directions (East, West, North and South) are shown in the figure. If you travel due east, your bearing is 90°.

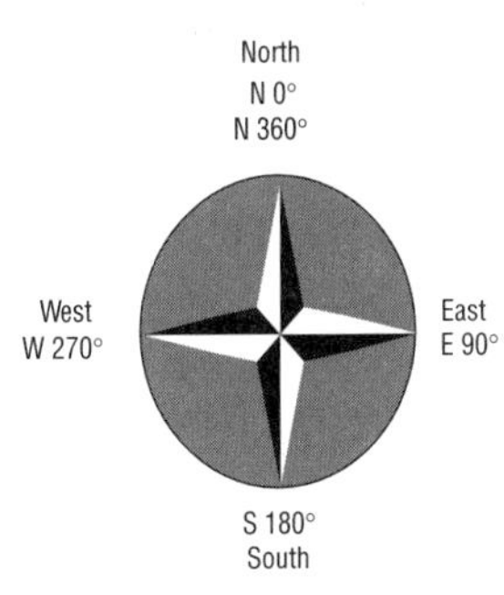

Cardinal directions.

The bearings between the waypoints MINE, CAMP and TOWN are:

Start	Destination	Bearing
MINE	CAMP	30°
MINE	TOWN	295°
CAMP	TOWN	240°
CAMP	MINE	210°
TOWN	CAMP	60°
TOWN	MINE	115°

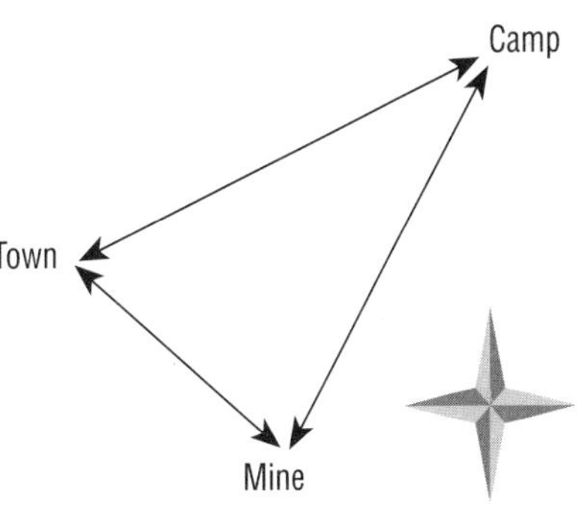

Receivers can report the bearing between your present position and any other waypoint or between any two waypoints. Bearings can be relative to the north pole or the magnetic pole, so be sure you know which is the one selected before you use a bearing. If the magnetic mode is set, the receiver automatically compensates for declination any place in the world. The difference between true and magnetic bearings is explained in the section titled North Settings.

Working with bearings, even calculating a return bearing, is easy, but if you need a refresher turn to Chapter 16. Mils are explained in the same chapter.

North Settings

There is more than one north and when the receiver reports a bearing, you need to know which north it references. Do not buy a receiver that does not provide both true north and magnetic north modes. A receiver may provide some or all of the following modes:

- True North
- Magnetic North
- User Defined North
- Grid North

Before explaining the various types of north, it is important to understand the difference between the two most important: true north and magnetic north. True north is referenced to the north pole, which is the axis through the center of the earth. Magnetic north is referenced to the magnetic pole, which is southeast of the north pole on Bathhurst Island in northern Canada. Magnetic declination is the difference, in degrees or mils, between the north pole and the magnetic pole from your position. The figure below shows declination throughout the

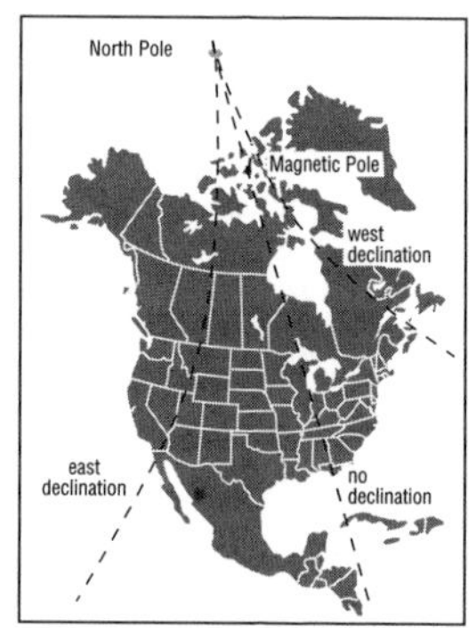

Magnetic declination in North America.

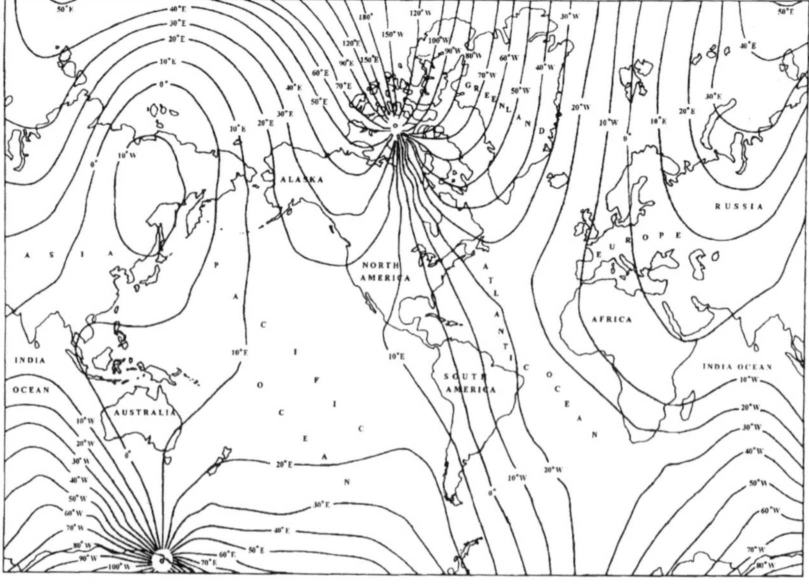

Magnetic declination around the world.

world, while the one above it shows how declination is measured. It is expressed as an east or west direction depending on whether the magnetic pole is to the right or left of your present position.

To manually convert a true north bearing (map bearing) to a magnetic bearing (compass bearing), remember the following phrase:

East is Least, West is Best

This means you subtract east declinations and add west declinations. Here are some examples:

- Map bearing = 50°, Declination = East 12°
  Compass bearing = 50° - 12° = 38°
- Map bearing = 276°, Declination = West 17°
  Compass bearing = 276° + 17° = 293°

In **True north** mode the receiver shows all bearings referenced to the north pole. When the receiver reports a direction of 0°, you are headed directly for the north pole. A bearing of 180° takes you directly to the south pole. Maps are oriented to the north pole, so set the receiver to the true north mode when using it with a map. A bearing is converted to magnetic simply by switching the receiver to the magnetic north mode or by using the manual conversion described above. Many receivers already know the declination for any area in the world and perform the conversion correctly.

Magnetic north mode references all bearings to the magnetic pole. When the receiver is set to the magnetic north mode, all bearings directly relate to the compass. If the receiver says the bearing to the destination is 109°, set your compass to 109 if you want to use it to get to your destination. To convert a magnetic bearing to a true north bearing, simply change the receiver mode to true north or use the inverse of the manual procedure described above.

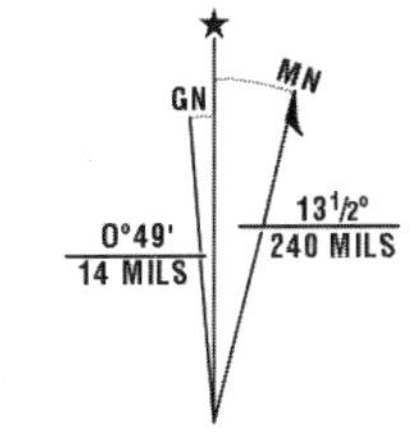

UTM GRID AND 1974 MAGNETIC NORTH DECLINATION AT CENTER OF SHEET

Declination diagram from a USGS 7.5 minute series map. The magnetic declination is E 13.5°. The difference between true north and grid north is W 14 mils.

User defined north allows the user, not the receiver, to specify declination.

Grid north is the direction to which the grid on the map is aligned. In most situations, grid north is the same as true north. Some receivers allow you to enter the grid declination if you are using a map that does not have the grid aligned with true north. Usually the difference between grid north and true north is so small that it can be ignored without consequence.

Data Formats

Make sure you buy a receiver that displays speed, distance and bearings in the units you prefer to use. Most receivers report speed, distance, altitude, CrossTrack Error, etc., in three different formats:

- Metric: kilometer, kilometers/hour
- Nautical: nautical mile, knots
- Statute: mile, miles/hour

It is important that a receiver be able to display information in all the above formats because each coordinate system is best suited to a particular unit. For example, UTM, UPS, MGRS and OSGB are best used with metric units as their grid is a kilometer-based grid. The latitude/longitude grid is based on nautical units, which is used on many marine charts, but most adventurers in the U.S. prefer to use statute units. Some receivers are capable of reporting speed, distance and altitude all in different units, which means you can mix and match units.

Some receivers provide two units for bearings:

- Degrees
- Mils

Bearings are more widely stated in degrees, but it is nice to have a receiver that can do the conversion between the two. Refer to Chapter 16 for more information on degrees and mils.

Selecting miles per hour for the speed unit.

Selecting statute miles for the distance unit.

The Garmin receiver selects the units in one command. You use the same units for speed, distance, altitude, etc.

Navigational Statistics

If you are on foot, it is nice to know the direction and distance to the destination, but information like speed, estimated time of arrival and other navigational statistics are not as important because you are moving slowly and the receiver probably is not on all the time. The picture changes when you are in a car, boat, plane, snowmobile or any other vehicle where you can leave the receiver on all the time and get a constant stream of data telling you where you are and when you will get to your destination. Your specific use of a GPS receiver will determine which navigational statistics are useful to you. Read the descriptions below of each measurement, then look for the receiver that has the ones you need.

The following navigational statistics are available on GPS receivers:

- distance, trip distance or odometer
- speed, average speed and maximum speed
- desired track (DTK)
- Course Made Good (CMG)
- CrossTrack Error (XTE) aka Course Deviation Indicator (CDI)
- estimated time en route (ETE)
- estimated time of arrival (ETA)
- trip time and elapsed time
- course to steer (CTS)
- Turn (TRN)

Distance

All distances reported by the receiver are straight line distances between the two points. The receiver does not have enough information to include any elevation changes in its calculation, so the actual walking or driving distance is not available. However, the electronic topographical maps described in Chapter 12 know about elevation changes for a given route and can calculate a true travel distance.

All distances are given in the units you select: statute, metric or nautical.

The distance between S-SHOP and REID is 4.87 miles.

Trip Distance or Odometer

Most receivers track the distance the receiver has traveled since the trip meter or odometer were last reset.

Speed

A receiver measures the time and distance between the point you were at a few seconds ago and where you are now, then it divides the distance by the time to get the speed.

There are two different ways to measure speed:

- speed over ground
- velocity made good

Both are explained below. Selective Availability does affect the speed measurement's accuracy, but newer receivers use averaging algorithms to make the calculation more precise. Even if a receiver averages, the receiver may report you are going some slow speed when you are standing still. At slow speeds, just ignore the random fluctuations. Higher speeds are measured more accurately because the variations caused by Selective Availability are a smaller part.

Receivers have upper speed limits, so if you plan on using it at really high speeds, be sure it will work at the speeds you want to go before you buy it. All speeds are reported in the units you select: miles per hour, kilometers per hour or knots.

Garmin compass screen showing both speed and average speed.

Speed Over Ground: Speed over ground (SOG) or ground speed is just like the speed given by the speedometer in a car; it simply measures how fast you are going at that very moment. SOG does not care if you are on course or off course, so it is a measurement of your speed irrespective of direction.

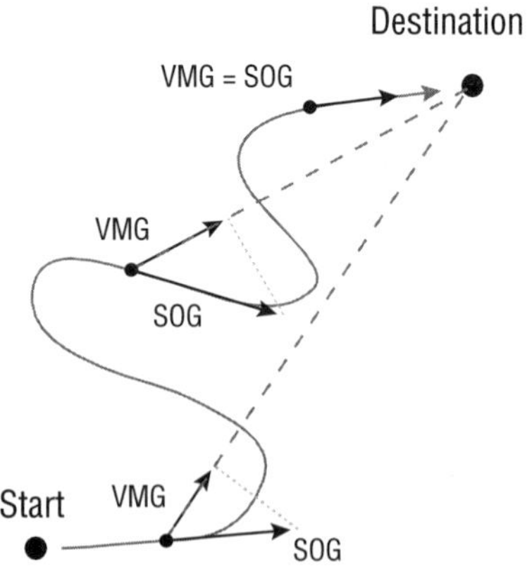

Relationship between SOG and VMG.

Velocity Made Good: Velocity made good (VMG) is the speed at which you approach your destination. VMG does take into account your present course and your destination. If you are directly on course, VMG is the same value as

SOG, but if you stray from course, VMG decreases and is less than SOG. The figure shows how VMG and SOG relate.

The calculations for ETA and ETE are based on VMG. If you are headed directly on course, ETE will decrease until it is zero at the destination. If you are slightly off course, the ETE will decrease until the receiver determines you will never arrive at the destination, then it either begins to increase or it disappears altogether. Refer to the section Estimated Times on page 61.

Average Speed: Average speed tells you how fast you really go in heavy traffic. It is not the same as speed over ground. SOG is your speed at any second in time. If one second you go 25 mph (40.2 kph), the SOG shows 25 mph. If a second later you go 50 mph (80.5 kph), the SOG instantaneously changes to 50 mph. Average speed divides the distance you have gone by the amount of time it took. Suppose you have driven your car for a long time and the average speed is 25 mph. When you suddenly accelerate to 50 mph, the average speed does not immediately change, but slowly starts to rise. After you have traveled 50 mph for as long as you did 25 mph, the average speed is only 37.5 mph (60.4 kph).

Any receiver that provides average speed must also measure the distance you have gone and the time in transit. Usually, the timer measuring the duration of the trip counts only when you are moving. In a traffic jam, the timer does not increment, so the average speed can be deceptively high if you go fast for a while then wait at a stop for even longer.

Maximum Speed: Maximum speed is the fastest instantaneous speed reached by the receiver. If you flail your arms with the receiver in your hand, the maximum speed represents how fast you moved your arms.

Direction Indicators

All directions calculated by the receiver are expressed as a bearing. Bearings are described above and in Chapter 16. Two directions are always provided by a receiver: the bearing of the direction you are currently heading and the bearing you should be going to get to your destination. The bearing you are currently going has names like:

- Course Made Good (CMG)
- track (TRK)
- heading (HDG)

The bearing you should be going to get to your destination may be called:

- desired track (DTK)
- bearing (BRG)

Deviation from Route Indicators

CrossTrack Error (XTE) and Course Deviation Indicator (CDI) both measure how far you stray from the direct course between two points.

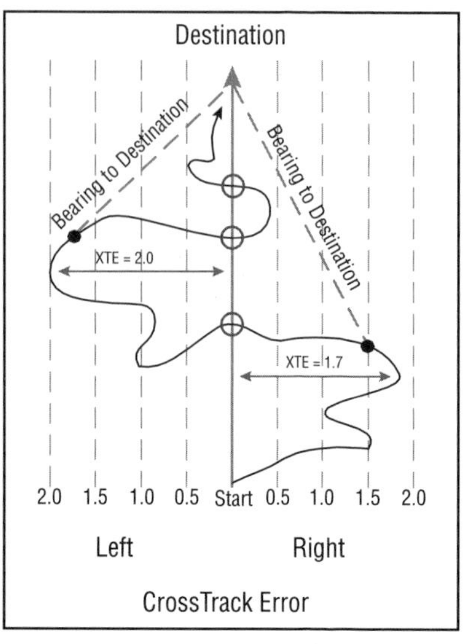

CrossTrack Error (XTE) measures the distance between you and the direct course between the point you started from and the destination you told the receiver. XTE is most helpful to pilots of boats or planes because they have the freedom of movement to maintain the direct course. Those on foot or in off-road vehicles usually have to go around many obstacles, so they are less concerned about how far they are from the direct course and more concerned about the bearing from their present position to the destination. However, there may be times when you can maintain a straight line and XTE is useful. If you use your receiver on roads, XTE is meaningless because you are confined to the roads. A good map screen is more useful.

The solid line in the figure is the direct course between Start and Destination. The receiver always tries to steer you on a straight line between two points. When you stray, the XTE is the perpendicular distance between the straight line and your current position. The dashed lines up the page show the CrossTrack Error to the right and left of the direct course. As you can see, it varies with your distance from the straight line. The point of maximum XTE is indicated for each major excursion. Whenever you are on the direct line, XTE is zero. Those points of no XTE are circled.

You can always return to the direct course by traveling the opposite direction of the XTE until XTE is zero. For example, if you have strayed to the left, you would travel to the right to return to the direct course. XTE is measured in the units you select for the receiver: kilometers, miles or nautical miles.

Regardless of how far off track you may be, the bearing reported by the receiver is the direction from your present position to the destination. If you get really far off track and it does not make sense to return to the straight line course, simply follow the bearing that leads from your current position to the destination.

A **Course Deviation Indicator (CDI)** graphically shows the amount and direction of CrossTrack Error. CDI displays are best utilized when your mode of travel permits you to go directly from the starting point to the destination like in a boat or a plane. In a situation where you are required to travel a certain corridor, like a pilot who must fly a designated flight path, CDI is very useful.

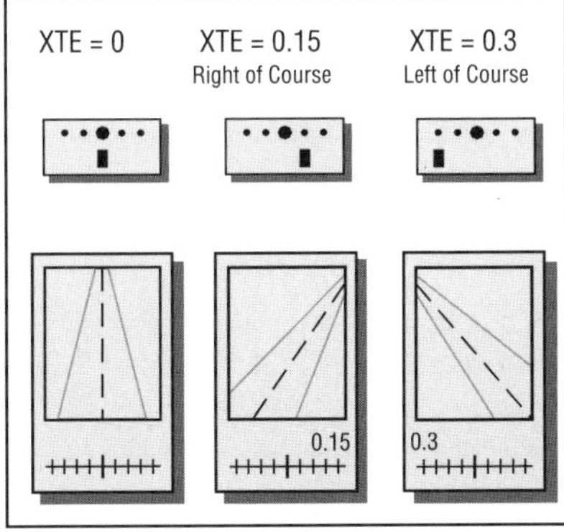

The two most common ways for showing XTE are indicated in the figure. In both cases, the display shows if you are off course to the right or the left and how far you are off course. The tolerance for the CDI can be set from very small to large. It is measured in the units you select, so it can be kilometers, miles or nautical miles. Most receivers have CDI ranges from 0.25 (kilometers, miles or nautical miles) to 5. If you want to stay strictly on the direct course, set the CDI limit to the smallest setting. A large CDI limit allows you to stray far from course and still be able to see how to get back.

The CDI display in the upper part of the figure uses dots to indicate the direction and amount of deviation. The small rectangle under the dots represents your position and the center dot is the direct line course. The dots to the right and left of center indicate the amount you are off course. In this example each dot is 0.15 units. When the rectangle is under the center dot, you are directly on the straight line course and your XTE is zero. If the rectangle moves under the first dot right of center, as shown in the figure, you are to the right of the direct course by 0.15 units. If the rectangle moves left of center, you have strayed to the left of the course. In the figure, the rectangle is below the second dot to the left, which means you are 0.3 units off course to the left.

The CDI screen based on dots can be combined with an arrow that points the direction to the destination along with numbers for bearing, distance, heading and speed.

The second CDI display is combined with what looks like a highway. The center line represents the straight line between the two points. The highway provides more information than the other display because it not only reports deviation from course, but also shows the direction from your present position to the destination. The upper display shows only XTE. However, many receivers combine the upper display with a small arrow that indicates direction to the destination. The tick marks under the display indicate the amount of XTE. The center mark represents your present position in relation to the straight line course. As you stray to the right of the course, the tick mark moves to the right of the center line as shown in the figure. The XTE is also shown numerically and in this case it is 0.15 and 0.3 units.

It is instructive to see what each display looks like along a path that is not even close to the straight line. The figure shows the displays at four different points. Note that the highway always indicates the direction you need to turn to head directly from your present position to the destination. At point P4, you gave up trying to get back to the straight course and simply turned until the highway pointed straight up and you traveled directly to the destination. At P4, there is still a CrossTrack Error, but as you are headed directly for the destination, the highway is pointing straight up.

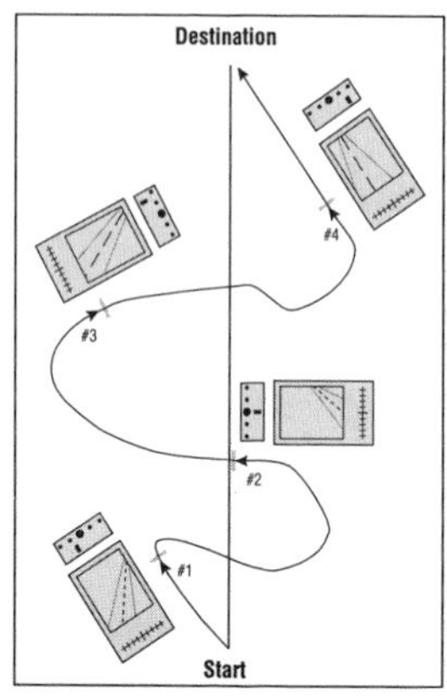

Course to Steer

When you happen to stray from the straight line course between two points, the receiver calculates the most efficient direction to return to course. Each brand of receiver determines the course to steer (CTS) bearing differently, but it is usually a compromise between returning to the straight line course and heading directly to the destination.

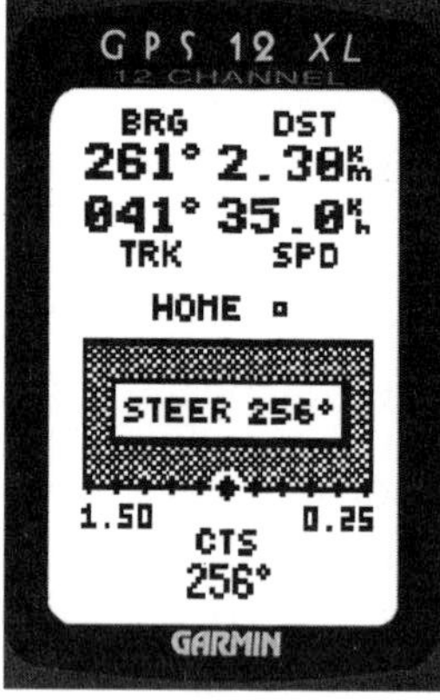

Course to steer is 256°.

Turn

The Turn navigational statistic reports how many degrees, to the right or to the left, you must turn to head directly to the destination. As the figure shows, Turn simply measures the angle between your present direction and the direction to the destination.

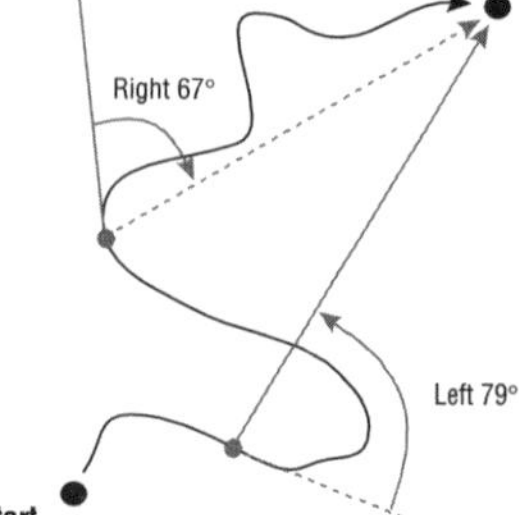

This figure illustrates Turn angles. Note that Turn is not a bearing, but rather the angular change in direction.

Estimated Times

Most receivers provide the estimated time of arrival (ETA), estimated time en route (ETE) or time to go (TTG), but they are accurate only if you are headed directly to the destination. ETA is the time of day when you will arrive, like 10:15 am. ETE and TTG tell you how much longer you must travel before arrival and is measured in minutes or hours. Both estimated times are calculated using velocity made good (VMG), which was explained earlier. The ETA and ETE are useful only in situations where you can travel directly, like in a boat or plane, to the waypoint without any detours. When a receiver is used on foot or in a car, it is possible to break up the trip into a route with lots of waypoints, but the ETA or ETE applies only between two successive points. When you reach one point in the route, the estimated times will apply only to the next point and not the ultimate destination.

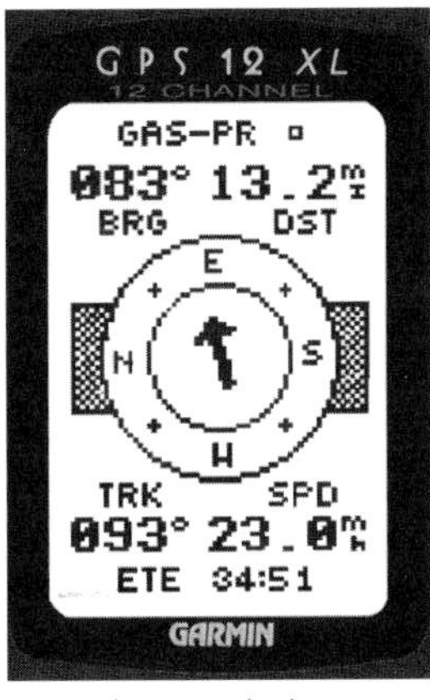

ETE is shown at the bottom of the compass navigation screen.

Timers

Many receivers provide timers. A common one is Elapsed Time. It simply counts the time since it was last reset. Another is a trip timer that records the amount of time you have been in motion. When you start moving it starts counting and stops when you stop. A good way to measure how much time you waste sitting at stop lights or parked on the freeway is to reset both the Elapsed and the Trip timers before you start your trip. At your destination, the difference between the two timers is the amount of time you sat motionless. Usually the Trip timer is used to calculate the Average Speed. Since it counts only when you are moving, the average speed can be artificially high if you were in heavy traffic and were forced to stop a lot.

Trip time is shown on left and elapsed time on right.

Navigation Screens

Position Screen

The position screen reports your current position, altitude and bearing. The position coordinate uses the grid format you chose. The time in Universal Time Coordinated (UTC) is also shown on the screen with any offset you have programed. If the receiver supports customizable screens, the position screen can show lots of other information like time, odometer, etc. See the section on Customizable Screens.

Steering Screens

There are three main types of steering screens.

A **Compass Navigation Screen** is the best screen to use when you have to go around obstacles and cannot travel directly to the destination. Hikers find it especially useful when used in conjunction with a compass. The receiver uses a circle or a semicircle to represent a compass with an arrow that continually points the direction from your present position to the destination. Most receivers also numerically show your bearing and the bearing to the destination.

The compass shows your direction as northwest. The arrow shows you must bear right to the destination.

The **Highway Navigation Screen** was designed for those who can go directly to the destination and who want to stay as close to the straight line between the two points as possible. It is simple to use because you just have to follow the road. If you are traveling directly to the destination, the highway will point straight up. If you stray to the right, the highway points to the left to steer you once more toward the destination. The highway screen was discussed in the Course Deviation Indicator section because it is usually combined with CrossTrack Error information.

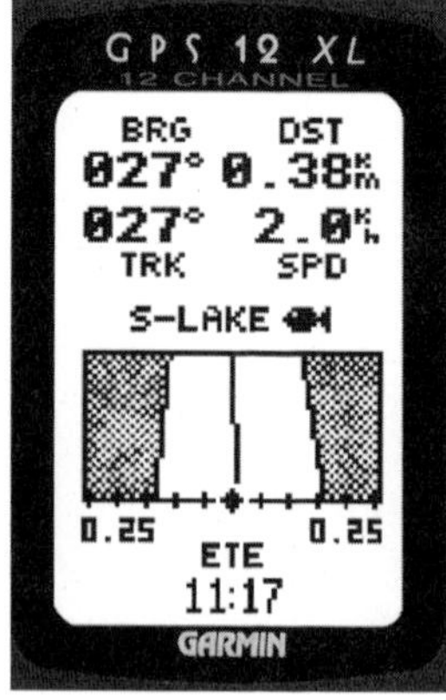

The destination lies 380 m straight ahead.

Some receivers use the **Course Deviation Indicator Navigation** screen discussed in the Course Deviation Indicator section to direct the user. See page 59 for a picture of the screen. It consists of dots, where the middle one is the straight line course from the start to the destination. Your position relative to the straight line is represented by a rectangle. If you stray from the direct course, the rectangle moves either left or right of center. You return to the course by moving in the opposite direction you are off course until the CDI is zero, then you turn to head directly toward the destination. Most CDI navigation screens also provide the bearing from your present position to the destination.

Map Screen

Map screens are powerful because they visually show where you are relative to waypoints stored in memory. If the receiver has built-in road maps like the one shown in Chapter 12, it makes navigation in a car simple. Most receivers offer a lot of options on the map screen.

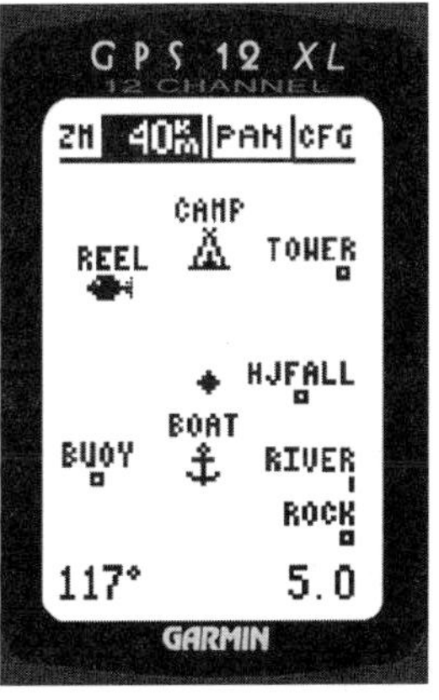

Map screen at 40 km scale showing waypoint names and symbols.

Orientation refers to how the map is shown on the screen. The three most common orien–tations are explained below.

North Up Orientation: The top of the receiver's screen represents north. Choose this orientation when you compare the map on the screen to a paper map of the area. North is always up regardless of your direction of travel.

Track Up Orientation: Your direction of travel is the track, so the direction you go is displayed as up on the receiver's screen. When you turn, all the waypoints on the screen move to show their position relative to your position and direction of travel. If you are in a car on a freeway and your destination lies to the right, it is shown to the right on the screen. Track up provides quick reference to where everything is around you, so if a point is shown at the top of the screen it is ahead of you; if at the bottom, it is behind, etc. Do not use the track up mode if the terrain forces you to twist and turn a lot because the waypoints or map on the screen are always changing position and sometimes it is confusing. Use the desired track up or north up in such a situation.

Desired Track Up Orientation: The destination is always shown at the top of the screen. If you need to get some place and the course is tortuous or if you have complete freedom of movement and can stick to the course, use this mode and watch your position relative to the top of the screen. If the symbol representing your position moves to the right of the screen, you are off course to the right and need to move left to get back.

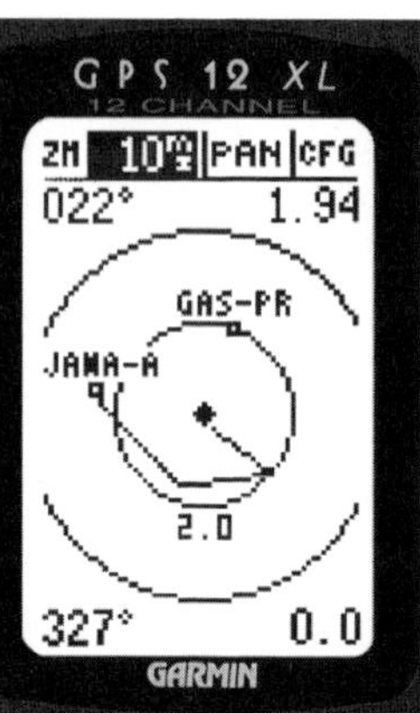

The track line extends from JANA-A to the diamond in the center.

Track Lines: Most receivers draw lines on the map screen to show your path of travel and the straight line course to the destination. Set the receiver to always log your track because it is useful to see where you have been in relation to the marked waypoints in the area. Allow the receiver to show the route to the destination if you can maintain the course and do not need to go around obstacles. If the screen gets too cluttered, you can always turn off the route line and erase the track log.

The track log is a list of positions stored in memory used to record and display your movements on the screen as described above. It works in two modes: wrap around or fill up. The track log memory is limited and can record only a certain number of position points. When the track memory is almost full, the fill mode tells the receiver to use the last bit of memory, then stop recording your movements. It fills the memory, then stops. On the map screen, the line representing your path stops when the memory is full. In the wrap around mode, the receiver does not stop recording your position when the memory is full, it simply wraps around to the beginning and starts to overwrite old data. On the screen, the line at the beginning of your journey disappears as the memory is used to record a more recent position.

It is foolish to depend on the track log to show the way back because data may be lost if it fills up or is written over. However, some receivers can convert the track log into a route. A route is permanent and will not be overwritten. If your adventure takes you on an unknown route, but you want to use the receiver to automatically guide you back, either mark waypoints along the way or buy a receiver capable of converting the track log to permanent memory.

Rings: Concentric circles around your present position make it easy to measure the distance to surrounding waypoints.

Scale: The map's scale can be set from tenths of miles to hundreds of miles, which is good because if there are a lot of waypoints in one area, the screen can get pretty crowded. If the screen still looks cluttered even after zooming in, turn off the waypoint names and turn on the route line to indicate your destination.

Customizable Screens

Most receivers allow the user to select the navigational statistics displayed on the screen. Your mode of travel whether it be foot, vehicle, boat or plane and your navigation preferences determines which information is important.

Flip Screens

Receivers with flip screen capabilities allow the user to determine if the display is portrait or landscape. The screens on handheld receivers are usually rectangular. The terms landscape and portrait refer to the screen's orientation when you view it. Most receivers present their information in the portrait format, which means the screen is held so it is taller than it is wide. Landscape means the screen is wider than it is tall. A flip screen allows you to decide how you want to hold, mount and view the receiver. A flip screen is convenient especially when using the map screen because it allows you to decide which aspect displays the information you want to see. If you place the map screen in the track up mode, the portrait mode allows you to see farther ahead and behind while the landscape mode shows more to each side. Some screens are also easier to see in one mode or the other. A flip screen offers greater viewing options.

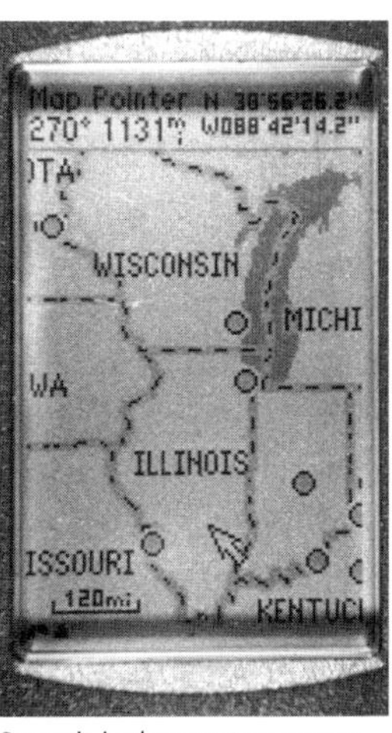

Portrait is the most common viewing aspect. A landscape perspective is shown below.

Multitone or Color LCD Screens

Most receiver screens offer two colors: black and white. Multitone and color LCD screens cost more, but they can also make the screen much easier to read because important information can stand out. Colors or even a gray scale can make the map screen much more realistic and aesthetically pleasing. The figure shows a map rendered in four shades of gray. Water is easily distinguished from land.

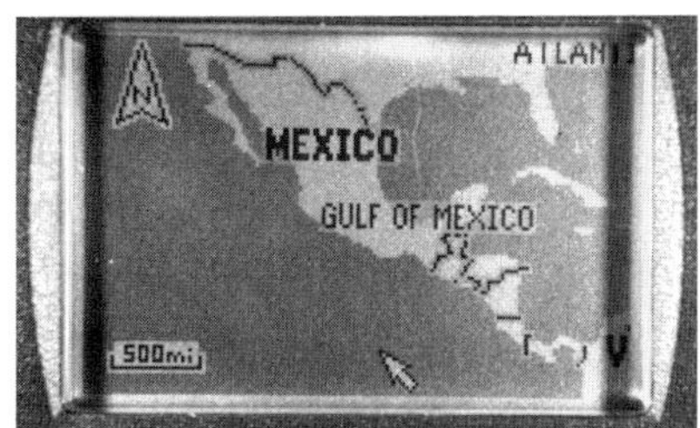

Water can be distinguished from land when you have a gray scale display.

Power Sources

Batteries

Although many newer receivers can last up to 24 hours on a fresh set of batteries, there are a few things you can do to conserve energy. If you are on foot, use the receiver only when you need a position fix to locate your position on a map. Most receivers use a type of screen called a liquid crystal display (LCD). If you want to see it at night, you have to turn on a small light bulb behind the screen called the "backlight." This drains the batteries quickly, so use the backlight sparingly. Purchase and use the cigarette lighter power cord whenever you are in a vehicle.

If you use your receiver in cold weather, replace your normal alkaline batteries with lithium, because they last longer when it is cold.

Changing the Batteries

Do not worry about losing data when you need to change the batteries. Some receivers have a small internal battery that will maintain the data even if the AA batteries are removed for an extended period of time. Other receivers have an internal capacitor to maintain the data for several minutes while you make the change.

External Power

If external power is available, like a cigarette lighter in a vehicle, use it. You have to purchase the external power cord, but it allows you to leave the receiver, and even the backlight, on all the time. External power saves you the expense of replacing batteries frequently and allows the receiver to become a true navigational aide that you will really appreciate the more you use it.

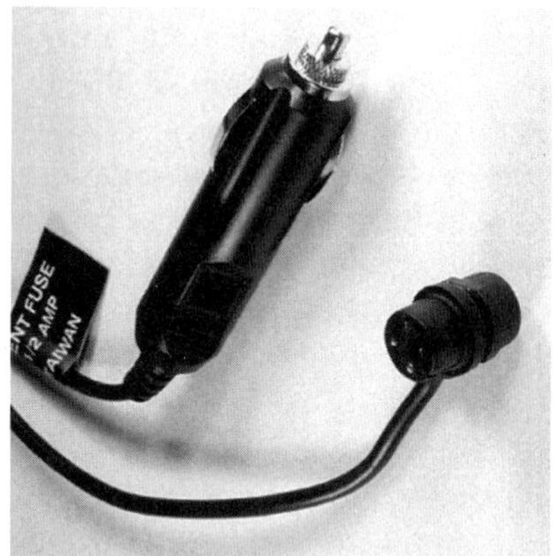

One side of the power cord connects to the receiver, the other to the cigarette lighter.

Miscellaneous Functions

Initialization

When a receiver is turned on for the first time or after it has been off for several months, it needs to know its approximate location to be able to lock onto the satellites. Most receivers make initialization simply by allowing you to select your approximate position from a list of countries in the world and their corresponding states or cities. It is also possible to enter the approximate coordinate of your position.

Temperature Range

Receivers have maximum and minimum temperature ranges and are not guaranteed to work outside of their stated range. If you work in extreme temperatures, buy a receiver designed for the range it will experience.

The limiting component of a GPS receiver is the liquid crystal display (LCD). Cold temperatures make them fade and work sluggishly and if it is cold enough it will freeze. Graphical displays perform worse in cold weather than simple alphanumeric displays, so do not be disappointed if the cold weather receiver you need for your extreme temperatures has a simple, straightforward display.

Man-Over-Board (MOB)

The man-over-board function is useful if you have to quickly mark a spot, so you can return to it later. Imagine you are in your boat, traveling across a lake at night, when suddenly you hear a cry that indicates someone just fell overboard. Being a quick thinker, you press the MOB button. The receiver immediately records your present position, then it instantly switches to the navigation screen to direct you back to the location just recorded. By the time you slow down and get the craft turned around, the receiver is already pointing the direction and distance to return. When you arrive at the MOB waypoint location, you start the search.

The usefulness of the MOB function is not limited to boats. Imagine you are an archaeologist. You just spotted something resembling an ancient Mayan temple when the base camp calls on the radio. It is a dire emergency and there is no time to lose in getting back to camp. You press the MOB button, jump in the jeep and rush back. Later the receiver will guide you back to the ruin.

Mounting

All manufacturers sell hardware to mount their receivers. It has been mentioned before that most receivers can be set on a car's dash and pick up the satellite signals through the window, but mounting hardware fixes the receiver to the vehicle, so sudden turns or stops do not send it flying. Mount the receiver within reach of the driver or pilot so they can press the buttons and in a position that provides the best viewing angle. A receiver mounted deeper inside the vehicle will make it impossible to pick up the satellite signals without an external antenna, so be prepared to purchase both the mounting hardware and the external antenna.

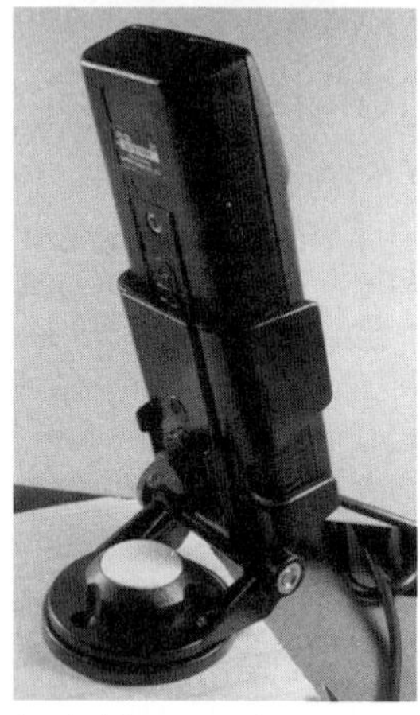

A mounting bracket holding a receiver.

Data Entry Keys

Some receivers can be set to beep each time a key is pressed. If you use a receiver in the dark, the backlight illuminates the screen, but not the keys. If the receiver beeps with every button press, you can be sure you really hit the key even when it is dark and you cannot see it.

The keypads on handheld receivers are small. If you use a receiver in cold weather while wearing gloves, use a pencil or something else to actually press the keys because your gloved hand will not be able to do it.

Small buttons on most keypads require care when used with gloves in cold weather. Magellan 2000 XL keypad.

Calculations

Solar and Lunar Calculations

Many receivers can calculate the times of sunrise, sunset, moonrise, moonset and moon phase based on the date and location. If you are planning an expedition months in advance or to an unfamiliar area, it is nice to know when it will be light or dark or if the moon will provide any light at night.

The moon will give you little light during the trip.

Coordinate by Reference or Projection

The coordinates of a waypoint can be calculated by specifying the bearing and distance from any other waypoint. Suppose you are on the safety patrol at a ski resort when a scared, exhausted skier arrives at the lodge. There has been an accident and all the skier can tell you is that he came from "that" direction and skied for about an hour to get to the lodge. You get out your compass to get a bearing of the direction indicated by the person and make a rough estimate of the speed and distance traveled. The lodge's coordinate is already stored in the receiver, so you create a new waypoint for the accident site that is the distance you estimated at the bearing you measure from the lodge. The receiver calculates the location's waypoint based on that information. Now you can use the calculated coordinate to easily find the location on a map and start a rescue operation close to the probable accident site.

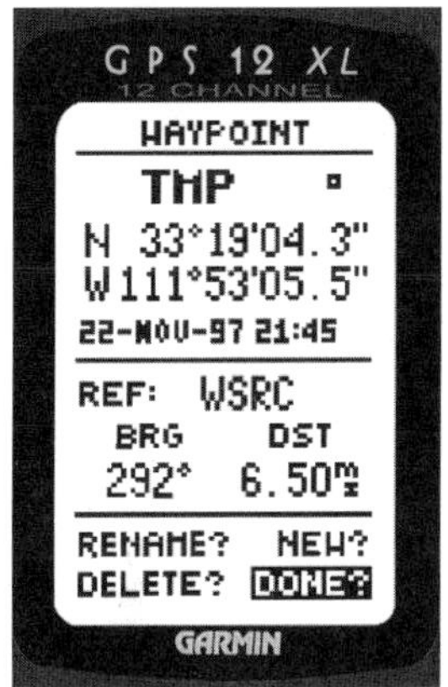

The waypoint TMP is 6.5 mi. (10.5 km) from WSRC at a bearing of 292°.

Point-to-Point Calculations

A receiver can tell you the distance and bearing between any two points. Some receivers have a separate screen that allow you to specify any two points and it performs the calculation. Any receiver that has a route function will at least calculate the distance between the beginning and the end of the route. Some receivers report the distance and bearing between each point in the route. This capability is handy if you want to know which part of the journey will be the longest and hardest.

Another good use of point-to-point calculations is as a training aid. If you want to use a GPS receiver, but do not have any manual navigation skills in case of an emergency, you can use the receiver to help you learn to use a compass and a map. When you measure a bearing between two points from a map, enter their coordinates into the receiver and have it calculate the bearing to see if your manual measurement was correct. When you use a compass to sight and walk a bearing, you can carry a receiver along to have it tell you the bearing you are traveling as a check on your proficiency. When you convert a bearing from the map to the compass or vice versa, you can use the receiver to do the same conversion to see if you applied the correction for declination properly.

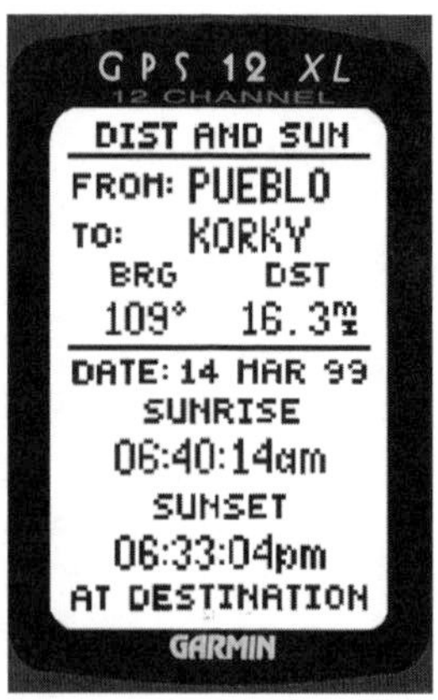

Point-to-point calculation shows distance and bearing from PUEBLO to KORKY.

Area Calculation

Only a few receivers are capable of calculating the area enclosed between any set of waypoints. Area calculations and their uses are discussed in Chapter 12. Professional users would find this powerful capability useful.

Time

The importance of accurate synchronization between the GPS satellites was discussed in Chapter 1. The time tolerances are so tight that every satellite has ultra-precise atomic clocks. The time maintained by the satellites is called GPS time, but each receiver is told how to convert GPS time to Universal Time Coordinate (UTC), which is really Greenwich Mean Time. There is a difference between GPS and UTC time. In December 1992, the difference was 7 seconds, which does not seem like much for most situations, but do not mistake GPS time for UTC when making celestial observations. Most receivers allow the user to provide an offset from UTC time to their local time zone, which makes the receiver's clock convenient to use. The time can also be expressed in a 12 or 24 hour format.

The time is set to a 12 hour clock with a -7 hour offset to UTC.

Data Entry

Handheld GPS receivers are designed to be as small as possible, so they do not have a keyboard like a computer. Unless data is downloaded from a computer into the receiver, everything must be typed in one number or letter at a time. Data entry is straightforward and fairly fast because receivers cycle quickly through the alphabet when the buttons are continuously held down.

Data entry was briefly described under the heading Waypoint or Landmark Manipulation. An example of entering a new waypoint is given here.

You want to mark your present location and give it the name CATLAN. When you press the mark button, some receivers are immediately ready to accept data input while others require that you also press the ENTER button. Once the receiver is ready to accept characters, press the up arrow once and the display will show "A" as the first letter. The display becomes:

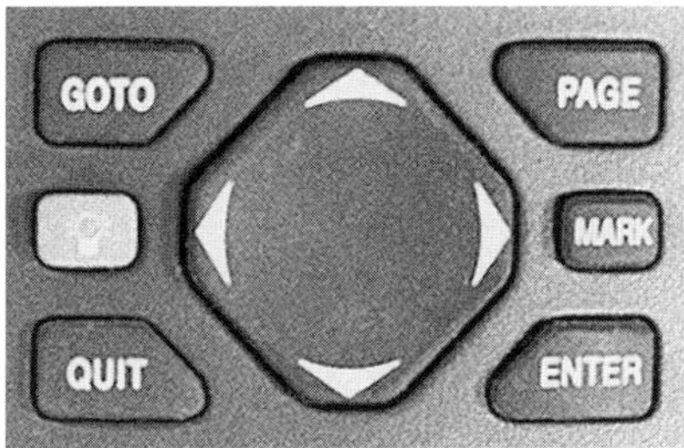

There are usually five buttons used for data entry: four arrow keys and a key to conclude the entry. In this case, ENTER concludes the Garmin 12 XL keypad.

A _ _ _ _ _

Each time the up arrow is pressed, the display advances to the next letter in the alphabet. If the down arrow is pressed, the display digresses to the previous letter. Press the up arrow one more time to get the letter "B," then once again to get the letter "C" as the first character. You now see:

The first letter is now the one you want, so press the right arrow button to move to the place where the second character will appear.

Use the up and down arrows to select the second letter. Because the second letter is an "A," selecting it requires only one press of the up arrow. Press the right arrow again to move to the location of the third letter.

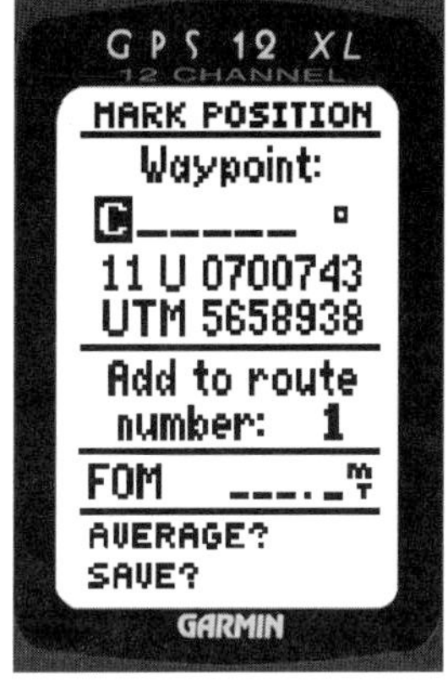

When the first letter is correct, press the right arrow and repeat the procedure to display the second letter.

The third letter is a "T," so to get it to appear on the screen you have to press the up arrow 20 times. Data entry would be very slow if you really had to press the button once for every advance in the alphabet, but fortunately all receivers are designed to advance rapidly through the alphabet if you press and hold down the up or down arrow buttons.

You know that "T" is close to the end of the alphabet, so instead of pressing the up button and advancing from "A" all the way down to "T," you press and hold the down arrow to move through the alphabet in reverse. When you press the down arrow, the receiver counts from 9 down to 0 before it reaches "Z," then starts up the alphabet in reverse. As you hold the button down, the letters zoom by, but as you get close to "T," you let up on the button. In this case the receiver stops on the letter "U," so you press the down arrow one more time and the letter "T" appears. The display now looks like this:

C A T _ _ _

The rest of the letters are entered in exactly the same manner.

1. **Use the up or down arrows to cycle through the alphabet. Press and hold the button to advance quickly.**
2. **Use the right button to move to the next position.**
3. **Return to step 1 and repeat until the entire name appears on the screen.**

Once all the letters appear on the screen, press the button that tells the receiver to accept the waypoint name.

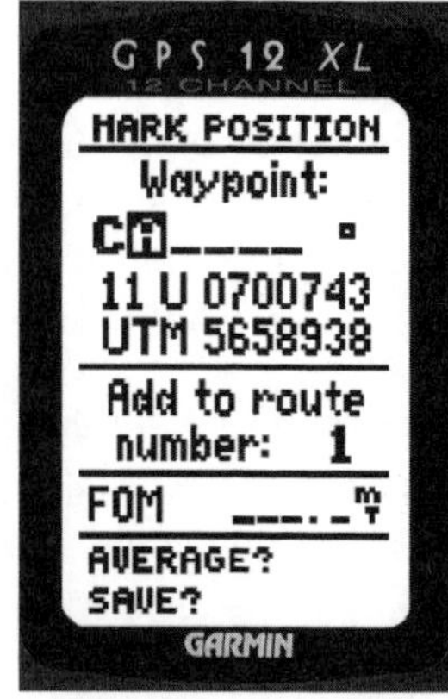

Some receivers allow you to add the new waypoint to a route. Use the arrow keys to move down the screen, enter the route number and press ENTER to save the waypoint in the receiver's memory.

5 Using UTM Coordinates on a Hiking Trip

Planning any excursion in the outdoors starts with using a map to decide where you want to go and the route you will take. In unfamiliar country you cannot always tell from the map if the route is feasible, so you consider alternatives. You follow the same process when using a GPS receiver for navigation. You take the coordinates of significant locations from the map and store them into the receiver. When you are out on your trip you combine the information from the GPS receiver with traditional navigational skills to find your way. After introducing you to the UTM grid, this chapter concentrates on how to enter waypoints, how to form a route that your receiver can use and finally, how to use the receiver while hiking.

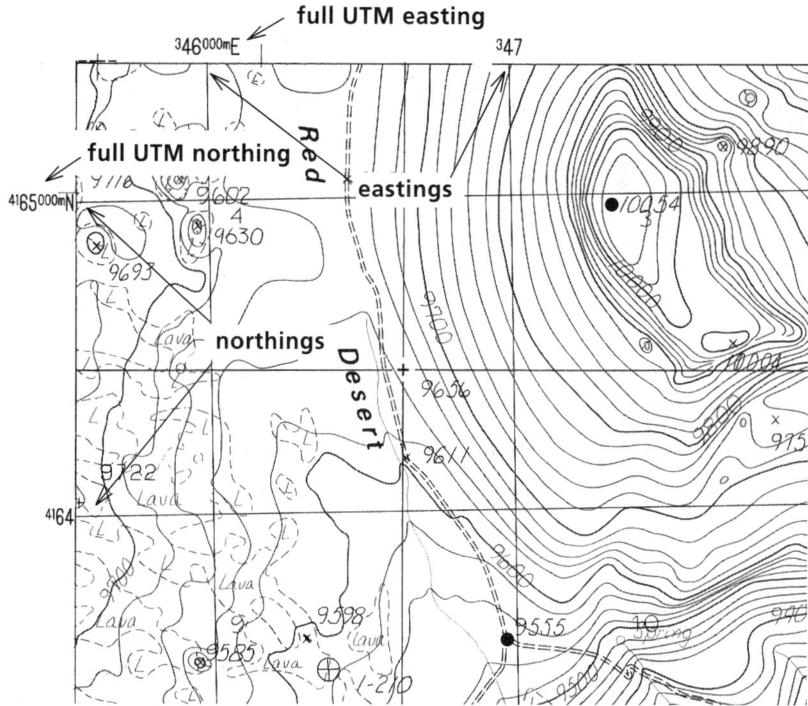

Introduction to the UTM Grid

Enough information on UTM coordinates is given in this chapter for you to determine the coordinate for any point on a map and to use the coordinates with a GPS receiver. Additional information on the UTM grid is given in Chapter 6. The latitude/longitude grid is explained in Chapter 8.

All maps have a grid that uniquely defines every point on the map. The topographical map shown on page 73 is the northwest corner of Henrie Knolls quadrangle, Utah (7.5 minute series, scale 1:24,000). It is printed with the UTM grid and has tick marks for the latitude/longitude and state grids.

The lines that are indicated with arrows form the UTM grid. The numbers along the top of the map are called eastings, which provide an east–west position. The numbers on the left side of the map are called northings. They give you a north–south position. Here is a quick introduction to eastings, northings and UTM coordinates.

Eastings

- Increasing easting numbers means you are going east.
- Full easting coordinate number: 3**46**000m.E.
- Distance between 3**46**000m.E. and 3**47**000m.E. is 1000 m (1 km).
- The large numbers are an abbreviation. On this map:

  46 means 3**46**000m.E.
  47 means 3**47**000m.E.
  Distance between 46 and 47 is 1000 m (1 km).

- The last three numbers stand for meters.
  Distance between 3**47**180m.E. and 3**47**721m.E. is 541 m.
  Distance between 3**47**180m.E. and 3**52**721m.E. is 5.541 km.

Northings

- Increasing northing numbers means you are going north.
- Full northing coordinate number: 41**65**000m.N.
- Distance between 41**64**000m.N. and 41**65**000m.N. is 1000 m (1 km).
- The large numbers are an abbreviation. On this map:

  64 means 41**64**000m.N.
  65 means 41**65**000m.N.
  Distance between 64 and 65 is 1000 m (1 km).

- The last three numbers stand for meters.
  Distance between 41**64**300m.N. and 41**64**560m.E. is 260 m.
  Distance between 41**64**300m.N. and 42**02**560m.E. is 38.260 km.

The UTM grid is based on meters and the grid lines are always 1 km (0.62 mi.) apart on large scale maps. It is easy to estimate distance on a map with the UTM grid because there is a known distance between each grid line. As you will see in Chapter 8, the latitude/longitude grid does not correlate so directly to physical distance.

UTM Coordinates

- The form of a UTM coordinate is zone, easting and northing.
- The zone is printed on the map. For this map it is 12.
- For some receivers, the zone is "12 S" or "12 N." See Chapter 6.
- The complete UTM coordinate of the hill 10,054 ft. is

  12 3**47**400m.E. 41**64**900m.N., or including the zone letter,
  12 S 3**47**400m.E. 41**64**900m.N.
  Abbreviated: **47**4 E. **64**9 N.

- The complete UTM coordinate of the junction between two unimproved roads with the elevation 9555 ft. is

  12 3**46**900m.E. 41**63**600m.N., or including the zone letter,
  12 S 3**46**900m.E. 41**63**600m.N.
  Abbreviated: **46**9 E. **63**6 N.

For an explanation of the zone letter "S" see pages 89-91.

Guidebooks that utilize maps with a UTM grid sometimes identify unnamed features by their abbreviated UTM coordinate. Accordingly, the intersection of the roads would be referred to as Grid Reference (GR) 469636 and the hill GR 474649.

Accuracy of UTM Grids

Some recreational users question the accuracy of UTM grids. The UTM grid is a projection of the earth's curved surface onto flat sheets of paper, and as a result there are some inaccuracies across each of the 60 zones (see the explanation of zones in Chapter 6. However, the error is so small that it is of no concern to users of civilian handheld receivers. The inaccuracies of GPS receivers due to Selective Availability, ionospheric interference and satellite geometry described on pages 31-33 far outweigh the inaccuracies of the UTM grid.

If you really need to correct for inaccuracies in the grid, some receivers allow you to enter a value for grid declination, which is the difference between grid north and true north. Some maps, including many of the USGS 7.5 minute series, have the angular difference between grid and true north printed on the map (see figure on page 53).

UTM and a GPS Receiver

You now know enough about the UTM grid to read coordinates from a map, however, there are a few points about using UTM coordinates with a receiver.

- GPS receivers need the complete coordinate numbers. Abbreviations are too map specific. For example, the coordinate for RIVER is entered as

  12 N 0544296E 3629614N

- When entering the coordinates, you do not enter the "m.E." or "m.N." If they are displayed by the receiver as part of the coordinate, they show up automatically without you doing anything.
- Some receivers require seven digits for both easting while others require only six digits for the easting. The first digit in a seven digit easting should always be zero.
- Selective Availability limits the receiver's accuracy to 100 m, so it is alright to round the coordinate to the nearest 50 or 100 m. For example, if the exact coordinate of a landmark is

  12 **S** 5**06**913m.E. 46**15**672m.N.

  it can be entered into the receiver as

  12 S 506900 4615700

  or

  12 S 506900 4615650

- When measuring coordinates off a map, you can either use a ruler to measure the easting and northing down to the last meter or you can just eyeball-estimate the coordinate to the closest 50 or 100 m as described above. The use of a ruler on a UTM map is demonstrated in Chapters 6 and 10 while the sources of several useful rulers are listed on page 200.

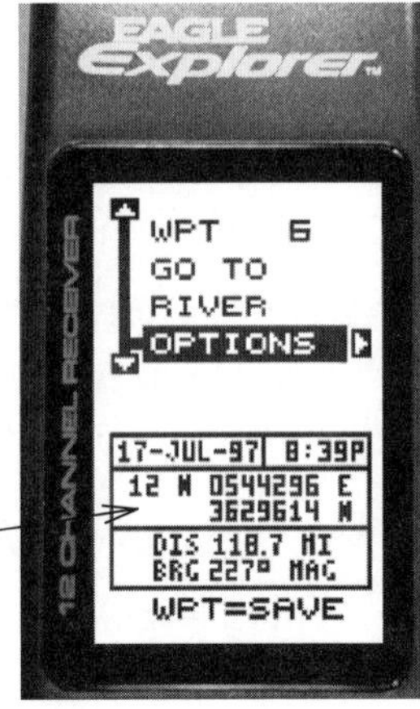

Eagle screen showing coordinate for RIVER.

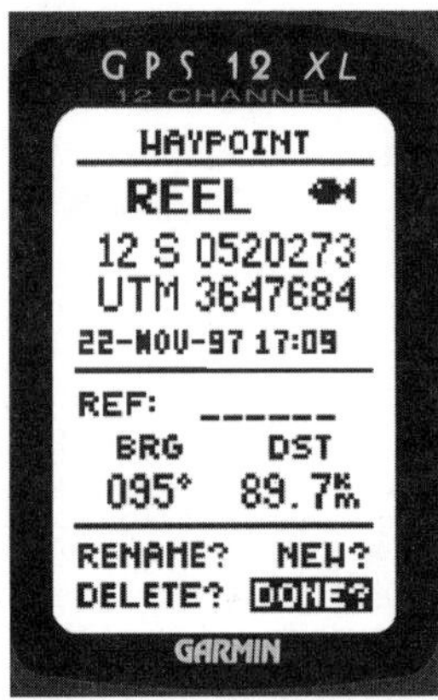

Garmin screen has leading zero before the easting.

Magellan screen does not.

A Hiking Trip in the Mountains

Navigation Plan

The route used in this example could be navigated using compass alone because of the easily visible landmarks such as mountains and streams. However, it illustrates how a GPS receiver complements your present navigation skills and provides increased accuracy. The scenario shows when and why you should rely on the receiver alone, and when it is appropriate to use a compass and altimeter. The example also demonstrates that all aspects of a trip cannot be planned in advance. At one point you have to cross a stream, but you have never been there before and do not know the best place to cross, so your plan allows you to search for a crossing place and still stay on course.

The trip's waypoints are marked on the map on the next page. You will arrive by helicopter at the lake near point #1 in late June. You will arrive late in the afternoon and will want to set up camp before the sun goes down, so you use your receiver to calculate the sunrise and sunset. You discover the sun rises at 4:30 am and sets at 9:28 pm. You arrange the helicopter to drop you off two hours before sunset and plan to get up at sunrise the next morning to catch some fish in the lake. The ultimate destination is point #8, but you plan to take two days to get there because you will photograph wildflowers along the way and want to leave time to search for the rare Alpine poppy that grows on Calumet Ridge. The first day's hike will take you from point #1 to #6 where you will camp overnight. The next day you will continue to point #8 where you will join your colleagues for four weeks of botanical studies at a well-established camp. The bush in the area is a dense spruce, so you plan to stay above tree line as much as possible.

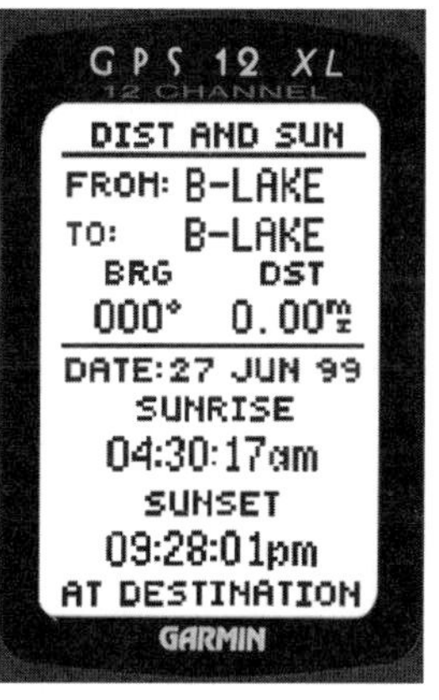

Garmin sunrise/sunset screen for point #1.

Your navigation plan combines your GPS receiver with a compass and altimeter for three reasons. The first is to conserve the receiver's batteries because you will be gone a month and will only have one fresh set for the return trip. The second reason is because part of the trip is through brush and you do not know if the receiver can pick up the satellite signals through the foliage. The third reason is to have a backup navigation method in case a caribou steps on your receiver or something else happens to break it.

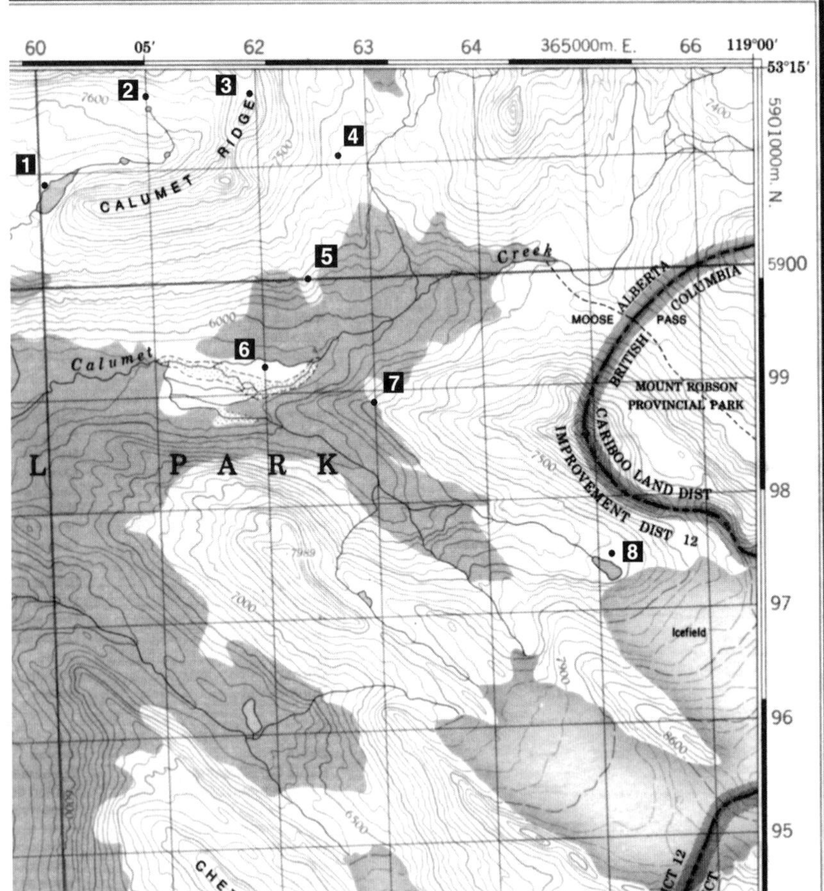

Northeast corner of Mount Robson, British Columbia, Canada (1:50,000 scale).

The terrain determines which tool you will use for navigation once you finally get there, but you have an advance plan all thought out.

- **Travel from point #1 to point #2:**
  Use the GPS receiver the entire way.
  Do not use a compass as you wish to go directly to the lake.
  The receiver will keep you on the right course thereby saving energy and time.
- **Travel from point #2 to point #3:**
  Use the GPS receiver the entire way.
  You want to go directly to the top of the ridge.
  The receiver will keep you on the right course thereby saving energy and time.

- **Travel from point #3 to point #4:**
  Use the compass and altimeter.
  You do not need to get exactly to #4.
  You will be descending steep scree with intermittent cliff bands. In mist this will be tricky and time consuming.
  Use the compass to walk toward #4 until you reach an altitude of 6,800 ft.
- **Travel from point #4 to point #5:**
  Use the altimeter with the GPS receiver occasionally.
  You want to travel almost in a straight line from #4 to #6. Point #5 is situated just before you enter the trees. You want to arrive as close to #5 as possible.
  Use the altimeter to drop gradually to an altitude of 6,400 ft. until you approach the trees.
  Once you are close to the trees, check your position with the receiver. If necessary, use the receiver's Goto function to guide you the last part of the leg to #5.
- **Travel from point #5 to point #6:**
  Use the compass.
  You have to walk through trees and you do not know if your receiver will work, so you plan to rely on your compass.
  Walk the bearing between #5 and #6.
  When you reach the clearing at the creek, use the receiver to verify your position.
- **Travel from point #6 to point #7:**
  Use the compass and altimeter.
  You are not sure where you can cross Calumet Creek as the runoff is high. Follow it upstream until it can be crossed.
  Cross the creek and try to get a new location reading using the receiver.
  If it can lock onto the satellites, get a position fix and walk the bearing from your present position to the tree line at #7.
  If the trees block the satellite signals, travel southeast, true north reference not magnetic, to the tree line.
- **Travel from point #7 to point #8:**
  Use the compass and receiver.
  Contour along at tree line and the stream when you arrive at it, until you reach the upper valley where the terrain levels off.
  Use the receiver to get an occasional fix, but for the most part, follow the stream to the lake.
  In good weather the entire route could be navigated by sight. However, in thick cloud or driving rain the receiver is very useful.

Entering Waypoints

The plan looks feasible, so it is time to enter all the waypoints into the receiver. Even though the receiver is not used to guide you to every waypoint, there are several good reasons to enter them into the receiver's memory. The first is because the receiver automatically calculates the bearing between each point. Of course, you could measure the bearings from the map, but it is so much easier with the receiver, especially when it automatically compensates for declination. The receiver can also calculate the distance between each waypoint. Only the route between #7 and #8 is not direct, so the sum of the distances between each point, as calculated by the receiver, will be close to the actual distance traveled. Because the receiver does not include changes of altitude in its distance calculation, it is impossible to get a complete picture of the hike's difficulty, but the total distance does provide an indication. Many receivers also provide a map screen that shows your present position and any waypoints stored in memory. A final reason to store the coordinates of each point in the memory is to prepare for the possibility of bad weather, which would mandate more reliance on the receiver than anticipated.

Use the map to estimate the UTM coordinates for each point to the closest 50 to 100 m. One hundred meters is one tenth of the UTM square grid shown on the map. The waypoints are represented by the dot next to the numbers on the map. The UTM coordinate for each point, rounded to the nearest 100 m, is given below along with a name:

Point	Zone	Easting	Northing	Name
#1	11 U	3**60**100m.E.	59**00**800m.N.	B-LAKE
#2	11 U	3**61**000m.E.	59**01**600m.N.	S-LAKE
#3	11 U	3**61**900m.E.	59**01**800m.N.	CRIDGE
#4	11 U	3**62**700m.E.	59**01**100m.N.	FLAT
#5	11 U	3**62**400m.E.	59**00**000m.N.	WOODS
#6	11 U	3**62**000m.E.	58**99**300m.N.	STREAM
#7	11 U	3**63**000m.E.	58**98**800m.N.	ORIDGE
#8	11 U	3**65**200m.E.	58**97**500m.N.	CAMP

Before you enter the data, initialize the receiver to the following settings:

- **Map datum: North American Datum 1927 (NAD 27)**
  If your receiver splits NAD 27 into separate settings for Alaska, Canada, Central America, etc., select NAD 27-Canada, otherwise, select NAD 27.
- **Units: Metric**
  The UTM grid is based on the meter, so it is much easier to use the map if the distance is also set to metric units.

- **Coordinate grid: UTM**
- **North setting: Magnetic North**
  A compass is used to get between several points. If the receiver is set to report direction as magnetic bearings, they can be directly dialed into the compass without compensating for the declination.
- **CDI limit: small**
  If the Course Deviation Indicator's tolerance is selectable, set it somewhere between 250 to 500 m. The receiver's Goto function will be used to navigate to points #2 and #3. A CDI limit of 250 to 500 m means you will stray at most 250 or 500 m from course before the receiver will warn you.

At last, the coordinates of each point can be entered into the receiver. The points entered on this trip will be formed into a route, not because the route function will be used, but because the receiver automatically calculates the distance and bearing between each point in a route and you want to know the bearing to use with your compass. Each receiver displays routes differently, but the information that all of them provide is shown below. The desired track is the bearing of the straight line between the two points. The distance is expressed in kilometers because the receiver's units were set to metric.

Name	Point	Desired Track	Distance km
B-LAKE	#1		
		25°	1.2
S-LAKE	#2		
		54°	0.9
CRIDGE	#3		
		108°	1.1
FLAT	#4		
		172°	1.1
WOODS	#5		
		186°	0.8
STREAM	#6		
		93°	1.1
ORIDGE	#7		
		97°	2.6
CAMP	#8		

Each segment in a route is called a leg. The distance of the first five legs of the trip, from B-LAKE to STREAM, is 5.1 km (3.2 mi.), while the total distance, if hiked in a straight line between each point, is 8.8 km (5.5 mi.). The receiver is now ready for the trip and you are ready to test it in the field.

In the Field

The day finally arrives. After a spectacular flight, the helicopter lands near the lake and you disembark with plenty of time to set up camp. Just as planned, you are fishing the lake the next morning at 4:00 am and catch a fine breakfast. When it is time to go, you turn the receiver on, but it seems to take much longer than usual to lock onto the satellites. When a receiver loses its memory, has not been used for a few months or when it is moved more than 300 mi. from the location where it last locked, it can take up to 12.5 minutes for a single channel receiver to get a position fix. The time between turning the receiver on and locking on to the satellites is known as Time To First Fix (TTFF) and was described in Chapter 1. Multichannel receivers still take a while to lock on for the first time, but they are much faster than receivers with fewer channels because they can read the almanac information from several satellites in parallel. The next thing you notice is that the altitude is not even close to the value stated on the map. You knew that the accuracy of the altitude would not be good enough for reliable navigation, so you brought along an electronic altimeter that looks like a watch. From the map, you determine your altitude is about 7,200 ft. and you calibrate your altimeter by setting its altitude to 7,200 ft. Manufacturers of electronic altimeters are listed in the back of the book in the Resources section.

It is time to get going, so you activate the Goto function and tell the receiver to guide you to point #2, which is named S-LAKE. As you walk along, the receiver reports that the desired track, as you already knew from the route information above, is 25° and your track is also 25°. The compass navigation screen has the arrow pointing straight ahead, which means you are right on track.

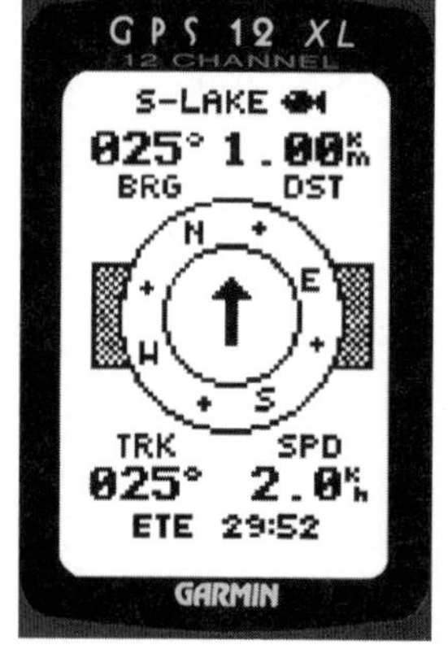

After a while, you start to look around for wildflowers and do not pay much attention to the receiver. Once you finally look, you notice your direction is now 38° and the arrow on the compass screen points to the left, which means you need to turn to the left to head directly to S-LAKE. You also notice that the bearing to get to the lake has changed from 25° to 24°.

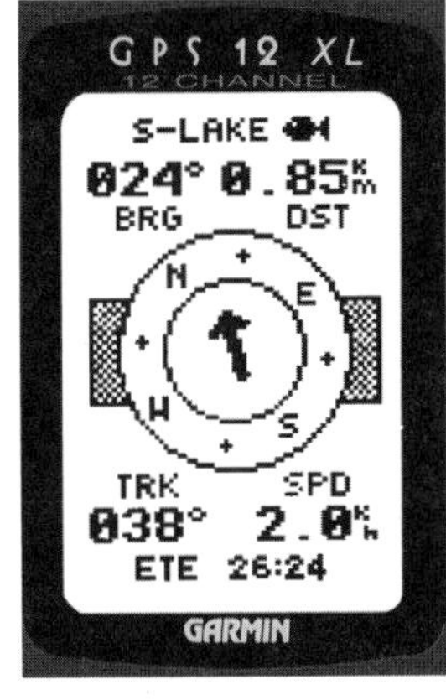

Before you correct your course, you switch to the highway screen and continue walking just to see what happens. After a short distance, the highway screen shows you are off the straight line course by 0.11 km. The diamond shape, above the "T" of ETE, represents your position. It lies to the right of the line going up the highway a distance of 0.11 km. The darker, hatched areas represent being off course by 250 m (820 ft.)—the value set for the CDI limit. You also notice you have wandered so far afield that the bearing to S-LAKE is now 16° and not 24°.

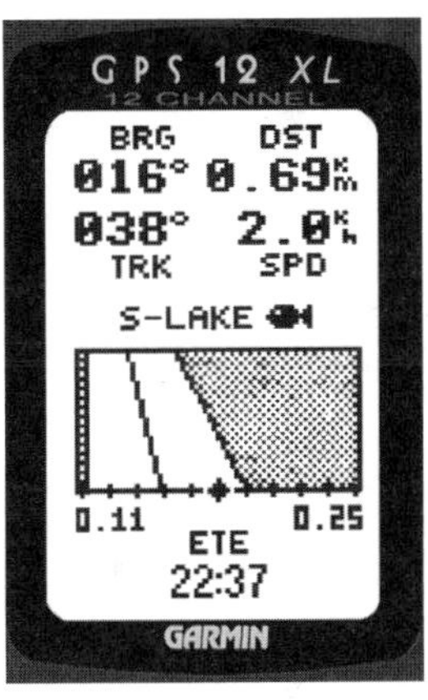

Then you switch to the map screen. It shows both B-LAKE and S-LAKE. Your position, marked by the diamond, is to the right of the straight line between the two points. It is not really a problem, you simply adjust your direction to the new bearing of 16° and keep going. The arrow on the compass display points straight up again and your track (TRK) matches the desired track (BRG), so everything is fine. You note your estimated time en route (ETE) is about 18 minutes, so it will not be long before you arrive at S-LAKE.

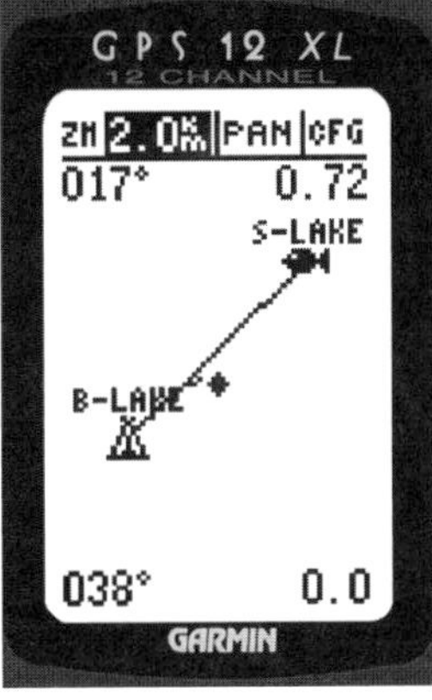

But then you start to wander again. There are more flowers with greater variety than you expected. With a few stops here and a quick picture over there, you soon find you are walking a bearing of 352° and the arrow on the compass screen points to the right, which means you need to follow the arrow to the right to travel toward S-LAKE. So much for going directly to the lake as you had planned. There is just too much to see and do.

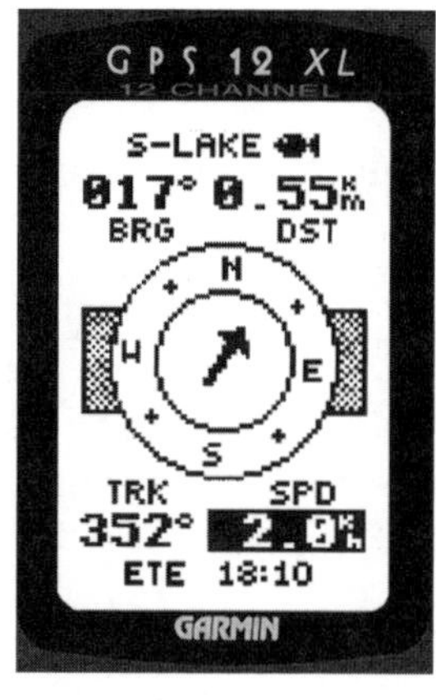

You switch to the highway navigation screen. As you continue to walk the same direction of 352°, your XTE decreases and soon you are only slightly to the right of the highway line. If you continue on your present course, you will cross from the right side of the highway line and be off course to the left with a quickly growing XTE.

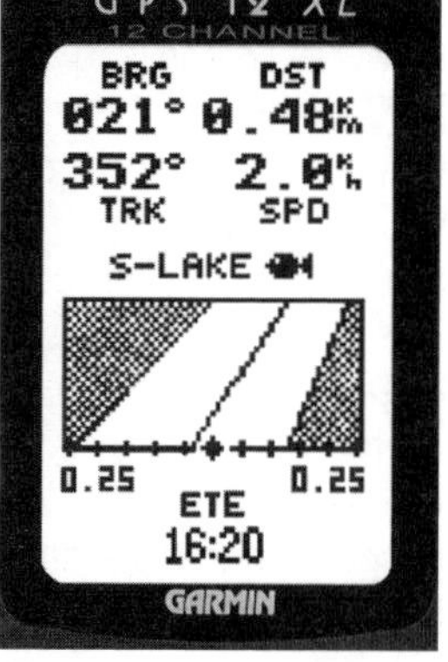

You continue on a bearing of 352° until the diamond is directly on the highway center line. Your XTE is now zero, but the bearing to S-LAKE is now 27°. You change your course to 27° and the highway points straight up. You are now right on course with no CrossTrack Error.

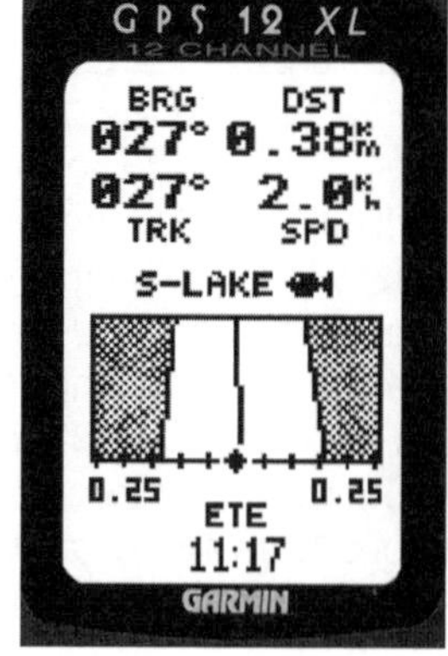

You decide to start paying more attention to the receiver. Within a few minutes, a line appears across the road on the highway display. It represents the destination and you are headed directly toward it.

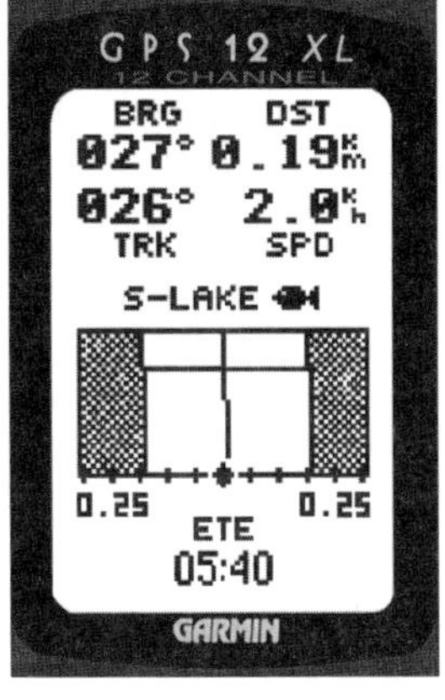

You stay on course and a short while later an alarm beeps along with a flashing message announcing your proximity to the destination. One minute later you arrive at point S-LAKE. You plan to use the Goto function to get from S-LAKE to CRIDGE, so you activate Goto and select CRIDGE as the destination. The navigation screen appears and points the direction.

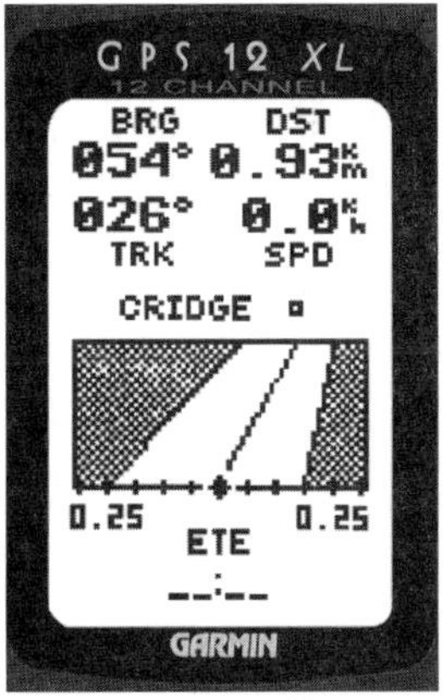

You now have a much better understanding of how to do basic navigation using your GPS receiver. You start by measuring the coordinate of the location you want to visit from a map, entering it into the receiver's memory and activating the Goto navigation function. The receiver guides you to the point along a straight line from your present position to the destination. If you do not travel directly to the destination, the receiver tells you not only how far you are off course, but what correction to make to head directly to the destination again.

You were walking a bearing of 26° when you arrived at S-LAKE, but the bearing to CRIDGE from S-LAKE is 54°, so the highway in the navigation screen points to the right showing that you need to change your course and hike off to the right.

On this leg, you pay a lot more attention to the receiver and you are able to hold the bearing exactly. You are progressing fine until you get about halfway to CRIDGE, when you encounter a very boggy section of ground. Your foot sinks so deep into the mud that you doubt you will be able to make it across without getting stuck, or worse, without falling down. You scan the horizon and notice solid ground far to the left that may provide passage.

You decide to leave your receiver on just to see what the navigation screen says as you take the long detour to get around the mud. To get to the solid ground, you travel at an angle of 90° off the straight line between S-LAKE and CRIDGE, which makes your bearing 324°. The arrow in the compass navigation screen signals a hard right, but there is nothing you can do to follow the course indicated by the receiver as long as you are walking around the mud. You switch to the highway screen to discover that you are so far off course that the middle of the highway does not even appear on the screen and a pop-up sign tells you to steer on a bearing of 90° to get back on course.

At long last you reach the rock and you switch to the map screen to see that you really went a long way off course to get past the mud, but the beauty of the GPS receiver is that you know exactly where you are and the bearing to CRIDGE is now 97°. Taking the detour with compass alone and still getting to CRIDGE would be much more difficult. The rest of the way is fairly flat and it all looks like solid rock, so you should be able to go from where you are directly to the destination. You look at the highway navigation screen and see only a small part of the highway in the upper right corner. The CDI limit is set to 250 m and it is clear you are off by much more than that.

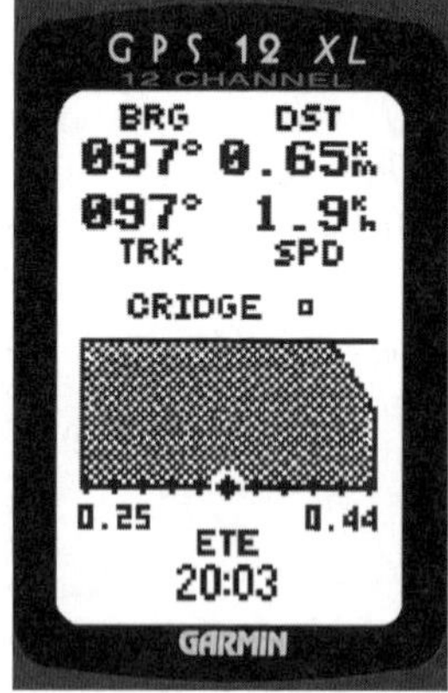

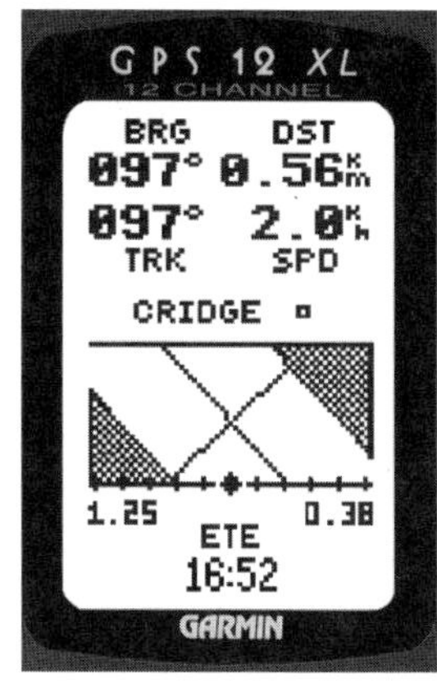

You increase the CDI limit to 1.25 km. The highway stretches off to the left and you can see that you are to the left of the middle of the highway by 0.38 km (0.24 mi.). The line across the road from one checkered side to the other represents the destination. You can see that you are getting closer to the destination, but the highway screen, as it looks right now, does not really tell you if you are on the right course. You can see the destination lies ahead and within the CDI tolerance, but the only way you know you are headed toward #3 is by the fact that your bearing matches the desired track.

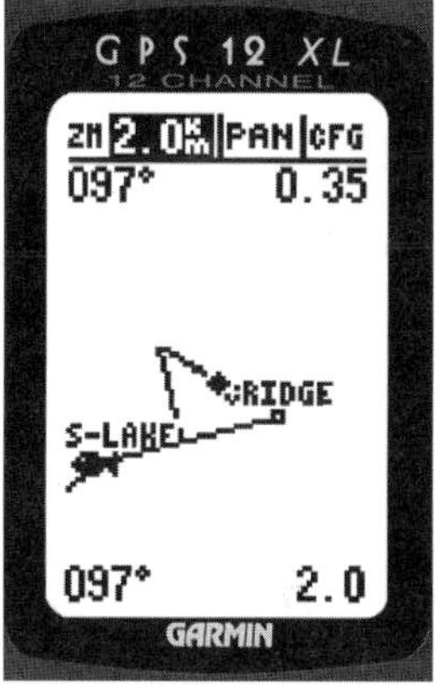

The compass and highway steering screens each play their part. The highway screen shows how close you are to the straight line between two points and the compass screen always tells you which direction to go regardless of your proximity to the direct course. The highway screen is best used in conditions where you have the freedom of movement to always maintain the direct course to the destination, like on water or in the air. The compass screen works well in situations where you have to go around obstacles that lie in the straight line path. Paying attention, you continue from your present position and quickly arrive at point CRIDGE. A look at the map screen also shows the detour you had to make.

The plan to get to FLAT is to walk in the general direction until you reach an altitude of 6,800 ft. The bearing between CRIDGE and FLAT is 108° with reference to the magnetic pole, so you turn the compass housing until the number 108 lines up with the direction arrow, you take a sighting and start to walk. Your altimeter reads 8,180 ft., which corresponds closely to the map. Point CRIDGE does not lie directly on any of the map's altitude lines, but you know it is somewhere between 8,100 ft. and 8,200 ft. The altimeter updates its electronic readout only once every two minutes, but the descent is not steep and the readout is generally up-to-date. When the altimeter reads 6,900 ft., you take a two minute break and when it updates you discover your altitude is 6,860 ft. The receiver tells you that you are within 100 m of FLAT. With your compass, you sight a bearing of 172° and hike keeping an eye on the altimeter. At 6,400 ft. you are close to the trees and the map screen shows your position very close to the waypoint WOODS, point #5 on the map. Next you sight a bearing of 186° and dive into the bush on the way to STREAM. The plant life is a lot thicker than you thought it would be and after a while you begin to wonder if it would have been faster to have gone around the trees and followed the stream up to the STREAM waypoint. You get out the receiver, but it will not lock because the foliage is so dense. There are no clearings where you might get a GPS fix, so you continue as close as possible on the bearing. Soon you are out of the trees, your receiver locks and the Goto function leads you to the STREAM waypoint, #6 on the map, where you spend the night.

The map screen on the receiver shows your position as a diamond and the locations of the other waypoints, but the line showing the direction you traveled between the waypoints does not appear like it did between S-LAKE and CRIDGE because you did not use the receiver to hike those legs.

In the morning you execute your plan by following the stream until you find a good place to cross. Once again the receiver will not lock in the bush, so you follow the contingency plan of walking southeast to get out of the trees, but you need to set your compass to get a sighting. You know the declination is east 22° and southeast in relation to true north is 135°. You repeat the phrase "East is least, West is best" to remind yourself that to convert from true north bearings to magnetic, you subtract east declinations and add west declinations. The declination is east, so you subtract 22° from 135° to get the southeast magnetic bearing for the area of 113°. You set your compass and you do your best to get through the bush as fast as possible. Once you are through, you follow the tree line then the stream directly to the lake without using either the compass, altimeter or the receiver. During the next month at the camp, you use the receiver to record the locations of wildflowers and to explore the icefields to the south and east.

When it is time to meet the helicopter, you use the map to plan a new route back to the lake that avoids traveling through the bush.

6 More UTM and Collecting Water Samples in the Desert

The beauty of the Universal Transverse Mercator (UTM) grid is its ease of use. It is simple to read eastings and northings directly from the map in the field without the aid of a ruler. However, there are elements of the UTM grid that need more explanation, such as the origin of the zone number and letter used in the previous chapter.

The UTM grid splits the world into 60 zones that are each 6° wide. Zone 1 starts at west longitude 180°, which is the same as east longitude 180°, as shown in the figure at the top of page 90.

The zone number increases by 1 for every 6° interval until the entire circumference of the world is covered and the last zone, number 60, is reached. As each zone is peeled off the globe and flattened, it loses its relationship to a sphere, so the UTM coordinates are called false coordinates, unlike the latitude/longitude grid, which is a geographic coordinate. The narrow width of the 6° zones reduces distortion when the strips are flattened. The Transverse Mercator projection provides a uniform grid for the entire earth. UTM maps do not cover the areas

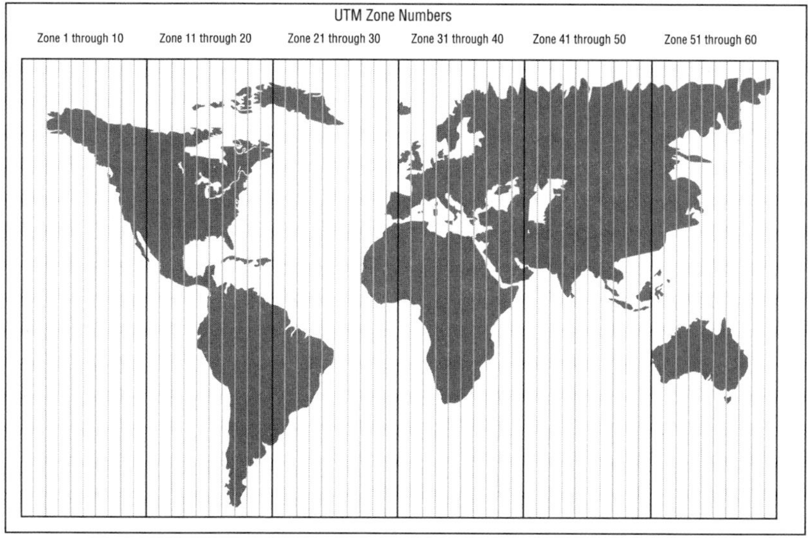

The 60 UTM zones.

around the north pole, above north latitude 84°, and the south pole, below south latitude 80°, because maps of the poles are drawn with the Universal Polar Stereographic (UPS) grid. The UPS grid is discussed in Chapter 14.

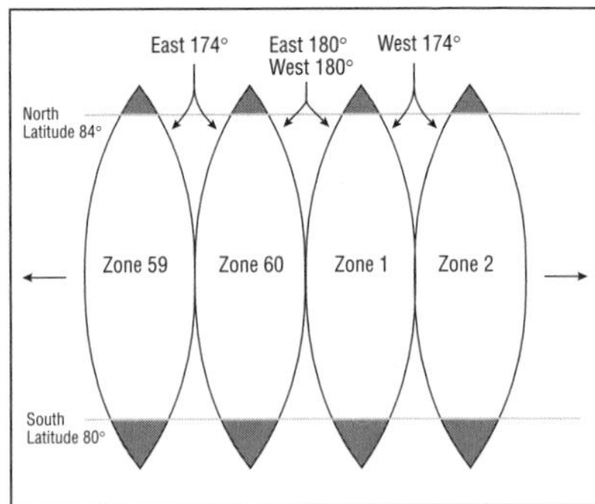

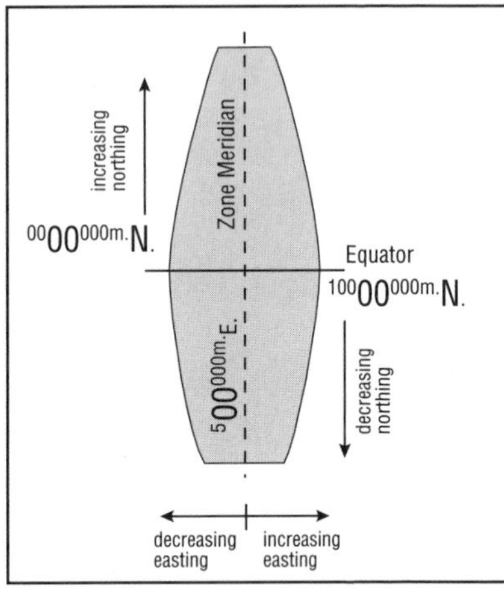

UTM zone meridians.

Each UTM zone has horizontal and vertical reference lines. UTM easting coordinates are measured from the line running down the middle of the zone called the zone meridian. Each 6° zone is split directly in two by the zone meridian. Zone 1, as shown in the figure on the right, is bounded by west longitude 180° on the left and west longitude 174° on the right. The middle of the zone lies on the W 177° longitude line, which is 3° toward the center from each side. Zone 2 is bounded by W 174° and W 168° with its zone meridian located at W 171° and so forth for each zone.

The meridian of every zone is always labeled 5**00**000m.E. An easting greater than 5**00**000m.E. lies east of the meridian, while anything less than that lies to the west. The value of an easting coordinate reveals its distance from the zone meridian in meters. The easting 5**01**560m.E. is 1560 m east of the meridian because it is 1560 greater than 5**00**000m.E.; whereas the easting 4**85**500m.E. is 500,000 - 485,500 = 14,500 m west of the meridian. A valid easting for a given zone will not be less than 1**66**640m.E. or greater than 8**33**360m.E. Easting coordinates always increase as you move east and decrease as you go west.

Northing coordinates are always measured relative to the equator, which is the horizontal reference line in each zone. The northing value assigned to the equator is 00**00**000m.N. for locations north of the equator and 100**00**000m.N. for places south of the equator. You have to know if the northing coordinate lies above or below the equator. The methods for describing if a location is above or below the equator are described below. A northing coordinate for a place north of the equator is simply its distance above the equator. A northing value of 58**97**000m.N. means the point lies

5,897,000 m north of the equator. A valid northing for a position above the equator will lie between 00**00**000m.N. and 93**34**080m.N.

The northing coordinates for locations south of the equator also define the position's distance from the equator, but the equator is assigned the northing value of 100**00**000m.N. The northing value 58**97**000m.N. lies 10,000,000 - 5,897,000 = 4,103,000 m south of the equator. Valid northing coordinates for the southern hemisphere lie between 11**10**400m.N., at the very southern end of a zone and 100**00**000m.N. at the equator. Regardless of whether you are above or below the equator, northing values increase as you go north and decrease as you travel south.

GPS receivers use three different ways to express the hemisphere of a UTM coordinate. The coordinates below all describe the exact same place in zone 11.

11 3**60**100m.E. 59**00**800m.N.
11 N 3**60**100m.E. 59**00**800m.N.
11 U 3**60**100m.E. 59**00**800m.N.

The first coordinate does not visually tell the user the hemisphere. When the coordinate was entered into the receiver, it asked for the hemisphere and recorded it in its memory, but it does not display it on the screen. The "N" in the second coordinate indicates that it lies in the northern hemisphere, whereas an "S" appears in the same place if the location is below the equator. In the third coordinate, the letter "U" is from the Military Grid Reference System (MGRS) and specifies position relative to the equator.

The MGRS divides each UTM zone horizontally into 8° sections and assigns letters as shown in the figure opposite. The letter "U" means your position lies somewhere between north latitude 48° and 56°. The word north starts with "N," which will remind you that in the MGRS system the letter "N" and every letter after it specifies a location above the equator. Do not mistake the letter "S" for the southern hemisphere if your receiver uses the MGRS letters.

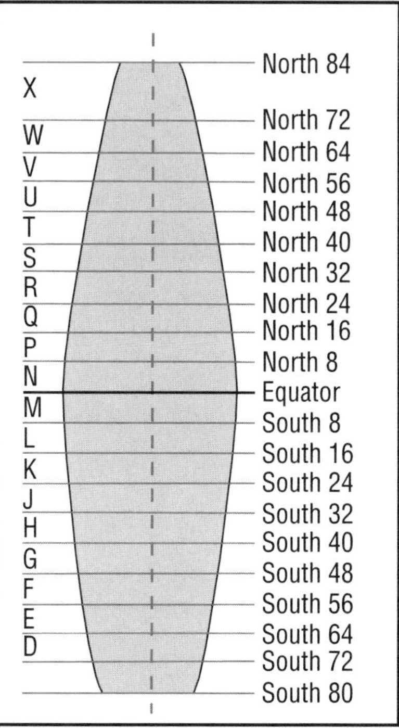

MGRS letters applied to a zone.

UTM Rulers

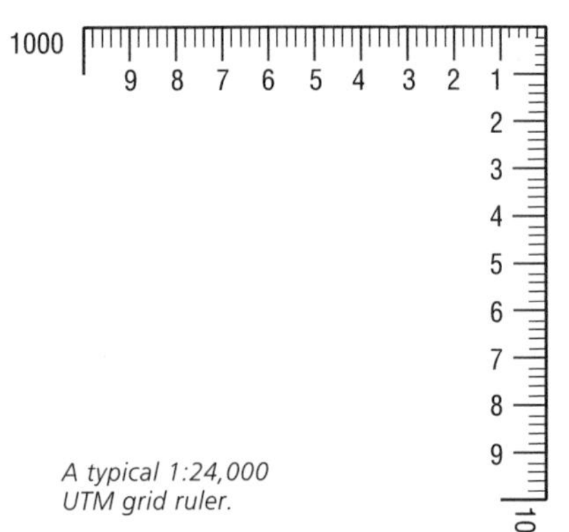

A typical 1:24,000 UTM grid ruler.

The point has been made several times that UTM coordinates on a large scale map can easily be read by the unaided eye. However, there are several rulers that make an already easy-to-use grid even simpler. The source of map rulers is found in the back of the book in the Resources section. The Topo Companion is used in Chapter 8 while the UTM Grid Reader is demonstrated in Chapter 10.

The corner of the ruler is placed at the location where you want to measure the coordinate. The lines of the UTM grid intersect both the vertical and the horizontal scales on the ruler. The figure shows how to measure the UTM coordinate of a building on the USGS Long Branch, NJ topographical map. Note that the horizontal scale is intersected by an easting grid line. The easting coordinate is found by adding the number where the grid crosses the scale to the base number of the easting grid line. In this case the scale is intersected at 480, so the easting coordinate becomes:

5**75**000m.E. + 480 = 5**75**480m.E.

A northing grid line intersects the vertical scale and the northing coordinate is found in the same way as the easting coordinate was found above. In this example, the vertical scale is crossed at 650 by the 44**58**000m.N.grid line. The northing coordinate becomes:

44**58**000m.N. + 650 = 44**58**650m.N.

The final complete coordinate is

18 T 5**75**480m.E. 44**58**650m.N.

The coordinates of any location are measured in the same way.

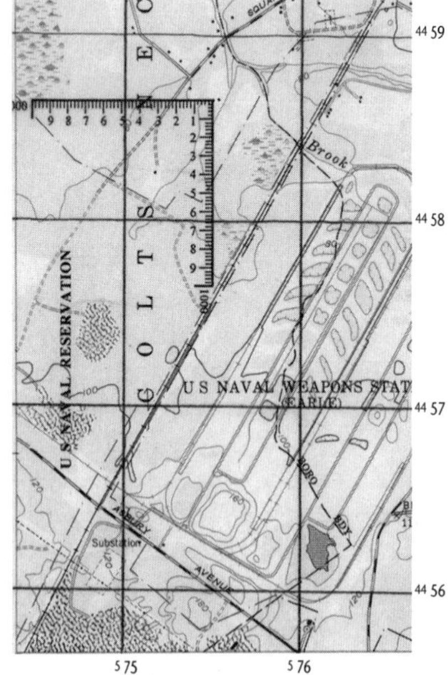

Long Branch, NJ USGS Topo.

Collecting Water Samples in the Desert

Now it is time to take another trip using the UTM grid. This time you need to collect water samples from springs in the Arizona Superstition Wilderness, which is an arid desert. There are distinctive landforms that could help in navigation, but much of the terrain looks similar making it easy to get lost. The GPS receiver will not only keep you from getting lost, it will help you travel the most efficient route.

Motorized vehicles are not usually allowed in the wilderness area, but you have been granted permission to use your four-wheel ATV, which is similar to a motorcycle, because the task needs to be finished fast. The receiver is mounted on the handlebars and is powered by the vehicle's battery, so it will be left on the entire time. The coordinates of all the places you need to go will be entered into the receiver's memory and linked together in a route. When you begin, you will activate the route and the navigation screen will steer you from one site to the next without you even touching the buttons, so you will be able to drive and navigate at the same time. You decide the compass navigation screen is the best for the job because you have to go around obstacles and cannot proceed directly from one point to the next. What you really need to know is the direction from your present position to the destination and the compass screen conveniently provides that information.

Once again, the trip starts with a map. The USGS topographical map of Pinyon Mountain, Arizona (scale 1:24,000) covers the area. Your map is old and does not have the UTM grid printed on it, so you draw the grid lines as indicated by the blue tick marks along the edges. Use a long ruler to line up the tick marks with the same numbers on opposite sides of the map and draw the line all the way across. As in the example of the previous chapter, the grid forms 1 km (0.62 mi.) squares. The zone number, 12, is printed on the map. However, if your receiver requires the MGRS letter to designate the hemisphere and you do not know what it is, you can either find the correct letter from the figure on page 91 or just use the letter "N" to tell the receiver the location is north of the equator. Once you enter the rest of the coordinate, the receiver automatically changes the letter from "N" to "S," which is correct for a receiver that uses the MGRS letter system.

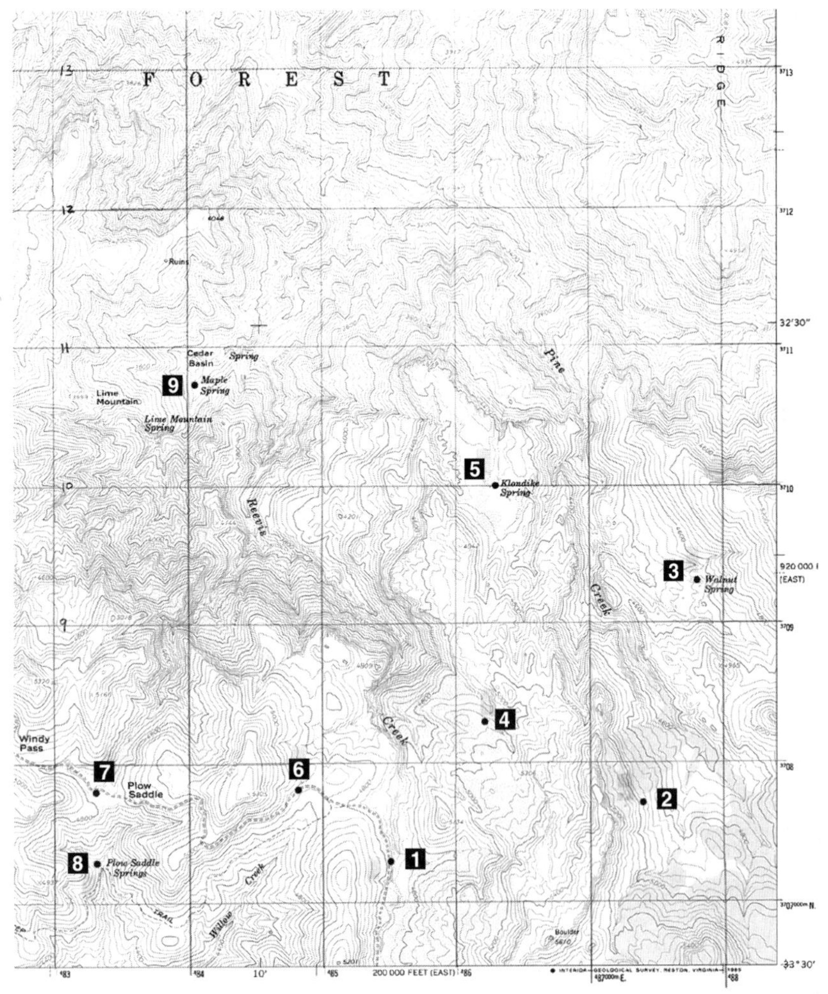

Point	Zone	Easting	Northing	Name
#0	12 S	4**85**410m.E.	37**04**000m.N.	W-00 off map
#1	12 S	4**85**510m.E.	37**07**300m.N.	W-01
#2	12 S	4**87**390m.E.	37**07**710m.N.	W-02
#3	12 S	4**87**800m.E.	37**09**300m.N.	W-03
#4	12 S	4**86**210m.E.	37**08**300m.N.	W-04
#5	12 S	4**86**300m.E.	37**10**000m.N.	W-05
#6	12 S	4**84**810m.E.	37**07**800m.N.	W-06
#7	12 S	4**83**300m.E.	37**07**800m.N.	W-07
#8	12 S	4**83**300m.E.	37**07**290m.N.	W-08
#9	12 S	4**84**050m.E.	37**10**740m.N.	W-09

As always, you must set the receiver properly before entering the waypoints.

- **Map datum: North American Datum 1927 (NAD 27)**
  If your receiver splits NAD 27 into separate settings for Alaska, Canada, Central America, etc., select NAD 27-CONUS (Continental US), otherwise, select NAD 27.
- **Units: Metric**
  The UTM grid is based on the meter and it is much easier to relate distances to the map if the receiver reports them in meters, so set the receiver's units to metric.
- **Coordinate grid: UTM**
- **North setting: Magnetic North**
  A compass will not be used to navigate, so set the north reference to true north so the bearings relate to the map.
- **CDI limit: Small**
  The receiver will guide you to all points, but you decided it does not matter how far you are off the straight line course just as long as you know the direction from your present position to the next point. Set the CDI limit to 5 km, so that just in case you decide to look at the highway steering screen, it will still look like a road even if you are a long way off course.

Using the map, you choose waypoints leading to the springs over terrain that looks passable with the ATV. On your ruler, you find the 1:24K UTM scale and measure the coordinates. The ruler makes it easy to get the coordinates to an accuracy of about 10 m (32.8 ft.). The coordinates for the numbers shown on the map along with their waypoint name are listed on page 94. Waypoint #0 lies on the road south of #1 just off the map. There are additional springs in the area that need testing, but the waypoints listed are enough for a morning's work.

The route for this trip is different from the previous chapter because some waypoints are used more than once. For example, the planned route takes you from #2 to #3 then back to #2 before continuing to #4. Each type of receiver displays routes differently, but the information they all provide is shown below. The desired track is the bearing between two adjacent points. When reading the bearing, remember the north reference was set to true north.

Name	Point	Desired Track	Distance km
W-00	#0		
		2°	3.3
W-01	#1		
		78°	1.9
W-02	#2		
		14°	1.6
W-03	#3		
		194°	1.6
W-02	#2		
		297°	1.3
W-04	#4		
		3°	1.7
W-05	#5		
		288°	2.4
W-09	#9		
		108°	2.4
W-05	#5		
		183°	1.7
W-04	#4		
		250°	1.5
W-06	#6		
		270°	1.5
W-07	#7		
		180°	0.5
W-08	#8		
		0°	0.5
W-07	#7		

The total trip as planned from W-00 to W-07, including all the back-and-forth between the waypoints, is 21.9 km (13.6 mi.). The altitude does not change much over the route, so the distance calculated by the receiver will be close to the actual distance traveled if the terrain allows you to travel directly between the waypoints.

The navigation plan is to use the receiver the entire trip because it will help you finish much faster than if you navigated with compass alone. You will travel on the road shown on the map wherever possible. When traveling from W-00 to W-01 and from W-06 to W-07, stay on the road regardless of where the navigation screen points. When you arrive at W-01, turn off the road and follow the direction indicated by the receiver as closely as possible and do the same when you arrive at W-07. You will carry the map and compass for backup navigation just in case something happens to the receiver.

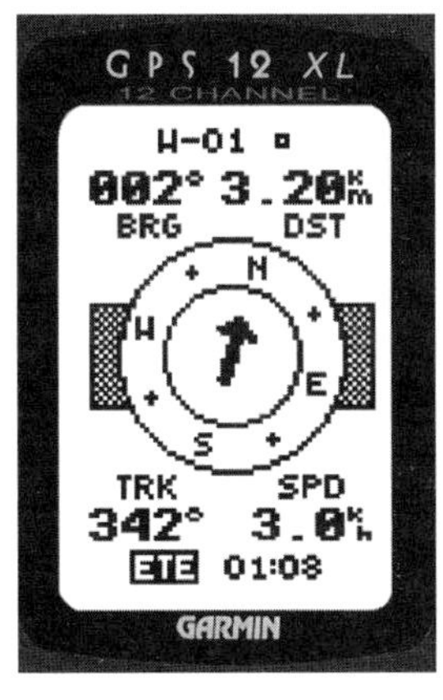

The day of the trip arrives and after a good night's rest at W-00, you start the ATV and turn the receiver on. The sun is just rising over the horizon making the saguaro cacti cast long shadows. It is going to be a scorcher of a day because there are no clouds in the sky. You find the route where you stored the waypoints and activate it. As you start up the road, the arrow on the compass navigation screen points straight up, which means you are right on course, but soon the road curves to the left. Your direction changes to 342° and the arrow turns slightly to the right showing that you need to turn to the right to go directly to W-01.

You ignore the arrow because you know you need to stay on the road until you reach W-01. The road curves to the right and the compass arrow swings left showing you how to return to the desired course, but you ignore it and press on. Within 0.25 km (0.16 mi.) of W-01, a message flashes on the screen that you are approaching the waypoint, so you slow down and get ready to follow the steering arrow. As soon as you arrive at W-01, the arrow on the navigation screen swings hard to the right and the bearing you are supposed to follow changes to 78°. You turn to the right and begin to go off the road toward W-02. You are able to maintain almost a direct course until you are about halfway there when you notice the terrain to the right is much flatter than the route you planned. You stop to consult the map and decide to veer to the right until the bearing to get to W-02 is 0°, which will put you due south of the waypoint. Then you will turn directly north to get to W-02 before heading off to W-03. You follow the easiest path possible and note your new bearing is about 106°. You had thought about moving W-02 farther south when you were planning the route, but you decided to put it where it is because you thought you could make it up the incline. Now that you are in the field, you see that the southerly route is better. You keep an eye on the bearing to W-02 and when it reaches 0° you make a hard left turn until the arrow in the compass points directly up showing you are headed directly to W-02.

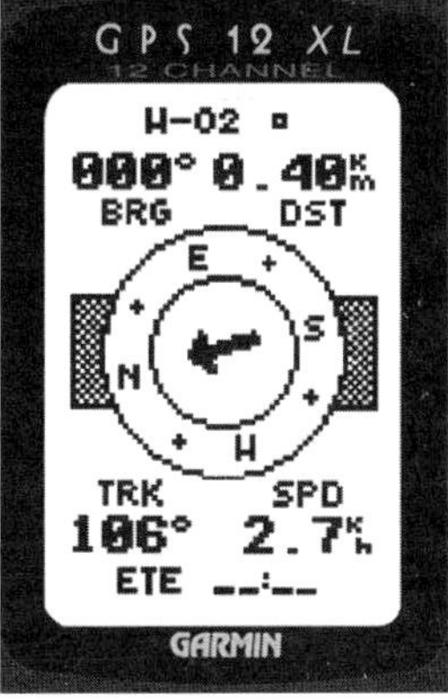

You cannot resist looking at the map screen, so you stop to see the map drawn by the receiver. This shows your present position, a diamond shape, directly south of W-02. It is exactly what you wanted.

Once you arrive at W-02, the receiver automatically starts steering toward W-03, so the bearing you are supposed to follow changes to 14° and the arrow points to the right. As you adjust your course by turning to the right, the arrow in the compass moves until it points straight up and your track is 14°. A third of the way to W-03, you see that the terrain to the east is more easily passable, so you do the exact same thing as before: you will veer to the right until the bearing to get to W-03 is 0°, then you will turn directly north to get to the waypoint. You turn to the right and watch the screen occasionally until the bearing to W-03 is 0°, then you drive due north. A quick look at the receiver's map show your deviation from course to be small and W-03 lies directly ahead. Within minutes you arrive at Walnut Spring and take the necessary samples.

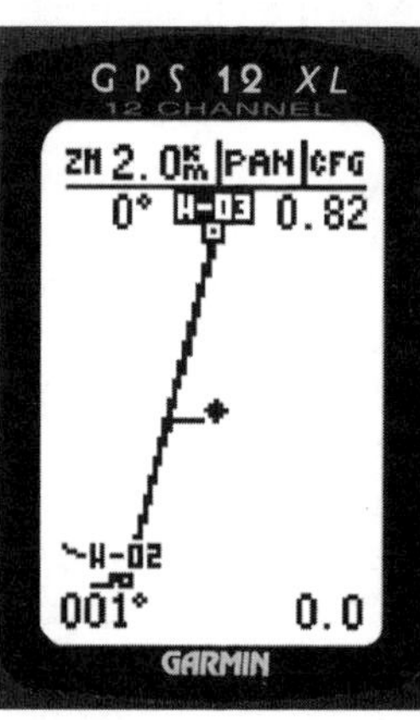

The receiver is already pointing the way back to W-02 at 194°, but you head due south on a bearing of 180° until the terrain looks passable, then you turn to follow the arrow to W-02. Until you turn to travel directly toward W-02, the arrow increasingly points more to the right. When you arrive at W-02, the receiver directs you to take a right turn to go toward W-04, but you know by looking at the terrain and also from the trip up that you should go due south of W-02 to where the terrain is more level, then turn toward W-04. For now you ignore the arrow and watch your own bearing to make sure it is 180°.

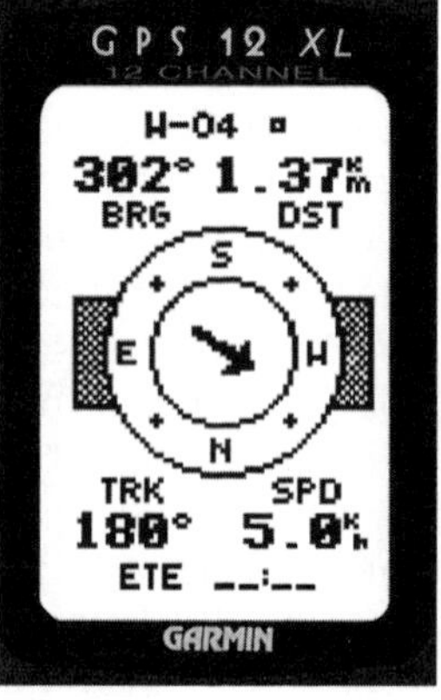

The receiver shows the distance to W-04 increasing, but as soon as you are off the small hill and can finally turn directly toward W-04, the bearing is 311° and you are 1.45 km (0.9 mi.) away. When you arrive at W-04, the receiver points the way to W-05. You adjust your course to 3° and notice that it is going to be a straight shot to Klondike Spring at W-05 because the terrain is fairly level.

After collecting water at the spring, you notice the terrain to W-09 is far rougher than you thought it would be from the map. You take another look at the map and decide to head due west to just past Reevis Creek, then turn almost due north to get to W-09. You will not be watching the compass arrow very closely until the bearing to W-09 is about 350°, but the receiver's map has been very useful during these maneuvers, so you decide to follow the terrain of least resistance and track your progress on the map screen. You travel for a while, then you look at the map. This shows you were headed west, then almost southwest. You are making progress because you are closer to W-09. The terrain is still passable, so you keep going.

When the bearing to W-09 is about 350°, you turn and head directly for the waypoint. Once you arrive at the waypoint, you look at the map to see the loop you had to make to get there.

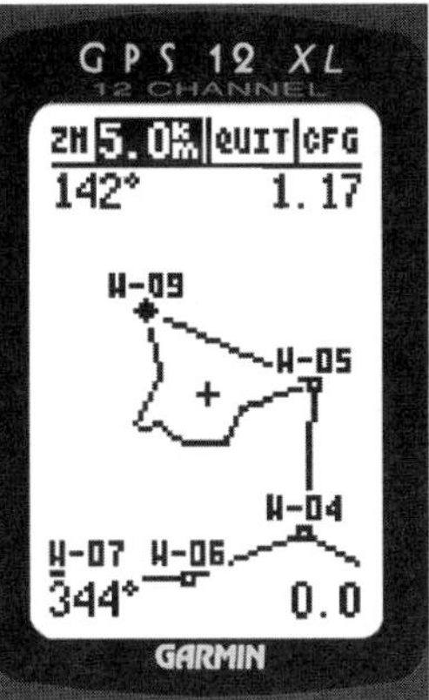

After you get the water sample from Maple Spring, the receiver is already pointed back to waypoint W-05. You want to take the same loop to return, so you use the receiver's map to follow the same route back. On the trip to W-09, the receiver's map was set to keep north at the top of the screen, but for the trip back you set it to display your direction of travel at the top. This "track up" mode allows you to easily see where you need to turn to stay on the track already drawn on the map.

The path from W-05 back to W-04 is a straight shot over easy terrain, so you switch back to the compass navigation screen and soon find yourself at W-04. The receiver now points directly to W-06. After surveying the terrain, you look again at the map to see that you have to cross Reevis Creek to get to W-06. The planned route might be a bit steep compared to the terrain farther south, but you decide to follow the receiver until you get to the creek and if you cannot cross there, you will travel parallel to the creek until the ground levels enough to cross, then you will follow the receiver's directions straight to W-06. When you get to the creek, you find the sides are really steep, so you drive alongside it in a southward direction until it becomes relatively flat and easy to cross. You look at the receiver's map and see you are almost headed straight for W-01. You could continue to W-01 using the receiver's map screen for guidance then take the road to W-06, but you decide to cross the wash and go directly to W-06. The arrow on the compass navigation screen shows the direct route, so you change your course to 272° and drive straight there. The plan is to take the road from W-06 to W-07, so once on the road, you stay on it regardless of where the compass arrow points until you arrive at W-07. From W-07 you follow the receiver's steering arrow directly to W-08 and take a sample from Plow Saddle Springs. The receiver then directs you back to W-07. The route is now complete, so you deactivate it. You do not really need the receiver any more because all you need to do is to follow the road back to your camp, but just so you know how long it will take to arrive, you activate the Goto function, select W-00 and watch the estimated time en route (ETE) as you zoom back to your tent.

7 GPS Navigation in a Whiteout

In the previous two chapters, you learned how to use a GPS receiver along with a map to plan your route. Another practical use of GPS technology is as a backup means of navigation in poor weather. You plan to take some friends to the top of Mount Columbia, located in the Canadian Rockies. To get to the peak, you need to cross the Columbia Icefields, which lie at an altitude of 3,038 to 3,353 m (10,000 to 11,000 ft.) and like any high mountain area, they are subject to whiteout conditions that make navigation extremely difficult. Clouds do not affect the satellite signals, so it is a perfect application for a GPS receiver.

Most people who climb Mount Columbia set up a base camp on the northeast side of the icefield. If the weather is bad when they arrive, they stay in camp and wait it out, but if it is clear they carry only their survival gear and hurry across the icefield to the peak. Even though it is clear on the trip to the mountain, it is not unusual for clouds to come up out of the valleys very quickly, resulting in whiteout conditions for the return trip. Preparations for finding your way back in conditions of poor visibility are made before leaving camp by sticking bamboo wands in the snow perpendicular to the proposed return route. The normal procedure for navigation in a whiteout, without a receiver, is to use a compass and dead reckoning. It is no easy task to travel 7 to 8 km (4.4 to 5 mi.) across an almost flat icefield in zero visibility. If your navigation is accurate, you cross the icefield, hit your wands and follow them back to camp. Navigation can be so difficult that parties are forced to spend a cold night dug into the snow while they wait for the morning sun to burn off the cloud.

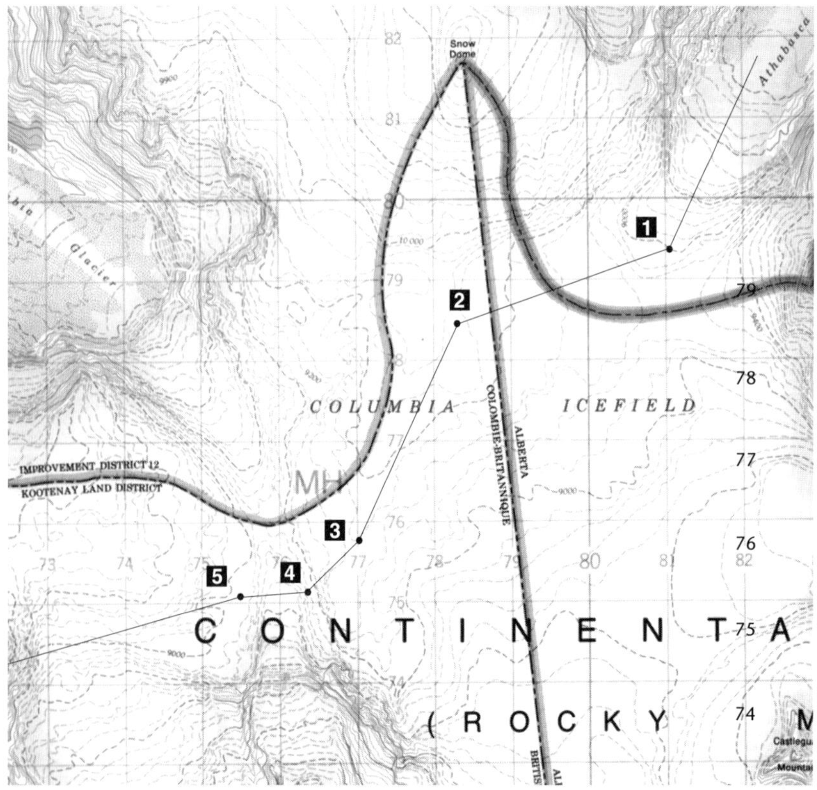

The first day of the trip, you will ski up the Athabasca Glacier to the Columbia Icefield via a snow ramp up a headwall between large crevasses and set up base camp. The camp is located where it is easy to find the top of the ramp even in poor weather. The second day you will cross the flat, featureless icefield to the base of the summit where you leave your skis and climb to the top. On the way to the peak, you have to cross a "trench," in the icefield formed where two heavily crevassed glaciers drop away on each side. In order to easily and safely cross, it is critical to find the highest point of the trench where the crevasses are the smallest. You have made the trip several times before and are intimately familiar with the way, so you do not enter waypoints in advance. However, you will store critical points during the trip to the peak just in case you need to use the receiver to retrace your steps in bad weather.

The day of the trip arrives and after a long drive you arrive at the staging area. You take a map along even though you are familiar with the route and of course you have your compass, just in case the receiver fails to perform. Before you leave your vehicle, you initialize the receiver to the following settings:

- **Map datum: North American Datum 1927 (NAD 27)**
  If your receiver splits NAD 27 into separate settings for Alaska, Canada, Central America, etc., select NAD 27-Canada, otherwise, select NAD 27.
- **Units: Metric**
  The UTM grid is based on the meter and it is easier to relate to the map if the receiver reports distances in meters, so set the receiver's units to metric.
- **Coordinate grid: UTM**
- **North setting: Magnetic North**
  A compass may be used to get between points. If the receiver is set to report bearings between points as magnetic bearings, they can be directly dialed into the compass without additional compensation for the declination.
- **CDI limit: Small**
  If the Course Deviation Indicator's tolerance is selectable, set it somewhere between 250 to 500 m. The receiver's Goto function will be used to navigate if there is bad weather. A CDI limit of 250 to 500 m means you will stray at most 250 or 500 m from course before the receiver will warn you.

After you initialize your receiver, you return it to your backpack and clip on your skis. You do not bother to mark the car's location because there is no difficulty finding your way down the Athabasca Glacier back to the staging area even in horrible weather. You and your friends start off and in no time reach the top of the ramp at the headwall, which is the first point you need to record. You need a breather here anyway. You get the receiver out of your backpack and after it locks onto the satellites, you record the first point of the trip:

#1 11U 4**81**019m.E. 57**79**434m.N. RAMP

From the top of the ramp, you ski onto the Columbia Icefield to a flat area just south of the Snowdome. You set up camp and place a line of wands for tomorrow's trip as a safety precaution. You also record the position of your camp:

#2 11U 4**78**327m.E. 57**78**541m.N. CAMP

The rising sun finds you and your friends equipped and starting across the icefield. The weather is beautiful. As a precaution you have an extra set of batteries in your backpack. If the weather turns bad and you need to use your receiver to get back, you will have to use the energy-eating backlight. You also carry an extra bundle of wands. The error introduced by Selective Availability will get you close to the best part of the trench, but not exactly where you need to cross, so you will place wands at both ends of the trench and along the best passage to make the crossing easier. The second day of your trip is going as planned and you make rapid progress to the top of the icefield where you make a right turn to head to the trench. You take a short break and record the turning point as another waypoint:

#3 11U 4**77**016m.E. 57**75**836m.N. R-TURN

Soon you reach the trench, where you spend some time finding the narrowest part. Once you find the best place, you strategically place wands and mark it as another waypoint:

#4 11U 4**76**328m.E. 57**75**207m.N. TREN-E

As you cross the trench, you continue to place wands to indicate the best passage. It dawns on you that the wands increase the accuracy of the GPS receiver in the same way that Differential GPS works. When you encounter a wand, you know exactly where you are even if the receiver tells you differently. The receiver can lead you close, but the wands provide the increased accuracy necessary for a safe crossing. The important function the receiver performs is to get you close enough to the trench that you can find the wands—something you would not dare try with compass alone. Once on the other side of the trench, you record another waypoint:

#5 11U 4**75**542m.E. 57**75**023m.N. TREN-W

Now both the east and west sides of the trench are marked. If a whiteout occurs, the receiver will be able to help you enter and cross the narrowest part of the trench. You have to travel 5 km (3.1 mi.) and an elevation gain of 610 m (2,001 ft.) before you reach the base, so you put the receiver away and start off again. When you reach the base of Mount Columbia, you leave your skis and mark their position:

#6 11U 4**70**518m.E. 57**74**345m.N. BASE-C

You climb the last 370 m (1,214 ft.) to the summit pyramid, taking care not to fall through the double cornice on the summit ridge. At the top, you enjoy the marvelous view of the surrounding mountains, with Mount Robson a glistening white fang to the north. You take the receiver out of your backpack and mark the summit—not that you will need it for navigation, but as a memento of being at one of the most gorgeous places on earth:

#7 11U 4**69**906m.E. 57**74**327m.N. SUMMIT

You decide to make a route of the return trip, just to see the distances and bearings between the waypoints. The map shows all the waypoints except the last two. The information given from the route function is shown below. The distances are in kilometers and the bearings have a magnetic reference.

Name	Point	Desired Track	Distance km
SUMMIT off map	#7		
		68°	0.6
BASE-C off map	#6		
		62°	5.1
TREN-W	#5		
		56°	0.8
TREN-E	#4		
		27°	0.9
R-TURN	#3		
		5°	3
CAMP	#2		
		51°	2.8
RAMP	#1		

You add up the distances of the journey's legs from SUMMIT to CAMP and get 10.4 km (6.5 mi.). You do not really plan on using the route function to get back, but you never really knew the exact distance from the base camp to the peak.

When you look up from the receiver, you notice the cloud from the valley below creeping up the glacier toward the icefield. It has already filled the trench, which means it is time to get moving—fast. You put the receiver into your backpack and start with your friends down to the base. By the time you reach your skis, you are in a thick cloud and the wind is filling your upward track with blowing snow, but you are not worried: With the receiver guiding the way, it will be a record run back to camp and not a cold night out.

Once your skis are on, you pull out the receiver, get it locked on, turn on the backlight for easier reading in the poor light and press the Goto function. You need to get from the base to the west end of the trench, so you select TREN-W as the waypoint you are going to. You select the compass steering screen that reports your current heading and the necessary heading to reach the trench. It will be just like using a compass, as you have done several times in the past, but better because you will always know the correct bearing to get to your destination even if you move off course.

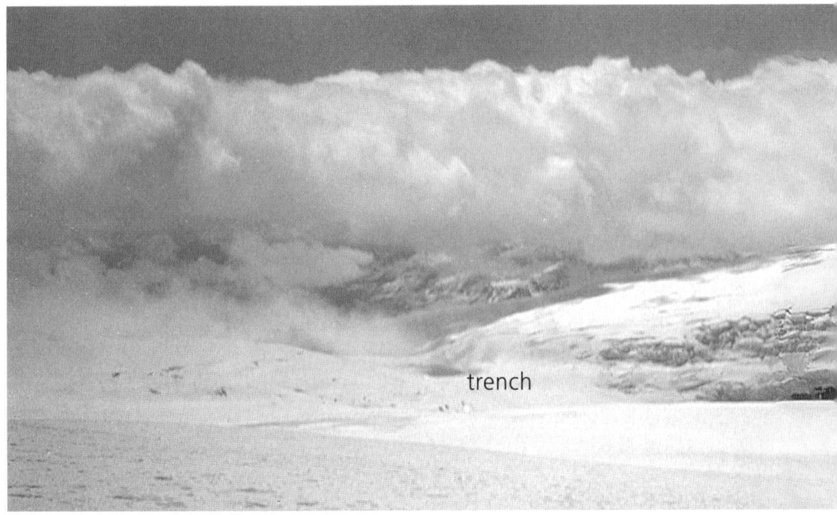

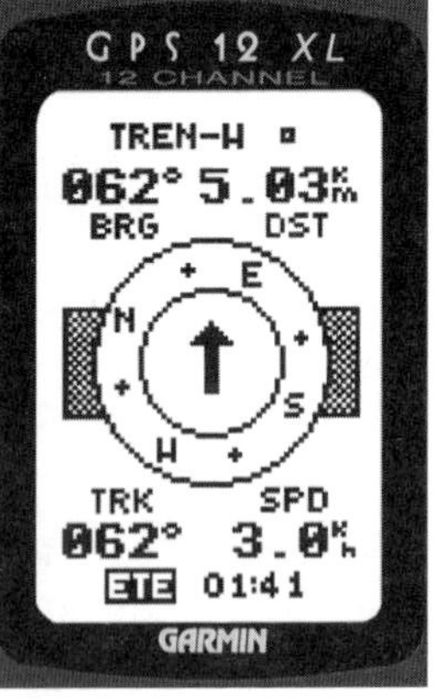

The steering screen shows the trench at a bearing of 62°, so you set course to match the bearing.

You look at the estimated time en route (ETE) at the bottom of the screen. At your present speed and if you stay on course, it will take about an hour and 40 minutes to get to the trench. As you cautiously ski down, you find that you can stay on course reasonably well, so you turn off the backlight and only turn it on for an occasional quick look to make sure you are still on course. It seems as though your plan to get back to camp using the receiver will work but only if you have enough batteries. Even though you have some spares, you know you had better conserve, just to be sure. Each time you look at the steering display, if your present course does not match the correct course, you check the highway steering screen to see your CrossTrack Error.

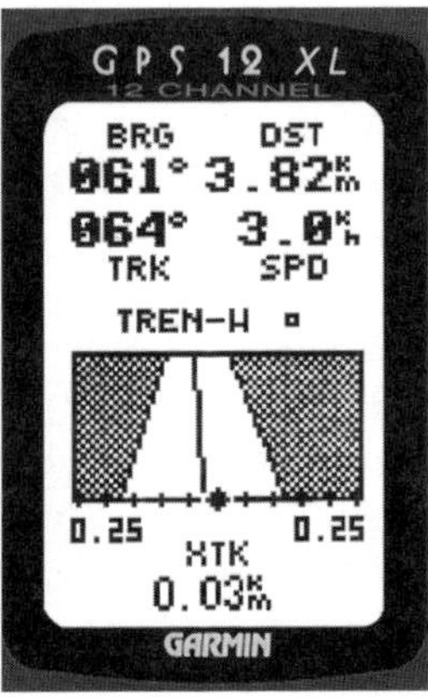

You can see you are 0.03 km (30 m or 98.4 ft.) to the right of the direct line to TREN-W and the highway is pointing to the left telling you to steer left to get on course. You are ecstatic because, before owning a receiver, you have never stayed so close to the correct bearing in a whiteout, and better than staying on the correct bearing, you also know exactly how far you have strayed and

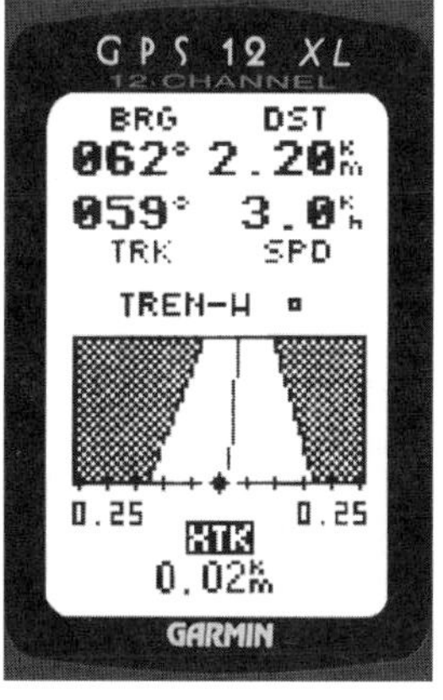

what to do to get back on course. You adjust your bearing to 61° and continue on.

The next time you look at the receiver, you notice you have strayed again, but this time you are to the left of the direct course by 0.02 km (20 m or 65.6 ft.).

As you have been off course for a while, the bearing to TREN-W has changed from 61° to 62°, so you steer slightly to the right to follow the new bearing. You also notice it is just over 2 km (1.2 mi.) to the trench—something you would have never known without a GPS receiver. You press on, making occasional course adjustments until finally, two hours after leaving the base of Mount Columbia, you arrive at the west end of the trench and find your wands.

You turn the receiver off while you rope in and prepare to cross. When you are ready to go, you turn the receiver on and activate the Goto function. You select the TREN-E waypoint. The steering screen shows the bearing to be 56°, so you leave the receiver on and watch the screen as you adjust your course to match. As you enter the trench, your pace really slows and you notice the receiver no longer gives you an ETE, but you know it can still accurately calculate the bearing from your present position to the other side of the trench. This juncture is critical, so you leave the backlight on and watch the screen continuously all while feeling for wands. Occasionally you check the map screen to verify your overall position in the trench and your course.

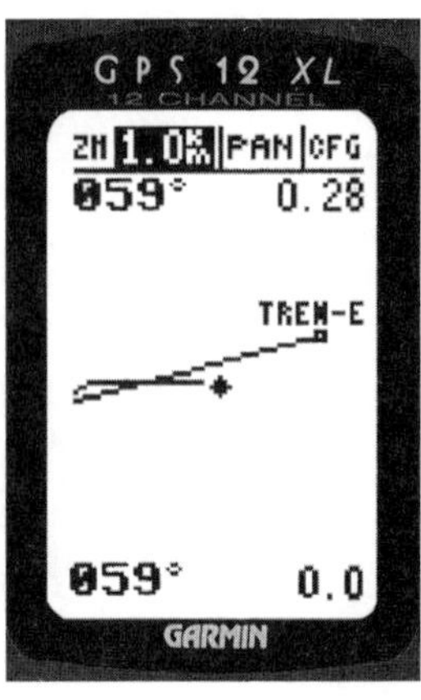

The first time you check the receiver's map, you see you are slightly to the left of the direct course. You also notice the bearing to TREN-E has changed to 59°. You are not sure if you walked off course or if Selective Availability made it seem like you did. You continue and adjust your course to the new bearing of 59°. When you hit your first line of wands, your confidence in the receiver increases. After traveling a short while, you check the map screen to see you have veered from the left of the straight course to the right.

You quickly change to the highway steering screen and see that your CrossTrack Error is 0.06 km (60 m or 196.9 ft.).

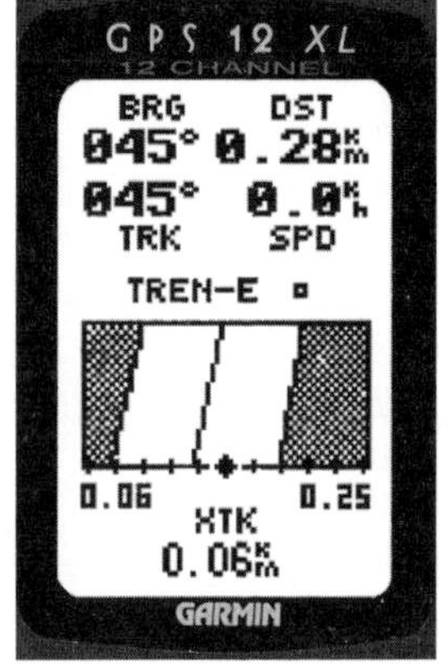

You are farther off course than you like or need to be and part of the problem is your own lack of vigilance. The bearing to the end of the trench is now 45°, so you watch the receiver more closely. A slow hour later, you find all the wands you placed and the receiver's map indicates you have successfully made it through the trench to the TREN-E waypoint.

This is a first. You have never gotten so far in such poor visibility and you would not have been able to do it without the combination of the receiver and wands. Now it is nearly a straight shot back to camp. You take off your ropes and activate the Goto function to lead you to R-TURN. The steering screen responds to your request and shows the bearing to be 27°. You start off, keeping an eye on the receiver.

Your vigilance on the leg to R-TURN results in a relatively quick trip of 40 minutes. After resting, you change the batteries and activate the Goto function to lead you to CAMP. Watching the receiver you adjust your course to 5°. The receiver calculates an ETE of approximately one hour at your present speed. With a bit of weaving back and forth to stay on track, you hit your wands an hour and 15 minutes later. Yeah! It is going to be a warm night. You follow the wands back to camp and as you unzip the flap to your tent, you discover someone else is already in it! They hit your wands and are taking refuge from the weather in your camp. You make a note in your journal: "Bring extra receivers to sell at the staging area."

8 Latitude, Longitude and a Kayaking Trip

The Latitude/Longitude Grid

The latitude/longitude grid is familiar to most people. It is printed on almost all maps even if it is not the primary grid. If you travel in a part of the world where your receiver does not have the local grid, do not worry because the map probably has latitude and longitude. The latitude/longitude grid is based on a sphere. The figure shows how the globe is divided by the lines of latitude and longitude.

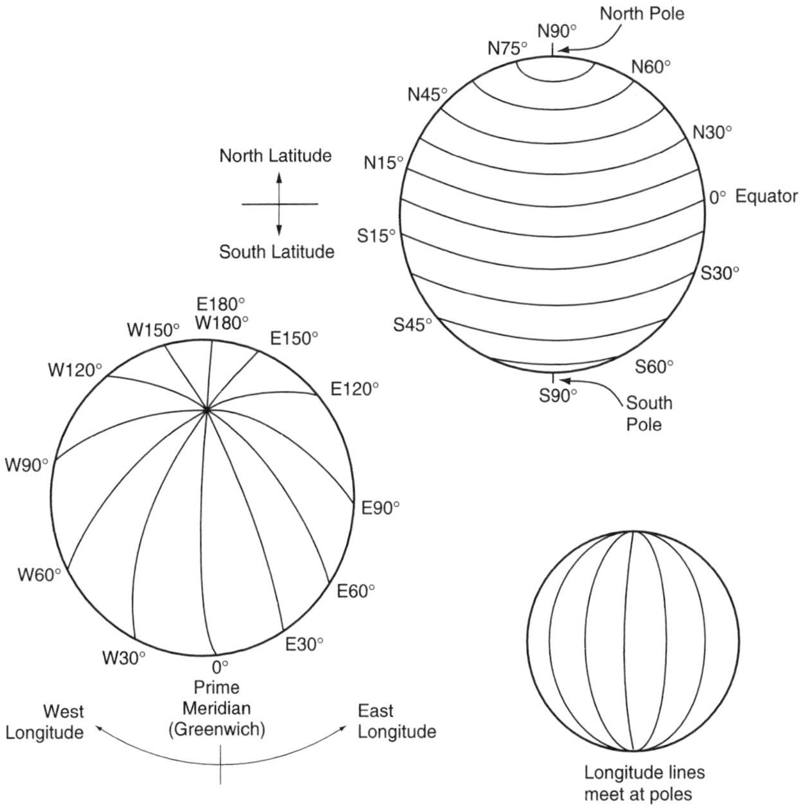

Lines of latitude go around the world parallel to the equator. Lines of longitude go from pole to pole. On a map, latitude lines are horizontal and longitude lines are vertical. If you need a review of degrees, minutes and seconds and how they relate to each other, turn to Chapter 16. Here are some interesting facts about latitude and longitude:

Latitude

- Lines parallel to the equator.
- Hemispheres designated North (N) and South (S).
  Equator is 0°.
  North pole is N 90°.
  South pole is S 90°.
- May be expressed in three formats.
  Hemisphere degrees minutes seconds: S 38° 27' 54".
  Hemisphere degrees minutes: N 23° 27.3'.
  Hemisphere degrees: N 58.385°.
- 1° of latitude is 111.12 km (69.05 mi.).
- 1' is one nautical mile (1.85 km, 1.15 mi.).

Longitude

- Lines run from pole to pole.
- Greenwich, England is the Prime Meridian.
- Hemispheres designated West (W) and East (E) of the Prime Meridian.
  Prime Meridian is 0°.
  International Date Line is W 180° (same as E 180°).
- May be expressed in three formats.
  Hemisphere degrees minutes seconds: E 140° 54' 09".
  Hemisphere degrees minutes: W 67° 28.75'.
  Hemisphere degrees: E 86.824°.
- Longitude lines converge at the poles.
- 1° of longitude is 111.12 km (69.05 mi.) only at the equator.
- 1' is not one nautical mile except at the equator.

Latitude and Longitude Coordinates

- Coordinate usually written hemisphere latitude, hemisphere longitude.
- N 47° 19.56', E 102° 42.84'.
- Called geographic coordinate because it is based on a sphere.

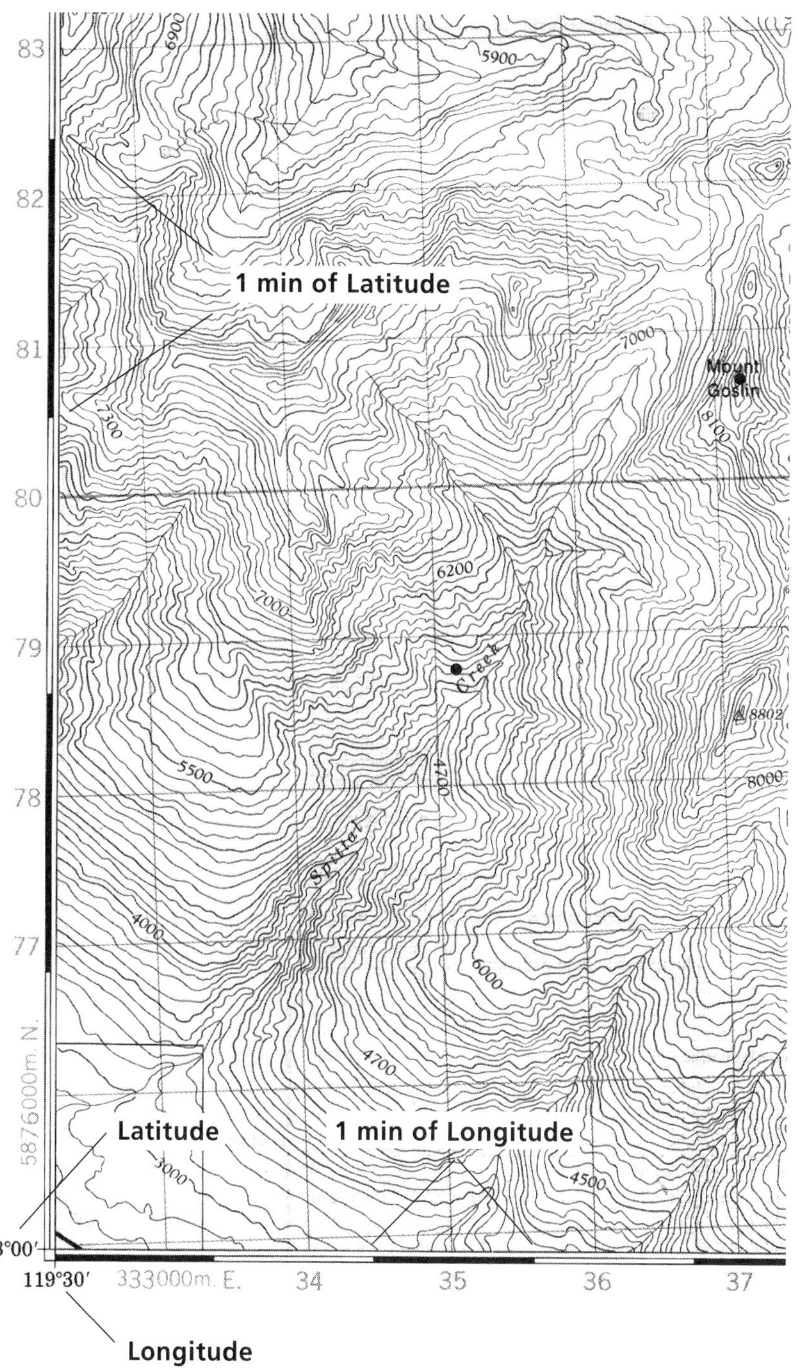

83
82
81
80
79
78
77
5876000m. N.
1 min of Latitude
1 min of Longitude
Latitude
Longitude
53°00′
119°30′
333000m. E.
34
35
36
37
Mount Goslin
Spittal
Creek
8802
6900
5900
7000
7300
8100
6200
5500
4700
8000
4000
6000
3000
4500

Finding the Latitude/Longitude Grid on Maps

Some maps make it easy to use the latitude/longitude grid. The map shown, a product of the Natural Resources Canada, is the southwest corner of the Mount Robson, British Columbia, Alberta, Canada topographical map. It has a 1 minute latitude/longitude grid.

The starting coordinates are shown in the bottom left corner. For this map, the latitude is N 53° 00' while the longitude is W 119° 30'. From the corner, the latitude/longitude grid is marked off in one minute intervals as indicated by the alternating black and white pattern printed on the map's edges. The numbers correspond to the UTM grid and have nothing to do with finding latitude/longitude coordinates. Up the left side of the map, the end of the white line, just below the 77 of the UTM grid, represents the latitude N 53° 01'. The end of the black mark above that is N 53° 02' and so forth. The longitude is measured the same way, but the minutes decrease as you travel east toward the prime meridian. The end of first black line at the bottom of the page is W 119° 29', the end of the white is W 119° 28, etc. For either latitude or longitude, one half of the alternating lines is half of a minute, one quarter is a quarter of a minute, etc. To get the coordinate of a location, place a ruler perpendicular to the side of the map for latitude or the bottom for longitude and measure to the closest tenth of a minute. Do not be confused by the UTM grid, which is printed on the map, just ignore it. Two examples of coordinates taken from the map on the previous page are:

- Mount Goslin:
  N 53° 3.2' W 119° 25.7'
- The letter "C" in Spittal Creek:
  N 53° 2.0' W 119° 27.4'

It is possible to measure coordinates with your eyes alone on a map with such clear, easy-to-use systems such as the one shown in the picture. Other types of maps require some preparation to use the latitude/longitude grid, but their use will be explained and demonstrated.

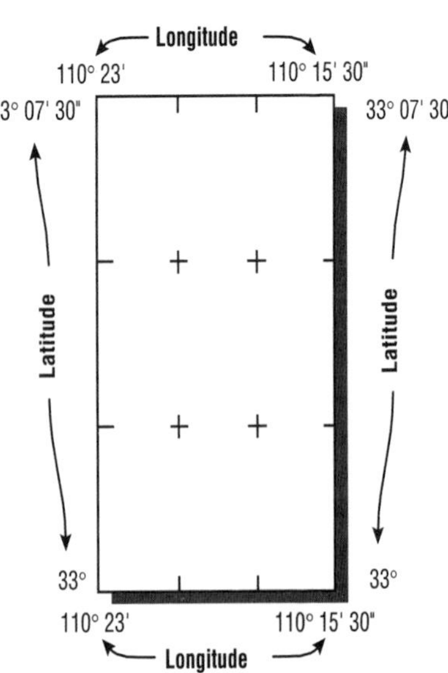

A USGS map before drawing latitude/longitude grid.

Preparing USGS 7.5' Maps

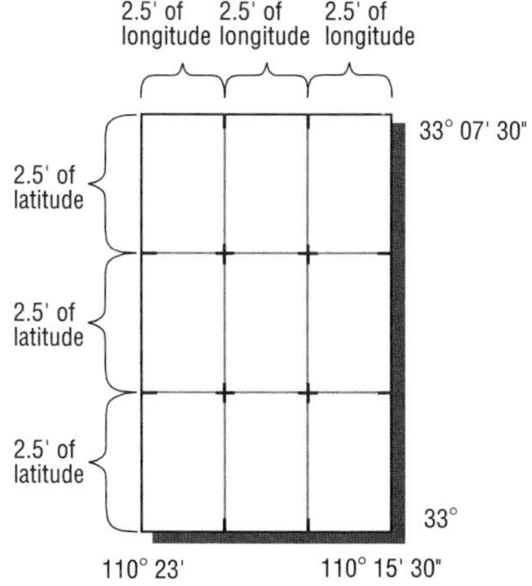

The 7.5' topographical maps printed by the US Geological Survey require some preparation when using the latitude/longitude grid. Tick marks on the side of the map and crosses inside the map, as shown in the figure, divide the maps into 2.5' rectangles. To draw the grid, use a ruler to draw from one side of the map through the crosses to the other side. A subdivided map appears similar to the figure.

A 2.5' rectangle of the southwest corner of the USGS Burrows Lake, Wisconsin topographical map on the next page demonstrates that an area 2.5' x 2.5' is much too large to accurately read a coordinate without taking further steps. Using your eyes alone, try to find the coordinate of the island in the southern part of Burrows Lake—labeled #1.

The longitude is just over half way between W 89° 50' 00" and W 89° 52' 30", which makes it about W 89° 51' 15". The latitude is about 1/5 of the way between N 45° 37' 30" and N 45° 40' 00", which gives it a latitude about N 45° 38' 00". The island's actual coordinate is N 45° 37' 55" W 89° 51' 23", which means visual measurement differed from the true coordinate by 8" in longitude and 5" in latitude. An error of 5" in latitude equates to 0.083', which is the same as 0.083 nautical miles or 506.34 ft. (154.3 m). The 8" error in longitude does not directly correlate to nautical miles since it is not at the equator, but the distance scale at the bottom of the map reveals that 2.5' of longitude at this latitude is 2 statute miles. Once all the conversions are done, 8" in longitude on this map is an error of 563.2 ft. (171.6 m). The error was not really that bad for an eyeball only measurement, but it is much easier to use latitude/longitude on a USGS 7.5' map if the 2.5' grid is further subdivided.

There are two easy methods to subdivide any latitude/longitude grid that is too large for convenient use. The first is to use an ordinary ruler and a pencil to draw more lines between the main latitude/ longitude lines, which in this case are the 2.5' lines. The second is to use a special ruler that is calibrated to minutes and seconds to directly read coordinates from the 2.5' X 2.5' rectangles. Both methods will be illustrated.

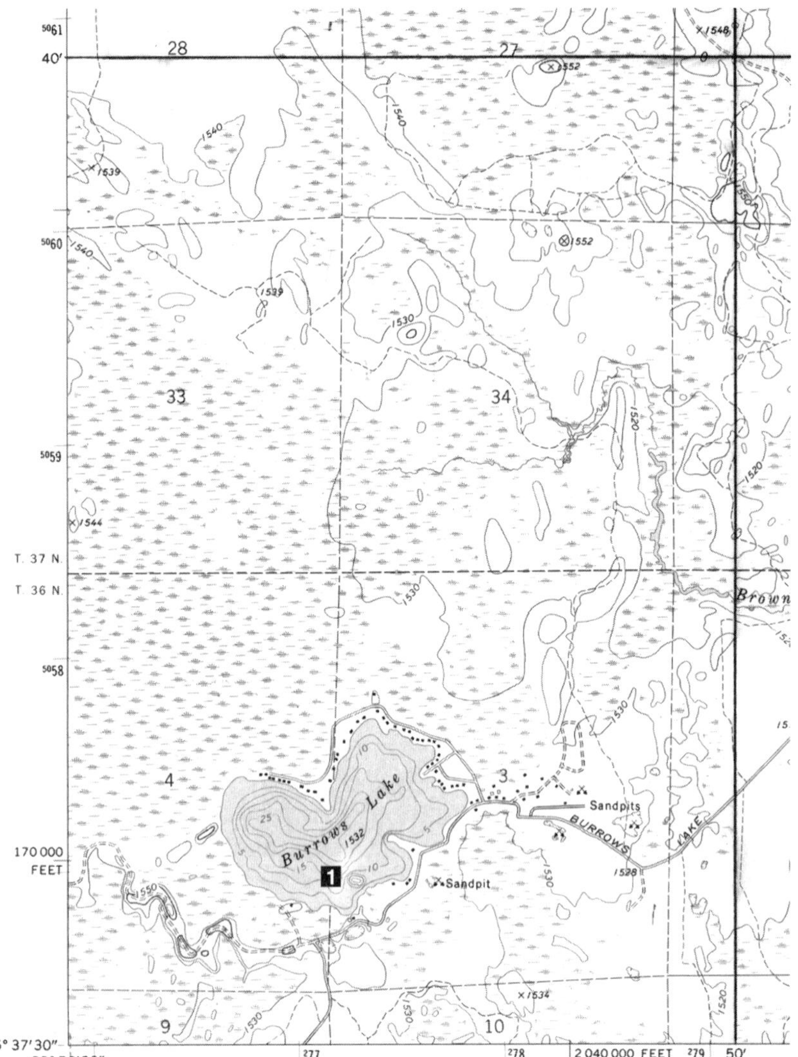
5061
40′
28
27
×1548
×1552
1540
1540
×1539
5060
1540
⊗1552
1550
1539
1530
33
34
1520
5059
×1544
1520
T. 37 N.
T. 36 N.
1530
Brown
5058
1530
4
3
Burrows Lake
Sandpits
25
1532
BURROWS
LAKE
170 000
FEET
15
10
5
1528
Sandpit
1530
1550
×1534
1530
1530
1520
9
10
45° 37′ 30″
89° 52′ 30″
277
278
2 040 000 FEET
279
50′

Drawing a Finer Grid

The key to subdividing a grid is to divide it by a number that results in a fraction that is easy to add in your head. It is easy to divide any grid into 4 equal parts, but in the case of a USGS 7.5' map, dividing the 2.5' rectangle by 4 means that each subdivision is 0.625' or 37.5" wide. It is not easy to perform mental calculates with units of 0.625, so the grid needs to be divided more sensibly. The 2.5' grid is best divided by either 5, which results in subdivisions of 0.5' each, or 10, which provides 0.25' between lines. It is easiest to work with 0.5' intervals because there are fewer lines to draw, so 5 is probably the best divisor to use. The southeast corner of USGS Burrows Lake is shown with the 2.5' rectangle subdivided into 5 equal parts in both latitude and longitude.

The finer grid makes it much easier to find latitude/longitude coordinates to the tenth of a minute. For example, using the map on the next page, the "S" in the northern part of Swamp Creek, label #1 on the map, has a latitude that is 2/5ths of the way between N 45° 39.5' and N 45° 40', which is N 45° 39.7', and a longitude 4/5ths of the way between W 89° 46.5' and W 89° 47', which is W 89° 46.9'. The exact coordinate for point #1 is N 45° 39.63' W 89° 46.85'. The resulting error in latitude is 0.07' (4.2") or about 425.3 ft. (129.6 m) and the error in the longitude measurement is 0.05' (3"), which for the latitude of this map equates to about 211.2 ft. (64.4 m). The measurement is only slightly more accurate than the example of Burrows Lake where only the 2.5' grid was used, but the finer grid used in this example makes it much easier to accurately and quickly find a coordinate using the eye alone. The exact coordinates of the four locations marked on the map are given below. See how close you can come to getting the same coordinate without using a ruler.

Point	Latitude	Longitude
#1	N 45° 39.63'	W 89° 46.85'
#2	N 45° 38.68'	W 89° 47.16'
#3	N 45° 37.83'	W 89° 46.11'
#4	N 45° 39.36'	W 89° 45.66'

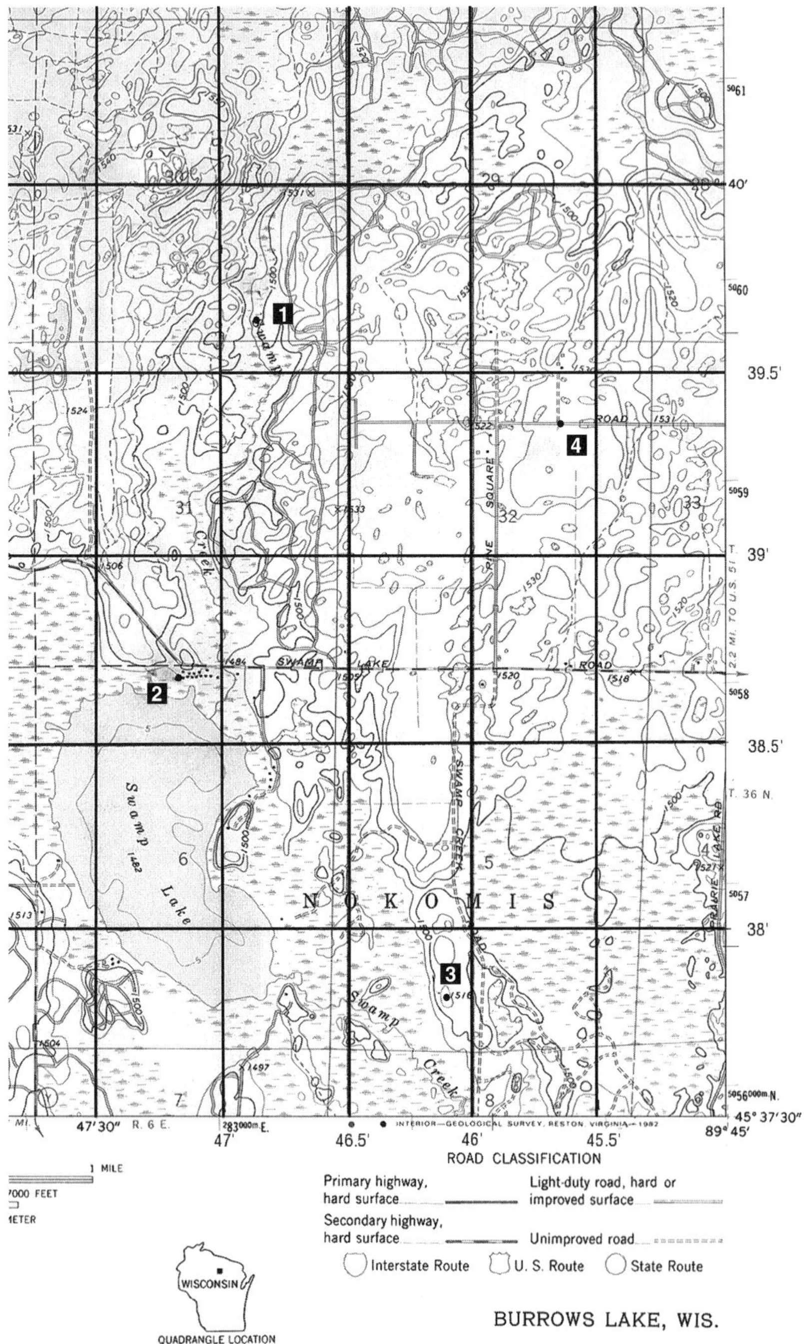

NOKOMIS
Swamp Lake
Swamp Creek
ROAD CLASSIFICATION
Primary highway, hard surface
Light-duty road, hard or improved surface
Secondary highway, hard surface
Unimproved road
Interstate Route
U. S. Route
State Route
WISCONSIN
QUADRANGLE LOCATION
BURROWS LAKE, WIS.

Using a Minute/Second Calibrated Ruler

The easiest and most accurate way to measure latitude/longitude is to use a minute/second calibrated ruler. It provides a method to measure coordinates to an accuracy of about 1" on a 1:24,000 scale map, which translates to an accuracy of approximately 30.9 m (101.3 ft.) or better and the time it takes to prepare the map is minimal. On a USGS 7.5' map, using a minute/second calibrated ruler requires that you draw only the lines for the 2.5' rectangles as described earlier. The ruler does the additional subdividing to make reading coordinates simple and accurate. An example of such a ruler is the Topo Companion shown here.

The numbers along the bottom of the rulers correspond to map scales: 1:24,000, 1:25,000, 1:50,000, 1:63,360 and 1:250,000. The USGS 7.5' topographical maps use the 1:24,000 scale on the minute/second calibrated ruler. The numbers on the 1/24K of the ruler represent tens of seconds while the lines between the numbers are individual seconds. How the numbers correspond to the 2.5' rectangle is shown in the figure. The ruler measures a full minute whenever it starts at a given number and ends on a number of the same value. The figure shows a full minute from 00 to 00 or 30 to 30. However, a full minute is also traversed going from 10 to 10, or 20 to 20 and so forth.

The source of the Topo Companion calibrated ruler is given on page 200.

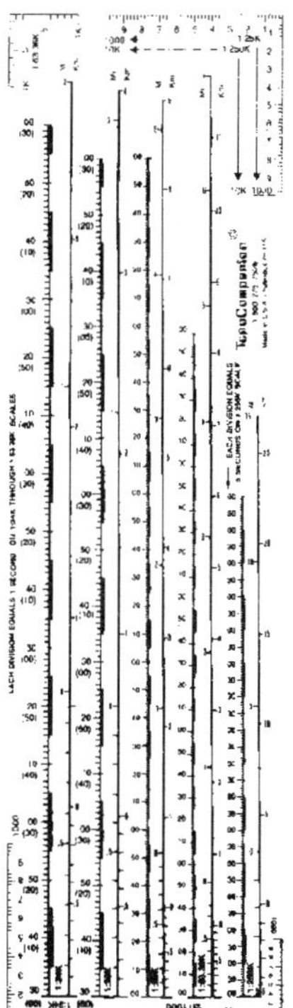

The Topo Companion minute/second calibrated ruler has several scales to measure latitude/longitude on most maps.

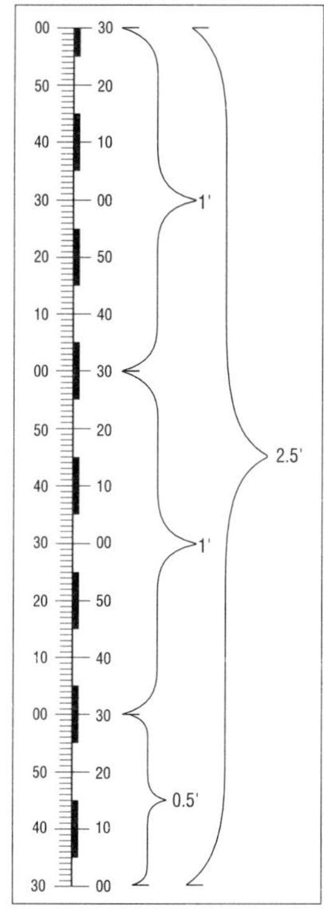

A closer view of a minute/second calibrated ruler for USGS topo maps at 1:24,000 scale.

Note the ruler starts at the bottom with 30 on the left and 00 on the right. The latitude or longitude of a 2.5' rectangle can start with either 00" or 30". The latitude of the southeast corner of the USGS Burrows Lake is N 45° 37' 30" while the longitude is W 89° 45' 00" (the 00" is not printed on the map, but it is shown here to demonstrate that it corresponds to the 00 on the minute/second calibrated ruler). If the coordinate ends in 30", use the numbers that start at 30 in your measurement. If the coordinate starts at 00", or if the seconds are omitted because they are zero, use the numbers that start with 00.

The key to using a minute/second calibrated ruler is to place the ends of the scale on adjacent latitude or longitude lines, then count off the seconds to the location. The map shown in the figure is the northeast corner of the USGS Four Peaks, Arizona map.

The horizontally and vertically drawn lines along with the top and right side of the map form the 2.5' rectangle. To measure latitude, one end of the ruler touches the bottom of the 2.5' rectangle while the other end touches the top. From the bottom of the ruler, count up the seconds to the location of Three Bar Cabin. The latitude of the bottom of the 2.5' rectangle is N 33° 42' 30", so use the numbers on the left of the scale that start with 30. The numbers on the left side of the scale and how they correspond to a latitude coordinate are given below:

Number on scale		**Corresponding latitude**
30	→	N 33° 42' 30"
40	→	N 33° 42' 40"
50	→	N 33° 42' 50"
00	→	N 33° 43' 00"
10	→	N 33° 43' 10"

Three Bar Cabin lies above 00, but below 10, so its latitude coordinate is between N 33° 43' 00" and N 33° 43' 10". The small tick lines between 00 and 10 must be counted to get to the exact coordinate. The cabin lies directly across from the 9th tick mark, so the final latitude coordinate is N 33° 43' 09".

It is just as easy to measure the longitude coordinate. The figure on the next page shows how the ends of the ruler are placed on the longitude lines of the 2.5' rectangle. Notice that the ruler is not completely horizontal because only at the equator is 2.5' of latitude the same physical distance as 2.5' of longitude. However, even though the ruler is at an angle, if the ends of the scale are on the longitude lines, the measurement will be accurate. Remember, the ruler measures minutes

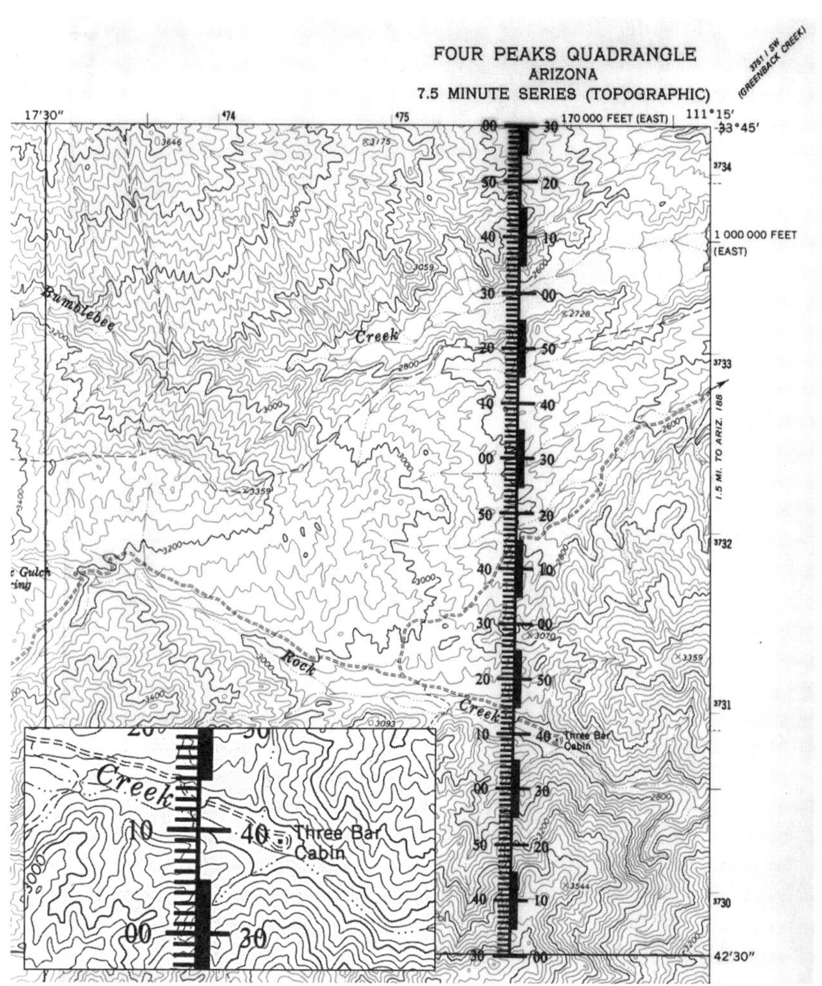

and seconds, not distance, so the spacing between the longitude lines is unimportant. The only requirement for the ruler to work on any scale is that the number of minute and seconds between adjacent latitude and longitude lines is the same. In this case, there are 2.5' between the latitude lines and the same amount between the longitude lines.

From the right-hand end of the ruler, count up the minutes and seconds to the point directly above Three Bar Cabin. The coordinate of the longitude line on the right of the 2.5' rectangle is W 111° 15', so use the numbers on the right, or in this position the top, of the scale because they start with 00. The relationship between the numbers on the scale and the corresponding longitude coordinate is given on the next page.

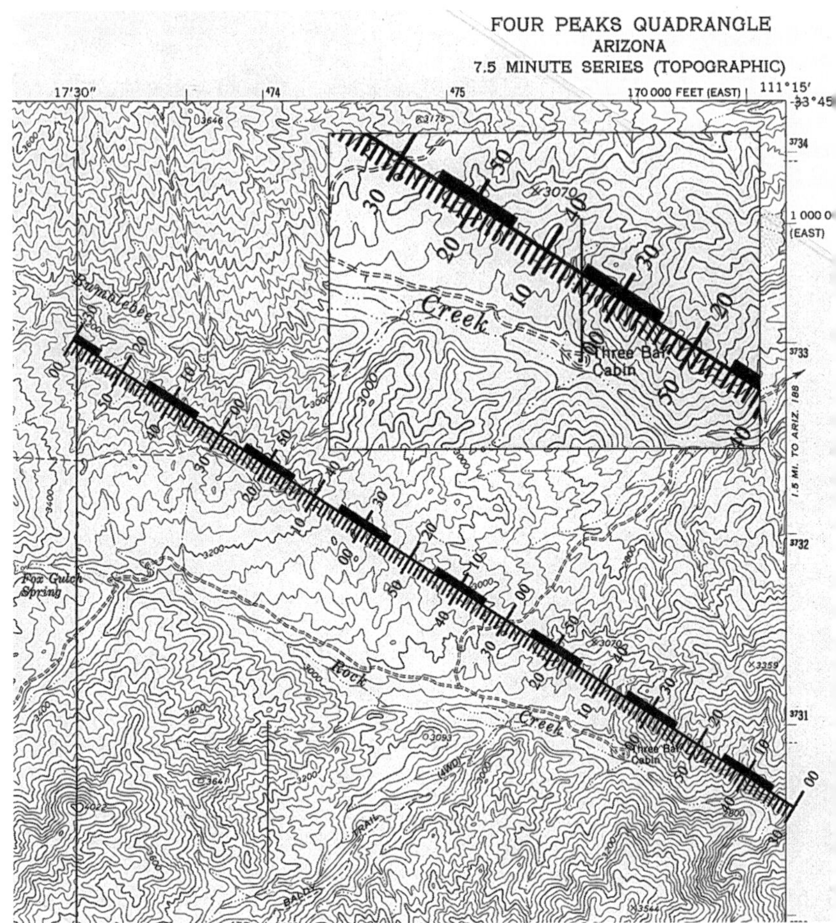

Number on scale		Corresponding latitude
00	→	W 111° 15' 00"
10	→	W 111° 15' 10"
20	→	W 111° 15' 20"
30	→	W 111° 15' 30"
40	→	W 111° 15' 40"

The location of Three Bar Cabin lies between 30 and 40 on the scale, which translates to a coordinate between W 111° 15' 30" and W 111° 15' 40". Count the small tick marks between 30 and 40 to get the exact coordinate of W 111° 15' 35". The final coordinate for Three Bar Cabin in latitude/longitude is

N 33° 43' 09", W 111° 15' 35"

A Kayak Trip

In May, your brother is coming to visit you in Dupont, Alaska and really wants to go to your cabin. When you describe how beautiful and peaceful it is there, he decides he wants to go as soon as he arrives and stay for the entire three days he will be in town. The only transportation you have between your house and the cabin is a kayak. It is only a 10.8 mi. (17.4 km) paddle, but your brother's plane arrives in Juneau at 10:30 pm and it will be dark before you can even start the trip. It is easy to navigate to the cabin by sight during the day and in the dark it is still possible, but much more difficult.

You decide your GPS receiver can guide you directly to the cabin, even in the dark, if you set it up so the navigation screens are continuously visible. It is impossible to hold the receiver and paddle at the same time, so you mount the receiver to the kayak. Another problem you need to overcome is powering the receiver. You will make the trip in the dark and will need the receiver's backlight continuously illuminated so you can see the screen. The backlight uses a lot of power, which means a lot of batteries, but you also need to attach lights to the kayak to be able to make it safely through the busy traffic of Stephens Passage. The lights are powered by a motorcycle battery and a quick look at the receiver's manual reveals that the battery's voltage lies in an acceptable range, so the battery will power both the receiver and the lights. You decide to use the route function to automatically guide you from one waypoint to the next without touching any buttons, thereby leaving your hands free to paddle.

Using your minute/second calibrated ruler, you measure the latitude/longitude coordinates for the trip's waypoints from the USGS Juneau, Alaska (A-1) map shown on the next page. The map is from the USGS 15' series and has a scale of 1:63,360. The latitude/longitude grid on the map forms 5' rectangles instead of the 2.5' rectangles of the 7.5' maps described above. The minute/second calibrated ruler is used in exactly the same way as demonstrated previously except you need to use the 1:63,360 scale to make the measurements.

The coordinates and names of the five waypoints are shown on the map:

Point	Latitude	Longitude	Name
#1	N 58° 13' 45"	W 134° 15' 55"	DUPONT
#2	N 58° 11' 53"	W 134° 14' 20"	TANTAL
#3	N 58° 08' 40"	W 134° 19' 45"	OLIVER
#4	N 58° 06' 35"	W 134° 18' 35"	P-TAGE
#5	N 58° 05' 50"	W 134° 18' 47"	ACABIN

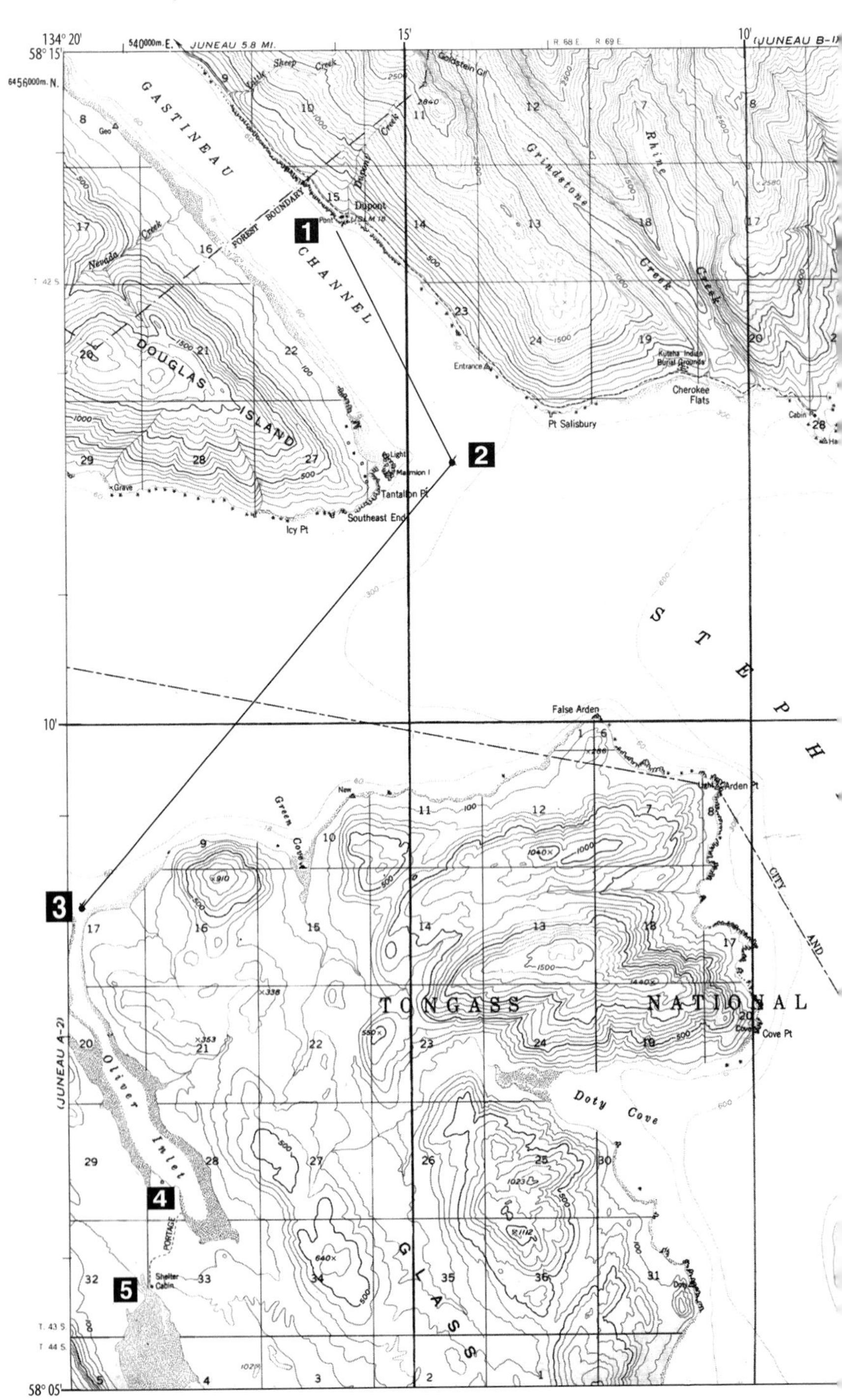
GASTINEAU
CHANNEL
DOUGLAS ISLAND
FOREST BOUNDARY
Dupont
Nevada Creek
Grindstone Creek
Rhine Creek
Goldstein Gl
Little Sheep Creek
Dupont Creek
Entrance
Pt Salisbury
Kuteha Indian Burial Grounds
Cherokee Flats
Tantallon Pt
Mamion I
Southeast End
Icy Pt
False Arden
Arden Pt
Green Cove
TONGASS NATIONAL
Cove Pt
Doty Cove
Oliver Inlet
PORTAGE
Shelter Cabin
GLASS
CITY AND
JUNEAU 5.8 MI.
(JUNEAU A-2)
134° 20'
58° 15'
58° 05'
10'
15'
1
2
3
4
5

Before entering the coordinates into your receiver, set it to the proper settings:

- **Map datum: North American Datum 1927 (NAD 27)**
  If your receiver splits NAD 27 into separate settings for Alaska, Canada, Central America, etc., select NAD 27-Alaska, otherwise, select NAD 27.
- **Units: Statute**
  Nautical units are best suited for latitude/longitude coordinates, but you have never used them before and can not relate to a nautical mile, so use statute.
- **Coordinate grid: Latitude/Longitude**
  Select the degrees, minutes and seconds format to correspond to the coordinates measured off the map.
- **North setting: True North**
  A compass is not going to be used to navigate, so it does not really matter if the receiver's bearings are oriented to the magnetic or north pole. You arbitrarily decide to make the bearings relate to the map and select the True North mode.
- **CDI limit: small**
  If the Course Deviation Indicator's tolerance is selectable, set it somewhere between 0.25 and 0.5 mi. On the water, there are no obstacles in the route you have planned, so a small CDI will allow the highway navigation screen to keep you on course.

Once the waypoints are in the receiver's memory, you set up the route that will lead you from DUPONT through all the intervening waypoints until you arrive at the cabin. The distance is expressed in statute miles and the bearings relate to true north as set above.

Name	Point	Desired Track	Distance km
DUPONT	#1		
		156°	2.4
TANTAL	#2		
		222°	5.0
OLIVER	#3		
		164°	2.5
P-TAGE	#4		
		188°	0.9
ACABIN	#5		

The plan to navigate the 10.8 mi. (17.4 km) is simple: use the receiver's route function to guide you the entire trip. You will paddle the kayak from DUPONT to P-TAGE where you will portage the kayak the remaining 0.9 mi. (1.45 km) to the cabin. While you are in the kayak and the receiver is connected to the battery, you will have access to the steering screens and other navigational statistics like speed, bearing, estimated time en route, etc. Your receiver uses averaging and smoothing algorithms to minimize the impact of Selective Availability on the speed measurements, so even at your slow speed the navigational statistics will be meaningful. You will also take a compass and a map, but if something were to happen to the receiver, you would use the compass to paddle due south to land, then either slowly follow the coastline west to Oliver Inlet or wait for sunrise to easily complete the trip.

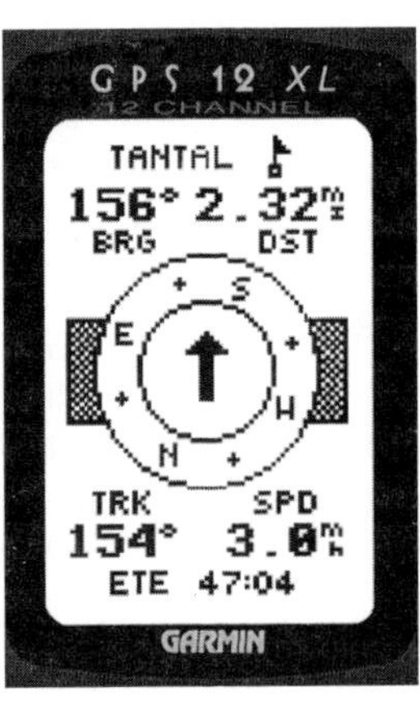

The day finally arrives. Your brother's plane pulls in at 10:40 pm and after several delays it is not until midnight that you are ready to shove off in the kayak. Before paddling, you turn on the lights and the receiver. Once the receiver is locked onto the satellites, you activate the route that leads to the cabin. The receiver instantly detects that you are already at the route's first waypoint, so it immediately starts pointing to the next waypoint, which is TANTAL.

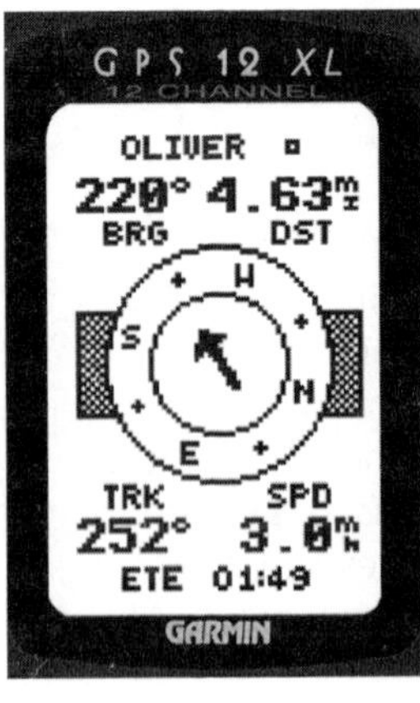

After paddling about halfway to TANTAL, you switch to the highway navigation screen and notice that you are slightly off course to the left of where you should be. You had been traveling at a bearing of 154° when it should have been 156°; as a result, your CrossTrack Error is 0.05 mi. (264 ft. or 80.5 m), which is not bad, but you also notice the bearing to TANTAL has changed from the 156° it was originally to 159°. You do not really want to steer deeper into Stephens Passage, so you adjust your course to 159° and continue. As you hold your course, you notice the CrossTrack Error steadily decreases. The receiver advises you of your arrival at TANTAL, then automatically switches and starts steering you across Stephens Passage to Oliver Inlet. You adjust your course to the new bearing of 222°.

As you paddle along, you and your brother get talking and you do not pay attention to the receiver. When you do look up, you see you have gone almost 0.4 mi. (0.64 km) at a bearing of 252°. The arrow on the compass navigation screen points to the left and the bearing to OLIVER is now 220°.

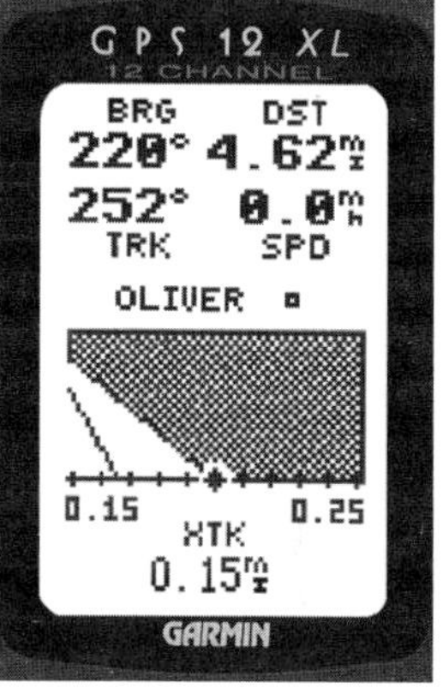

You switch to the highway screen. The direction of the highway also veers left indicating you need to steer left to get back on course. It also shows your CrossTrack Error to be 0.15 mi. (792 ft. or 241.4 m) to the right of the intended course.

You decide to try an experiment to get back to the direct line between TANTAL and OLIVER as fast as possible. The figure illustrates your position at the X. The direct course between TANTAL and OLIVER is 222°, but because you paddled on a bearing of 252°, you are 0.15 mi. away from the direct line course as indicated by the CrossTrack Error. The fastest way to return to the direct line is to follow the route indicated by the dotted line, which is perpendicular to the direct route. The dotted line bearing is

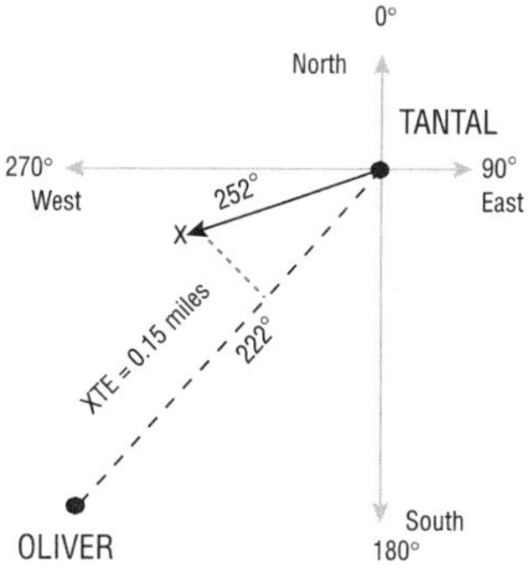

$$222° - 90° = 132°$$

You turn the kayak to the left until your bearing is 132° and paddle until your CrossTrack Error is zero. Soon you are back on the direct route and turn right to a bearing of 222° to head straight to OLIVER. Everything is smooth sailing without much traffic until you get halfway into Stephens Passage where you hear the loud sound of a fast motorboat. Fortunately they see you and give you plenty of room, but when the sound of the motor dies down, you hear something that sounds like a dog barking. No dog on land could sound that close, so you decide to investigate.

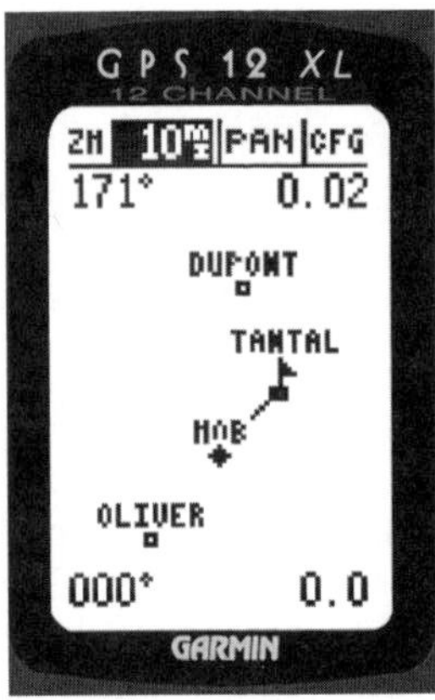

Before you start paddling toward the dog's bark, you activate the Man-Over-Board (MOB) function, which immediately marks your present position. You plan to investigate the sound, then return to where you are right now to continue the trip to the Oliver Inlet. The MOB function not only marks your current position, but it automatically activates the Goto function and steers you to the position just marked. While you are looking for the dog, you will ignore the receiver's screen. When you are ready to continue your trip, the receiver will lead you back to the MOB coordinate where you will disengage the Goto function and resume the route to the cabin. Out of curiosity you switch to the map screen and see that the MOB waypoint is about halfway between TANTAL and OLIVER.

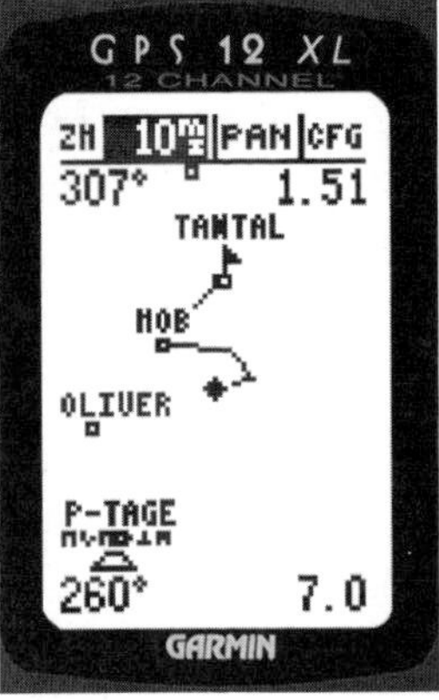

Because you are following the dog's bark and not the receiver you leave it on the map screen just to see where you are going in relation to the waypoints that lead to the cabin. Either the dog is afraid of you and is swimming away or you are having a hard time following the sound as it travels over the water because the receiver's map shows you paddling all over the place.

Sure enough, the dog is not on land and as you pull it on board, it seems really happy to see you. When you notice it does not have any tags, you are pretty sure the owners will not even know where to begin to look for their lost pet. You take another look at the receiver's map. You first check to make sure the map is pointing north up so everything looks like the map you used to plan the trip. If you return to the MOB waypoint, it will take a lot of extra paddling because the dog was so far away. You decide the best approach is to paddle directly from your present position to OLIVER, so you cancel the MOB Goto function. The method you use to continue your journey depends on your receiver. On some receivers you can simply activate the original route you were following. The receiver knows you are past TANTAL and will automatically begin to steer you to OLIVER. If your receiver does not have that capability, you can save your current position as the HERE waypoint and form a new route from HERE to OLIVER to P-TAGE, then finally to ACABIN.

Your receiver cannot pick up a route where it left off, so you store your position as HERE.

Using the new waypoint, you form a new route.

Name	Point	Desired Track	Distance mi
HERE			
		250°	2.8
OLIVER	#3		
		164°	2.5
P-TAGE	#4		
		188°	0.9
ACABIN	#5		

From where you are right now, it is still 6.2 mi. (9.98 km) to the cabin. You activate the new route, switch to the steering screen and swing the kayak around to a bearing of 250°. The trip continues with few course corrections until you arrive at the cabin.

Three glorious days later, when it is time to go home, it is easy to get the receiver ready for the trip back because you only have to press a single button to reverse the original route. When you told the receiver to reverse the route, it automatically formed the route shown below:

Name	Point	Desired Track	Distance mi
ACABIN	#5		
		8°	0.9
P-TAGE	#4		
		344°	2.5
OLIVER	#3		
		42°	5.0
TANTAL	#2		
		336°	2.4
DUPONT	#1		

Once more, in the dark with the receiver showing the way, you, your brother and new dog paddle from the cabin back to the house glad you were able to spend as much time there as you did.

9 More Latitude, Longitude and a Sailboat Rally

Every year, your sailing club has a timed race where the object is not to be the fastest, but the closest to a set time between points. The time is fixed to teach you how to better control the boat and you are docked points for every minute you are too fast or slow. Points are also given for the proximity you arrive at each location. Some of the places are fairly remote and it would be difficult for judges to monitor a boat's arrival, so each crew is given an instamatic camera to prove how close they got to each marker.

It is your fifth year in the race. You finally understand how to handle the craft and can sail proficiently in most conditions, but you are hopelessly inept at judging your speed in the water. Last year, you zoomed as fast as you could to get close to each point, then waited until the time was almost up before moving in the last little bit. Your method left a lot to be desired because you placed 45th out of 100 contestants. This year you need to be a bit more controlled. You search the rules carefully and find there are no restrictions on GPS receivers. You outfit your boat with an external antenna, power cord and mounting hardware because you plan to use the receiver's navigational statistics to help you arrive right on time.

The stopping points of the race have been published on the official chart, so you reach for your ruler to measure coordinates for your route. The coordinate grid on the chart is latitude/longitude, so you grab your minute/second calibrated ruler to start measuring, but none of the scales seem to work. You notice the scale at the bottom of the map: 1:40,000.

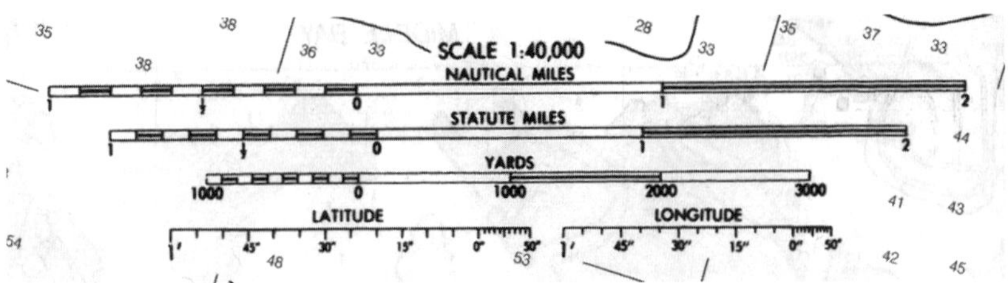

"Great!" you complain. The ruler you have does not have the scale you need. Then you notice the subdivided lines that have "LATITUDE" and "LONGITUDE" written above them. After comparing the lengths of the scales to the distance between the latitude and longitude grid lines, you realize that you can make your own minute/second calibrated ruler for the 1:40,000 scale. There are three ways to make the ruler:

1. **Make one ruler, based on the latitude grid line, and use it exactly like the Topo Companion ruler described in Chapter 8.**
2. **Make two rulers: one for latitude and the other for longitude. They would be different lengths and would not be interchangeable.**
3. **Make a ruler with longitude on the left side and latitude along the top as shown in the figure. This type of ruler makes it possible to place the ruler's corner on an object and easily read the coordinates.**

You decide to make a ruler like the one described in the third option above. To make the ruler, first measure the distance between two latitude lines. For this chart at this scale, the distance is 9.2 cm (3.62 in.). Use centimeters because it is much easier to divide a length that is based on a factor of 10. Inches are subdivided into 1/4, 1/16 or 1/32 increments, which result in difficult math when dividing. Draw a vertical line 9.2 cm long on a piece of paper. Because the latitude lines are 2' apart, the line represents 2' of latitude. Label the bottom of the line 2' as shown in the figure. Measure down from the top 4.6 cm, or halfway down, draw another line and label it 1'. The top of the line represents 0', but do not label it because it will get in the way of the longitude line when it is drawn later. There is enough room between each minute mark to make 10 subdivisions, which translate into 0.1' marks. The ruler shown in the figure has 0.1' subdivisions, but only every other mark is labeled so the ruler does not look cluttered.

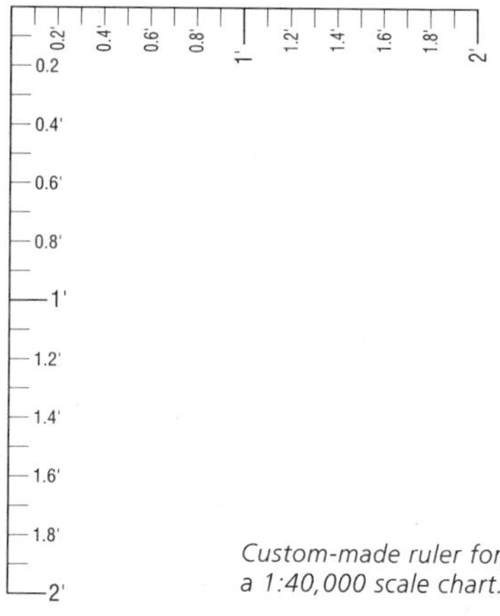

Custom-made ruler for a 1:40,000 scale chart.

Dividing each minute into 10 equal units translates to 0.46 cm between each line. To do the subdivision, place the top of the ruler at the top of the line. Measure down 0.46 cm and draw the first small line. Measure down an additional 0.46 cm, to 0.92 cm, and draw the second line, which can be labeled 0.2'. Continue down the ruler in

0.46 cm increments until the subdivisions are drawn and labeled as shown in the figure.

Back on the chart, the ruler measures 7 cm (2.76 in.) between adjacent longitude lines. On the paper you are using to make the ruler, draw a 7 cm horizontal line to the right from the top of the vertical latitude line forming a right angle. Just as with the latitude, the longitude grid lines are separated by 2'. Label the end of the line 2' and draw a line at the halfway mark, 3.5 cm, and label it 1'. The space between the minute lines can again be subdivided into 10 equal parts to provide 0.1' marks. Only 3.5 cm separate the longitude minute marks, so each 0.1' mark is separated by only 0.35 cm. To draw the subdivisions, place the ruler at the left end of the line. Move to the right 0.35 cm, draw a short line. Move right an additional 0.35 cm, to 0.7 cm, draw a short line and label it 0.2'. Continue moving right by 0.35 cm, drawing and labeling lines until your ruler looks like the one in the figure. Once you have drawn the ruler, copy it onto a transparency so the map's features are visible when you use the scale to measure.

Measuring coordinates is easy with the ruler. The way the ruler is drawn requires the latitude scale to always be on the left and the longitude on top. To measure a coordinate, place the corner of the ruler on the location and note where the latitude and longitude lines intersect the scales. Finding the coordinate to the mouth of Howells Creek is shown in the figure.

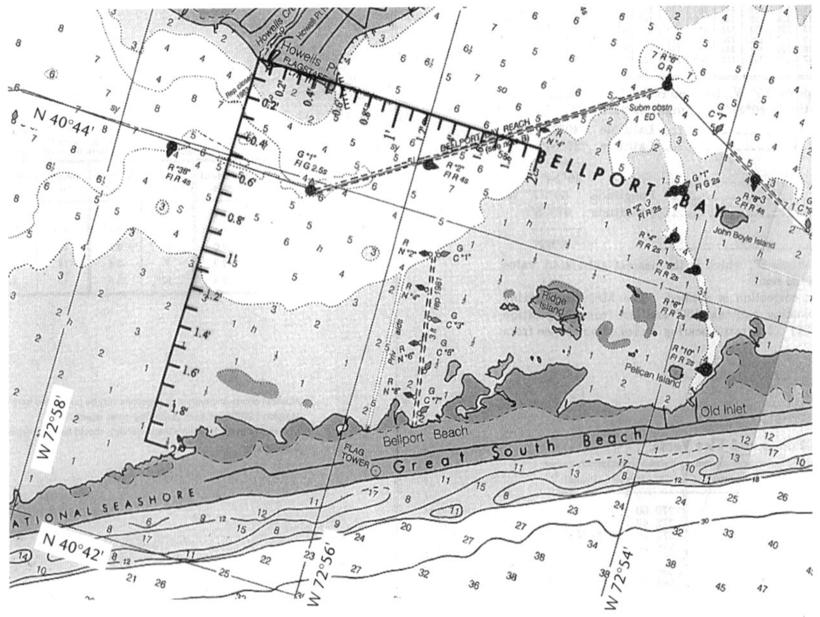

The ruler's corner is placed at the river's mouth. The N 40° 44' latitude line intersects the latitude scale (vertical) at 0.5'. The latitude is calculated by adding the number where the latitude grid line intersects the ruler to the grid line's coordinate value, so in this case the latitude becomes:

- N 40° 44' + 0.5' = N 40° 44.5'

The same approach is used with the longitude. The W 72° 56' longitude line intersects the longitude scale between the 1.2' and 1.3' marks. Use your eye to estimate the distance between the two marks to arrive at the number 1.23'. Add the number from the scale to the value of the longitude line to get:

- W 72° 56' + 1.23' = W 72° 57.23'

The final coordinate to the mouth of Howells Creek is:

- N 40° 44.5', W 72° 57.23'

Now it is easy to measure coordinates from the map, so you begin your work. This year's contest has four locations numbered 1 through 4.

A quick look reveals that the path from #1 to #2, #2 to #3 and #4 back to #1 are not straight lines. The receiver's estimated time en route (ETE) calculation is based on the Velocity Made Good (VMG) measurement. Refer to Chapter 4 for an explanation of VMG and Speed Over Ground (SOG). If you are headed directly for a waypoint, the ETE is the actual time it will take to get there. If you are off course or the course is not a straight line, the VMG and ETE both vary widely. The only straight shot on the sailing course is between #3 and #4, so you break up the route between each location into a series of straight lines. You will use the receiver's route function to lead you from one waypoint to the next and if you stay on course, the ETE will be the actual time between each point and you can use it to help meet the time requirements. You label the intermediate waypoints: 1A, 1B, 2A, 2B and 4A.

The coordinates of all the waypoints you will use along with their names are listed below.

Point	Latitude	Longitude	Name
#1	N 40° 42.38'	W 73° 13.2'	P1
#1A	N 40° 39.22'	W 73° 12.6'	P1A
#1B	N 40° 38.71'	W 73° 11.2'	P1B
#2	N 40° 38.46'	W 73° 11.43'	P2
#2A	N 40° 39.2'	W 73° 10'	P2A
#2B	N 40° 39.73'	W 73° 10'	P2B
#3	N 40° 39.57'	W 73° 10.55'	P3
#4	N 40° 42.05'	W 73° 10.68'	P4
#4A	N 40° 41.6'	W 73° 12.2'	P4A

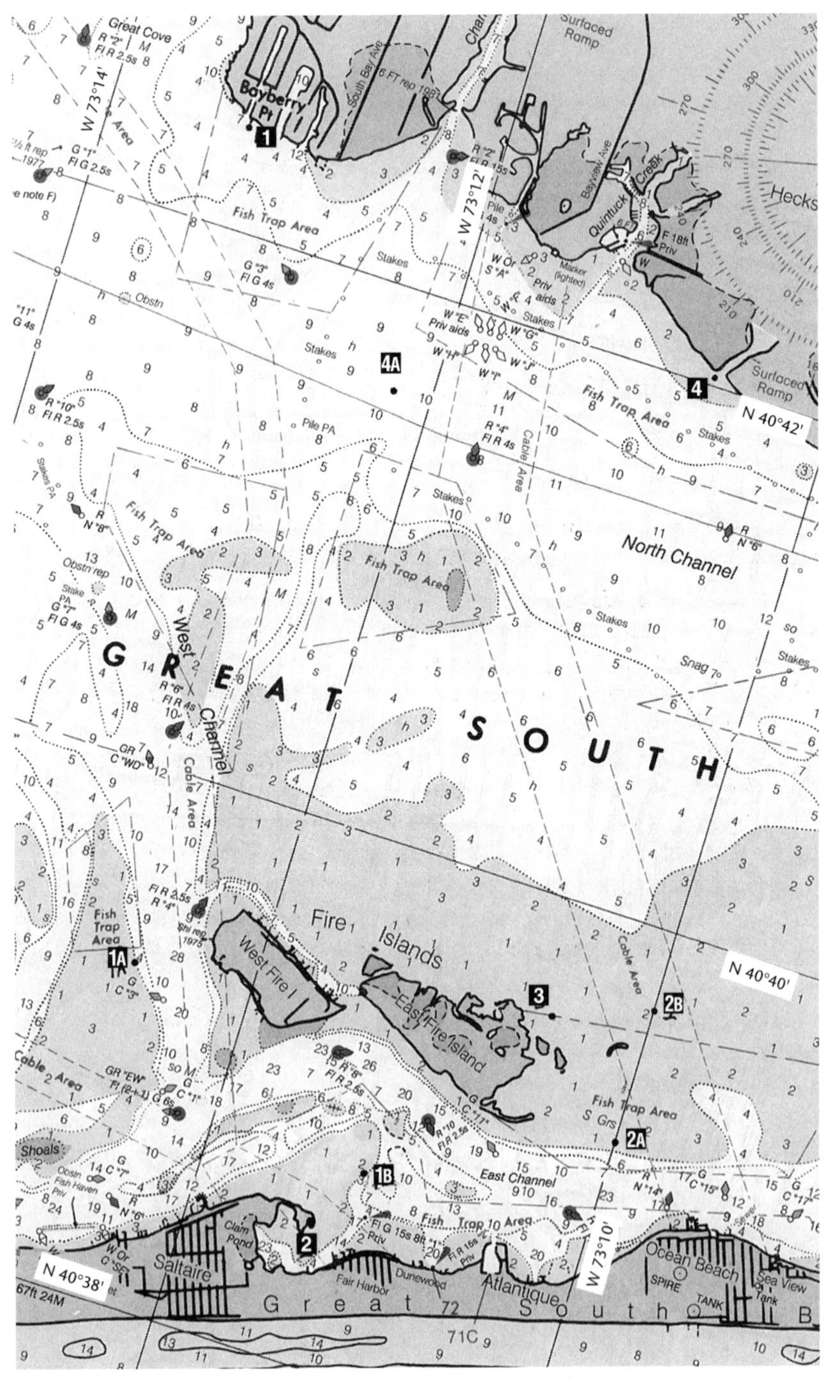
Great Cove
Bayberry Pt
W 73°14'
W 73°12'
W 73°10'
N 40°42'
N 40°40'
N 40°38'
Fish Trap Area
North Channel
West Channel
Cable Area
GREAT SOUTH
Fire Islands
West Fire I
East Fire Island
East Channel
Saltaire
Clam Pond
Fair Harbor
Dunewood
Atlantique
Ocean Beach
Sea View
Great South B
Quintuck Creek
Bayview Ave
South Bay Ave
Surfaced Ramp
Hecks
Shoals
1
1A
1B
2
2A
2B
3
4
4A

Before you enter the waypoints into the receiver, you need to specify the map datum. You search the official race chart in vain, but the datum was not included. You debate what to do. Never before have you had to know the datum for the race because navigation with a compass does not require it. If you ask the rally organizers, they will be suspicious and ask why you need it. You are not a very good liar, so you decide you will have to make an educated guess. The chart was made in the U.S., so the datum is probably NAD 27, NAD 83 or WGS 84. If you pick the wrong datum, the position error will only be a few meters. This will not pose a problem because you only have to get close to each point, not exactly on top of it. You decide to use NAD 27 because it is the datum used by most of the charts you own. Some of the newer charts use NAD 83, but you cannot tell from the copy if it is old or new. You set your receiver as shown below:

- **Map datum: North American Datum 1927 (NAD 27)**
  If your receiver splits NAD 27 into separate settings for Alaska, Canada, Central America, etc., select NAD 27-CONUS, otherwise, select NAD 27.
- **Units: Nautical**
  You have quite a bit of experience with charts and have a feel for nautical miles, so select nautical units.
- **Coordinate grid: Latitude/Longitude**
- **North setting: Magnetic North**
  The big, on-board compass is like an old friend and even though you are using a GPS receiver, you will turn to your own compass when actually trying to maintain a course.
- **CDI limit: A medium setting**
  You are proficient at holding an accurate course. The highway navigation screen may prove useful, so you do not want a CDI limit that is so large that it is meaningless, or one that is so small that you can never hold the course. Your receiver has a setting of 0.25, 1.25 and 5.0, so select 1.25 nautical miles.

After setting the receiver, you enter the waypoints and then form a route.

Name	Point	Desired Track	Distance n mi
P1	#1		
		186°	3.2
P1A	#1A		
		129°	1.2
P1B	#1B		
		229°	0.3
P2	#2		
		69°	1.3
P2A	#2A		
		14°	0.5
P2B	#2B		
		263°	0.4
P3	#3		
		11°	2.5
P4	#4		
		262°	1.2
P4A	#4A		
		330°	1.1
P1	#1		

The total trip is 11.7 nautical miles (13.5 statute miles, 21.7 km). The time for each leg was also sent with the chart, so you quickly form a table listing times and distances, and you calculate the constant speed required to cover each leg in the specified time.

Leg	Time min	Distance n mi	Speed knots
#1 to #2	36	4.7	7.8
#2 to #3	21	2.2	6.3
#3 to #4	13	2.5	11.5
#4 to #1	24	2.3	5.8

You can easily sustain the 11.5 knots needed for the jaunt between #3 and #4, so none of the legs appear to be excessively fast. Next you calculate the time that can be spent on each leg as you defined them on the map. You decide that last year's strategy still has merit, but this year you will not rush so fast then wait so long. You form the following table:

Leg	Distance n mi	Target Time min	Speed Required knots
P1 to P1A	3.2	23	8.3
P1A to P1B	1.2	8	9
P1B to P2	0.3	5	3.6
P2 to P2A	1.3	11	7.1
P2A to P2B	0.5	4	7.5
P2B to P3	0.4	6	4
P3 to P4	2.5	13	11.5
P4 to P4A	1.2	11	6.5
P4A to P1	1.1	13	5.1

Fortunately you do not have to sail the craft solo. You will stay at the helm, keep an eye on the instruments including the GPS receiver and tell the crew members what to do to keep on course and on schedule. You plan to use the estimated time en route (ETE) timer on the receiver to calculate the time it should take to get to a point. The ETE will help you sail the right speed to meet the time requirements of each leg, but ETE changes with speed and course, so you need an additional timer to keep track of the time elapsed on each leg. It would be nice to have a countdown timer that could be set at the beginning of each leg to keep track of the absolute time you have to get to the next waypoint. As long as the time on the countdown timer matches the ETE, everything will be alright. The only alternative to a countdown timer is to subtract the elapsed time from the time allowed for each leg, but doing the math is inconvenient especially when a timer countdown will do it for you. The receiver does not have one, but your watch does, so you plan to use it.

On the day of the race, you have the chart, the tables you made and your receiver. A boat leaves every 10 minutes and your turn finally arrives. You turn the receiver on and activate the route. The steering page shows the bearing to P1A as 186°, so you shove off and keep an eye on the compass until you reach that heading. According to plan, it should take 23 minutes to reach P1A, so you set the countdown timer and activate it. You tell the crew to put on sails until you reach the desired speed of 8.3 knots. You immediately notice that the ETE is not stable. It does not count down at one second intervals, but jumps down a few seconds, then up even more. Sometimes it suddenly changes by up to a minute. This type of behavior occurs only when your course meanders or your speed fluctuates. You check your compass and grip the helm sternly to bring the ship to a steady speed and course. After doing everything you know how, the seconds of the ETE still change unpredictably, but the minute reading seems stable and usable. You decide to rely on only the minute part of the ETE. The countdown timer says you need to be at P1A in 19:30 while the ETE is around 20 minutes, which is pretty close, but you still decide to compensate for your slightly slow start by putting on a bit more speed. When your speed reaches 8.9 knots, the ETE drops to about 16 minutes while the countdown timer is 17:31. It looks like a game of cat and mouse between the timers.

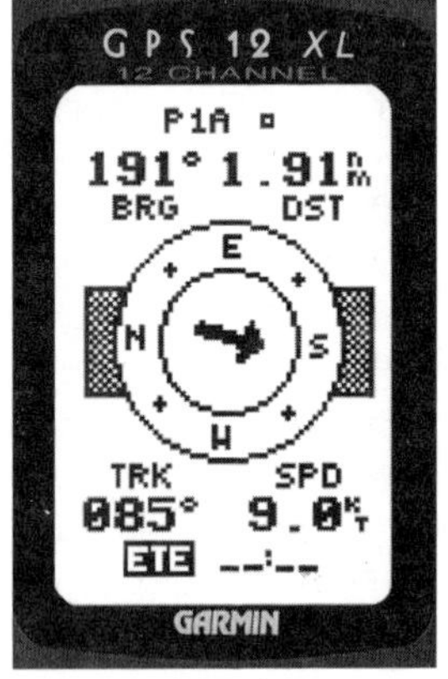

"Ship ahead!" one of the crew calls from the bow. You blast your horn because sailboats have right-of-way, but the other ship does not move. You blast again, but there is no response, so you take evasive maneuvers. As you steer your boat hard to the left, the arrow on the compass navigation screen points far to the right showing the direction you need to turn to get back on course. The ETE disappears and the screen shows your present direction as 85°.

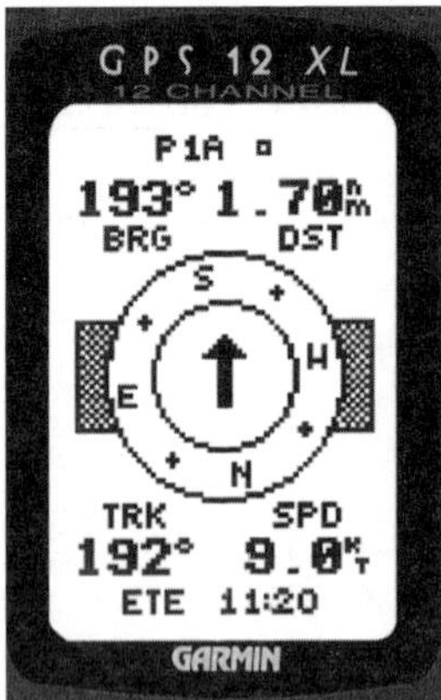

Once past the obstacle, you turn once more toward P1A, but the bearing to get there has changed from 186° to 193°. You bring the boat around and try to get as close to the correct bearing as possible.

The countdown reports 9:30 to arrive, but the ETE is bouncing around 10 minutes. You put on more sails and at 10 knots the two timers almost match. It is straight sailing until the receiver signals the change in direction to get to P1B. You make a quick note of the time it took to get to P1A and with an eye on the compass, you bring the boat around to 129°. You made it to P1A in 22:47, so you reduce your speed from 10 knots to the 9 the plan allows to get to P1B. You also set the countdown timer to 8 minutes and start it.

"Cable ship ahead!" you hear from above. You are in a cable area, but you did not know they would be working the weekend. They certainly will not move, so you had better do so. You veer hard to the right to get around then return to course. The countdown timer says 4:18, but the ETE is somewhere close to 6 minutes. More speed, but there is another obstacle. A group of fishing boats are bringing in their nets, so you steer around them too. Once clear you have 2:08 to get to P1B, but the ETE at your present speed is over 5 minutes. You take a look at the moving map. What a mess!

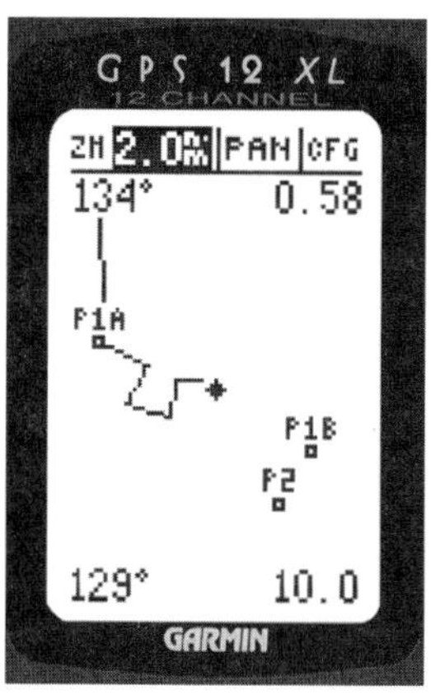

It took 10:15 to get to P1B, which means you have to subtract the 2:12 you went over from the time it takes to get from P1B to P2, so you have 2:48 left. You set the countdown timer and bring the ship around to 229° to head for P2. It is a short distance and fortunately the way looks clear. You find that 10 knots is too fast, so you slow down until the ETE is close to the countdown timer. When you arrive, you are ahead of schedule by 30 seconds, but after you snap the photo of the race marker and get started again, you note it took 2:31 seconds for the leg. The adjusted time was 2:48, so things are looking good.

A watch with a countdown timer complements the ETE time.

The next leg should take 11 minutes. You reset your timer and assume a heading of 69° as you try to get up to the target speed of 7.1 knots as fast as possible.

It is smooth sailing to get to P2A until you get close and can see there is more cable work going on in the area of P2B, so you decide to make a change in the route. Instead of going around the small island closer to P2B, you will sail between it and the main island. The time to go from P2A to P2B and P2B to P3 is 10 minutes. As you are now going directly from P2A to P3, you have 10 minutes to do it. It is not a straight path to P3, so you will set the timer and use the ETE as a guide, not as an exact measure. You will use the tactic of covering most the distance quickly and slowing down a lot once you are headed directly to P3 and the ETE can be compared against the countdown timer. You will ignore the bearing the receiver gives until you can go directly toward P3.

When you arrive at P2A, you start the timer, but you do not do anything to the receiver. Many receivers can figure out when you head to a non-adjacent point in a route that it too should skip and direct you to the next closest waypoint. You cover most the distance at about 7 knots, so when you come close to P3 you have about 2 minutes to go. By now the receiver is pointing to P3 and you slow your speed so the ETE almost matches the countdown timer. A quick look at the moving map shows the detour you took.

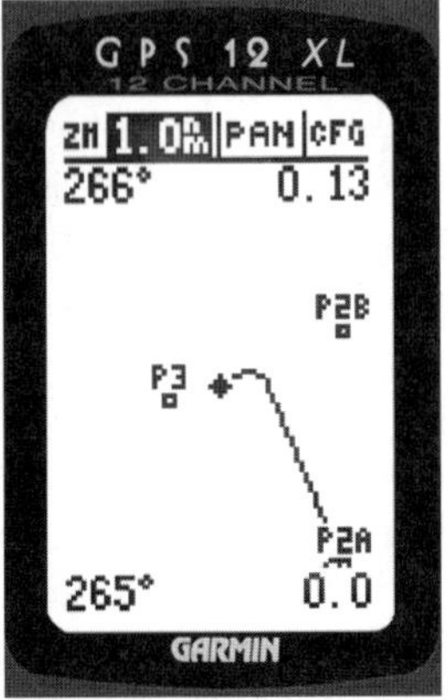

Your plan worked out great because you reached P3 in 10:22. You take the photo, set the timer, change your heading to 11° and try to pick up speed as fast as possible to reach your target of 11.6 knots. The total elapsed time from P1 to P3 is 56:50 while the allotted time is 57 minutes, so you are doing great!

The trip to P4 was not exactly straight because you had to get around a few obstacles, but the receiver's ETE calculation and the countdown timer keep you on schedule and you arrive a little under at 12:25. You and the crew are working like a finely tuned machine, at least until you try to take the picture. In an effort to get as close as possible, you lean over the side of the boat. You snap the photo, but when you try to get back your feet slip and you let go of the camera. You and the rest of the crew watch as it sinks to the dismal depths. You know the race is over—at least for your crew. Losing the camera means disqualification. Your time will not even be recorded.

You all decide to sail on as though nothing happened. Back at the helm you man the timer and receiver. It takes 11:48 to get to P4A and finally 13:18 to reach the finish line. Your total time is 94:21, which looks pretty good when compared against the 94 minutes set for the course. It is the closest you have ever come and if only you had not dropped the camera the first prize might have been yours.

10 Small Scale Maps and a Road Trip

All of the previous chapters demonstrated the use of a GPS receiver with large scale maps between 1:24,000 and 1:50,000. A receiver can also be used with small scale maps like 1:100,000 and 1:250,000, however, their use is different because it is impossible to pinpoint exact locations as with a large scale map. Small scale maps are useful for highway driving because a large area is shown on a single map and major interchanges are easy to mark. Large scale maps must be used in cities where the coordinates to individual intersections are important. A popular map series at the 1:250,000 scale is the DeLorme Atlas and Gazetteers, where each book covers an entire state. Light gray latitude/longitude tick marks appear along the side of the maps. The southeast corner from page 21 of the Arizona Atlas and Gazetteer is shown in the figure below.

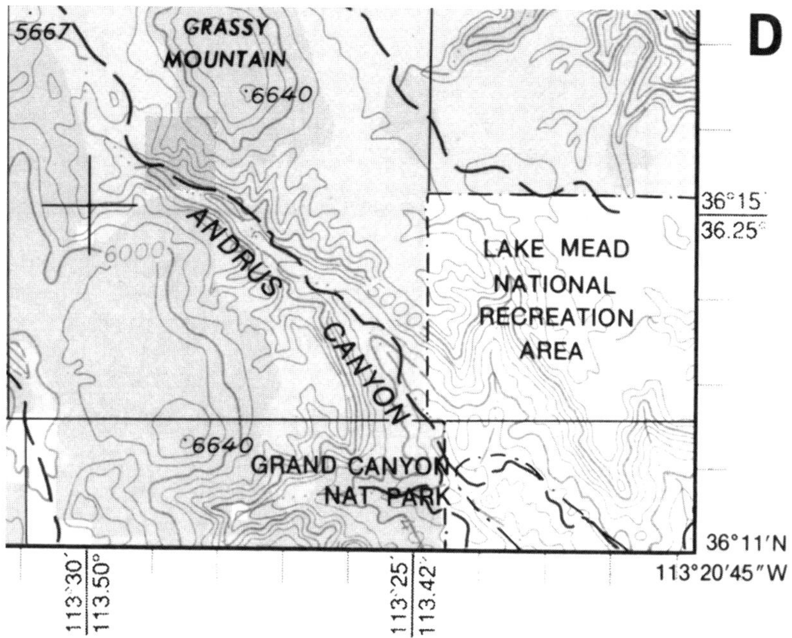

Map from Arizona Atlas & Gazetteer © DeLorme, Yarmouth, Maine. Reproduced with permission.

The latitude at the bottom of the map is N 36° 11'. The latitude for each gray tick mark going up the right side of the page increases by 1 minute for each mark. The first tick mark above N 36° 11' is 36° 12', followed by 36° 13', then 36° 14' until it reaches the tick mark labeled 36° 15' shown above the line and 36.25° below the line. The latitude 36° 15' is the same as 36.25°, which is expressed as degrees only. Refer to Chapter 16 if you need a quick review of degrees and minutes. On this map it is easier to use degrees and minutes (i.e. 36° 40.33') instead of degrees only (i.e. 36.67°), so you can ignore the degree only numbers. The grid actually covers two pages, so when the book is open, as represented in the figure below, the map on facing pages covers approximately 49' in latitude and 1° 22' in longitude.

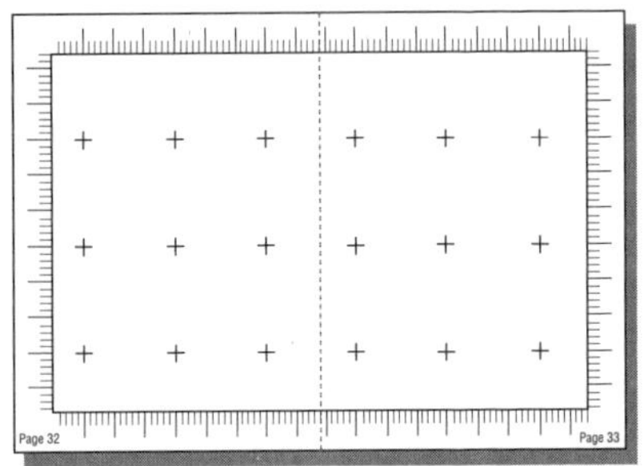

As you can see, the latitude/longitude grid is not printed on the map, so a little preparation is required before it can efficiently be used with a GPS receiver. The grid can be drawn and used with either a 1' X 1' grid or a 15' X 15' grid.

The 15' X 15' grid must be used with a minute/second calibrated ruler; whereas the 1' X 1' grid can be used with the eye alone, but it requires a lot of drawing. The grids are demonstrated and explained below to help you decide which is the best one for you.

1' X 1' Grid

If you want to draw a grid on the map that can be used with the eye alone, simply use a ruler to draw lines that correspond to the 1 minute tick marks. The 1' X 1' grid is about as fine a grid as you can profitably get on a 1:250,000 scale map, so there is no need to make any further subdivisions. Draw the latitude lines from one side of the two facing pages all the way to the other side and the longitude lines from top to bottom. The 1' X 1' grid is shown on the corner of a map in the figure opposite.

Coordinates can now be read directly from the map. The intersection between US Route 95 and Castle Dome Mine Road, label #1 on the map, lies almost on latitude N 32° 58'. The longitude is about 1/4 of a minute west of W 114° 17', so the intersection's coordinate is N 32° 58', W 114° 17.25'. The coordinates of a few points with their eyeball measured coordinates are given below. Each point is labeled with a number and a dot shows the points' exact location.

Point	Latitude	Longitude
#1	N 32° 58'	W 114° 17.25'
#2	N 33° 9.33'	W 114° 25.9"
#3	N 33° 0.4'	W 114° 20.66'
#4	N 33° 2.4'	W 114° 31.5'
#5	N 33° 2.4'	W 114° 10.33'

Easy use is the 1' X 1' grid's advantage, but its disadvantage is the time it takes to draw it on the map. The 1' X 1' grid is best used when drawn only on the areas where you need to measure coordinates. For example, draw the grid only at the road intersections you will travel and not over the entire page.

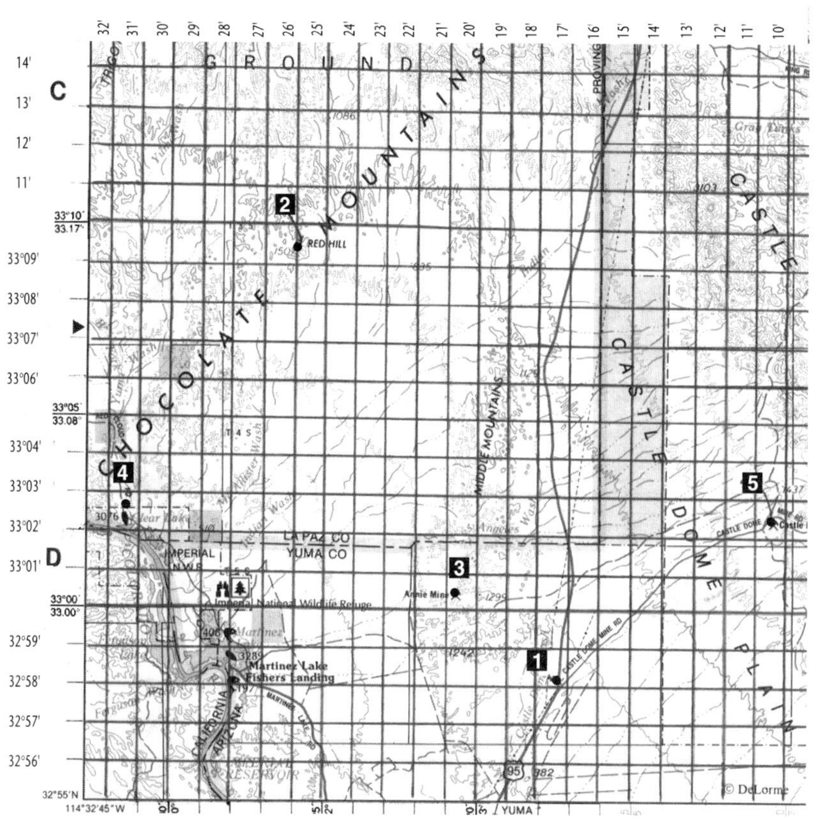

Map from Arizona Atlas & Gazetteer © DeLorme, Yarmouth, Maine. Reproduced with permission.

15' X 15' Grid

The 15' X 15' grid must be used with a minute/second calibrated ruler, but it provides the fastest and most accurate way to measure coordinates from any location on the map. There are two ways to draw the 15' X 15' grid on the map. The first method utilizes the crosses found on each page as shown in the figure below. To form the grid, draw lines through the crosses from one side of the page to the other and from top to bottom. The grid is shown as it would appear on two facing pages.

Not all the rectangles of the grid are 15' X 15', because the total minutes of latitude and longitude across the map is not a factor of 5. The minute/second calibrated ruler can measure latitude in any rectangle even if it is not 15' X 15'. However, longitude can only be measured on rectangles that are 15' wide regardless of their height. The shaded squares are not quite 15' X 15' and it is more difficult to use the ruler in those areas. The minute/second calibrated ruler is used exactly as shown in Chapter 8. Note that longitude cannot be measured on the right and left sides of the map because the rectangles are not 15' wide. The longitude can be measured on the sides of the maps by drawing the 1' X 1' grid in the areas where the ruler cannot be used or by using only a part of the ruler to measure, but fortunately the 15' X 15' grid can be shifted to cover the map more efficiently.

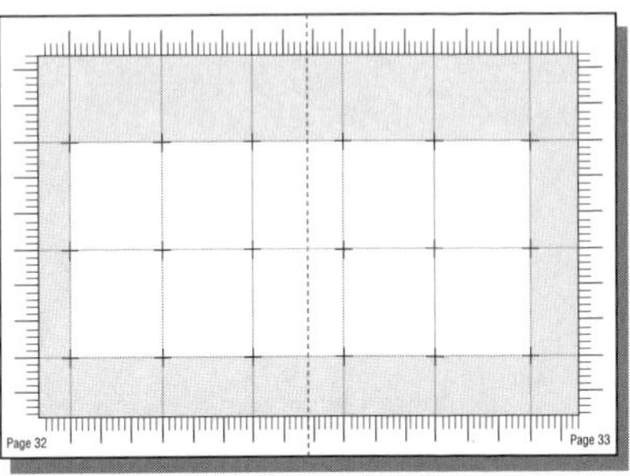

The calibrated ruler cannot easily be used in the shaded areas.

15' X 15' Grid Adjusted

When the 15' X 15' grid is drawn through the crosses printed on the map, it is difficult to measure longitude in rectangles that are not 15' wide. So instead of using the crosses to form the grid, start on either side of the map and draw a vertical line through the first longitude tick mark whose minute value ends in 0 or 5. For example, draw the first line through a longitude like 114° 15' or 112° 30', not through 111° 13'. From this first line, count over 15 minutes and draw the next vertical line and so forth until you reach the other side of the map. The same approach is taken with the latitude lines. Start with the first latitude tick mark, at either the top or bottom of the map whose minutes end in either 0 or 5, and draw a horizontal line across the map. Count off 15 minutes in latitude, then draw the next horizontal line and so forth until you run out of latitude tick marks. The grid will look similar to the one in the top figure opposite.

Notice that more of the map is covered by full 15' X 15' rectangles than when drawn through the crosses, which makes it easier to use the minute/second calibrated ruler.

There is one situation you need to consider when drawing the longitude lines on the map. Sometimes the longitude on the edge of a map has a minute value that ends in either 0 or 5, but it also has a non-zero second value. Such a situation is shown in the figure to the right. The edge of the map starts at 113° 10' 15", which raises the question of whether to draw the first vertical line for the grid on the edge of the map or to the left by 4' 45" at the 113° 15' tick mark. If you use the edge of the map as the first vertical grid mark, the width of the rectangle will not be 15', but 14' 45". If you use the 113° 15' as the first vertical grid line, then the area to the right of 113° 15' cannot be measured easily with the ruler. The most convenient solution is to use the edge of the map as the first vertical line and live with the slight inaccuracies introduced by a rectangle that is slightly less than 15' wide.

With the grid drawn on the map, the minute/second calibrated ruler can measure the coordinates of any location. Measurements must be done with the 1/250K scale, which is shown to the right. The 00 marks the start of a minute and the 30 represents 30" or half a minute. A full minute goes from 00 to 00 and the entire ruler comprises 15 minutes total, the same size as the rectangles on the map. The small tick marks are each worth 5 seconds.

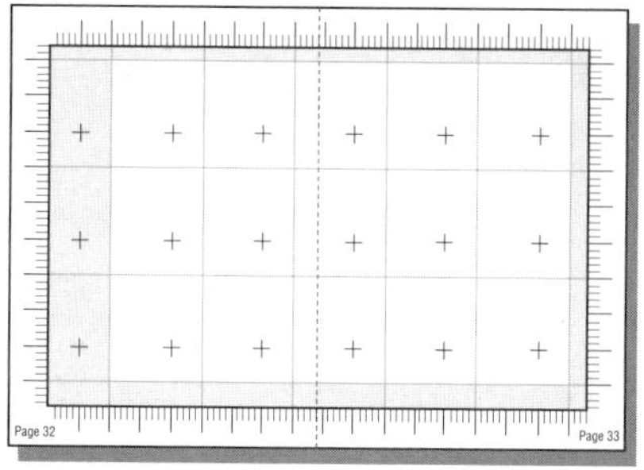

Adjusting the 15' X 15' grid results in more measurable area.

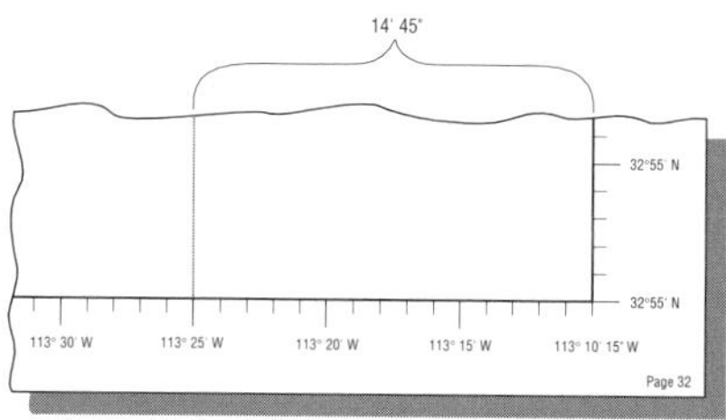

Ignore squares slightly short of 15' X 15'.

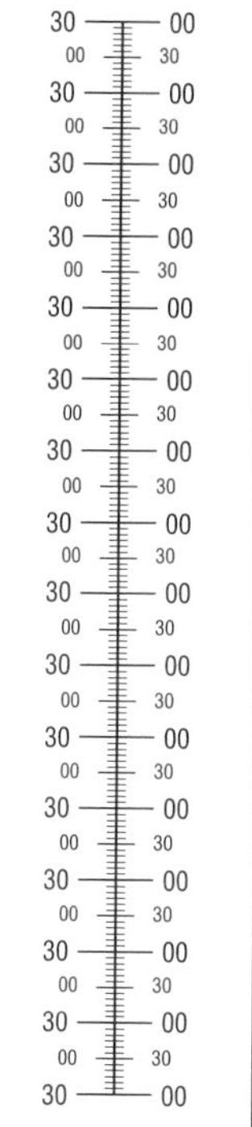

1/250K minute/second calibrated ruler.

To measure a latitude coordinate, place one end of the ruler on the bottom line of a grid rectangle and the other end on the top as shown in the figure. Count the number of minutes and seconds from the bottom latitude value to the location of interest. The figure shows how to place the ruler to measure the latitude of Needle Peak. Using the right side of the scale, the first 00 number on the ruler lies on the N 32°40' latitude line. The next 00 is N 32° 41', the next 00 is N 32° 42' and so forth. The 30 number just below Needle Peak is N 32° 45' 30" and the point for the peak is three small tick marks above the 30 number, so the final latitude is N 32° 45' 45".

The longitude is measured by placing each end of the minute/second calibrated ruler on adjacent longitude lines, refer to Chapter 8. The longitude line on the right-hand end of the ruler is W 111° 55'. Count up the minutes from the right side of the ruler and stop at the 00 just to the right of Needle Peak, which represents W 112°. Then count off four small tick marks to the one directly below the point for the peak. The final longitude is W 112° 0' 20". The final coordinate for Needle Peak is N 32° 45' 45", W 112° 0' 20".

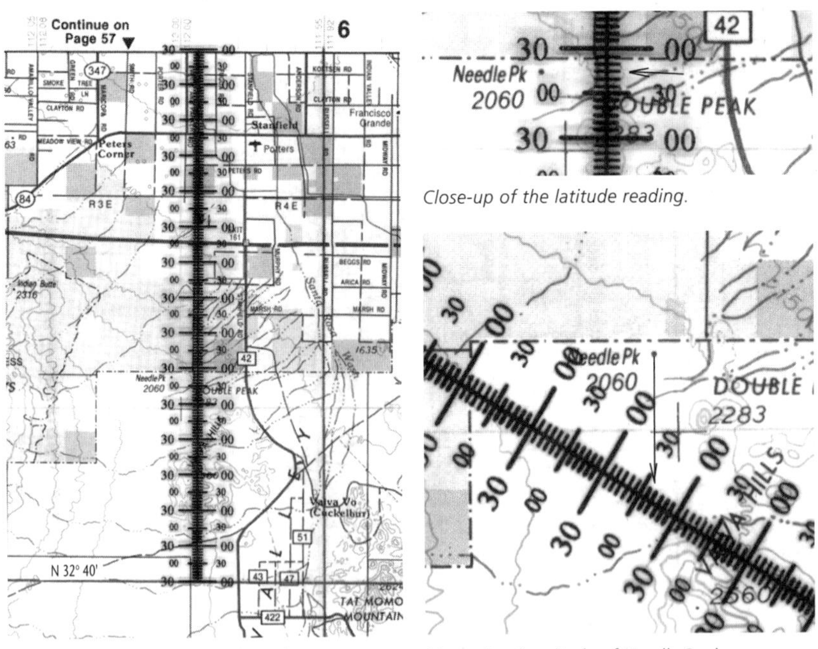

Close-up of the latitude reading.

Measuring latitude of Needle Peak.

Measuring longitude of Needle Peak.

A Road Trip

You are a mine engineer and you need to do some inspections near Sif Vaya and the Vekol Mountains. You have never been in that part of the state and decide to use your GPS receiver to keep you from missing the turn-offs. You are not too concerned about finding the mines once you get in the area because they are well marked, but it is getting to the area that has you concerned. You have been told that the road leading to both mines is difficult to see from the highway.

From Gila Bend you will travel east on Interstate 8 to Indian Reservation Route 42 where you will travel south to the turn-off for the dirt road to Sif Vaya. The same road eventually leads to the Vekol Mountain mines. As your first waypoint, you choose the intersection of Interstate 8 and Route 42, labeled #1 on the map. The receiver will give notice as you approach a waypoint, so you will have plenty of time to slow down to turn off. The second, labeled #2, is the intersection for the turn-off to Sif Vaya. Once again, the receiver will warn you of your approach, so you know when to slow down to start searching for the road. The third waypoint leads you straight through the intersection just before the Sif Vaya mines. You do not want to turn left at the intersection, so a waypoint at any place on the road beyond the mines will make the receiver point the direction you need to travel to get through the intersection correctly. The last waypoint is in the area of the Vekol Mountain mines. After passing waypoint #3, the only time you need to look at the receiver for direction is at the intersection where you need to turn right to get to the mines. Because of the position of waypoint #4, the receiver will point right when you need to turn right.

You use the minute/second calibrated ruler to measure the coordinates of each waypoint and give them a name as shown below.

Point	**Latitude**	**Longitude**	**Name**
#0	N 32° 57' 00.0"	W 112° 44' 45.0"	GILA-B off map
#1	N 32° 49' 35.5"	W 111° 57' 40.0"	EX-161
#2	N 32° 35' 15.0"	W 111° 59' 40.0"	KOHATK
#3	N 32° 36' 15.8"	W 112° 03' 35.0"	S-VAYA
#4	N 32° 33' 15.5"	W 112° 06' 10.0"	VEKOL

You know that you must select the map datum on the receiver before you enter the waypoint coordinates and you are correct in not assuming it is the NAD 27 datum. You search the atlas and find on the inside of the front cover that the datum is WGS 84. You are ready to configure the receiver:

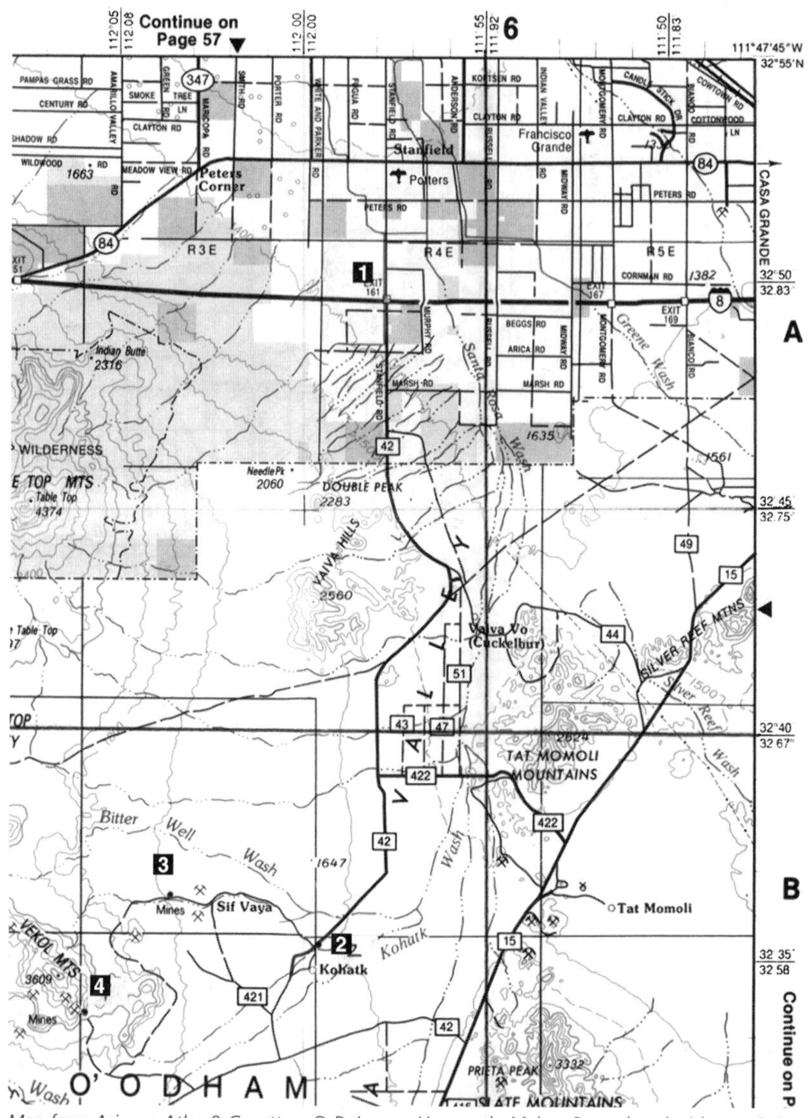

Map from Arizona Atlas & Gazetteer © DeLorme, Yarmouth, Maine. Reproduced with permission.

- **Map datum: World Geodetic System 1984 (WGS 84)**
- **Units: Statute**
  You will be using the receiver in your truck and want the speed and distance statistics to match the speedometer and odometer.
- **Coordinate grid: Latitude/Longitude**
  Select the degrees and minutes format to correspond to the coordinates on the map.

- **North setting: True North**
  You have a compass, but probably will not use it, so set the receiver to true north. When looking at the map the bearings reported by the receiver will make sense.
- **CDI limit: not important**
  You will be in your truck and must follow the road. Most of the time you will be far off the straight course the receiver wants you to follow. Only at intersections will the receiver supply information that will help you make a decision as to direction and then you will only look at the arrow on the navigation screen that points the way. You set the CDI to its largest limit and do not even look at the highway navigation screen that displays the course deviation.

After setting the receiver, you enter the waypoints and form a route.

Name	Point	Desired Track	Distance km
GILA-B	#0		
		100°	46
EX-161	#1		
		187°	17
KOHATK	#2		
		287°	4
S-VAYA	#3		
		216°	4.3
VEKOL	#4		

The receiver reports the total distance from Gila Bend to the mines at Vekol Mountains as 71.3 mi. (114.7 km). You are ready to make the trip, so you put the receiver into its mounting bracket in the truck, plug its power into the cigarette lighter, and connect it to the external antenna mounted on the roof.

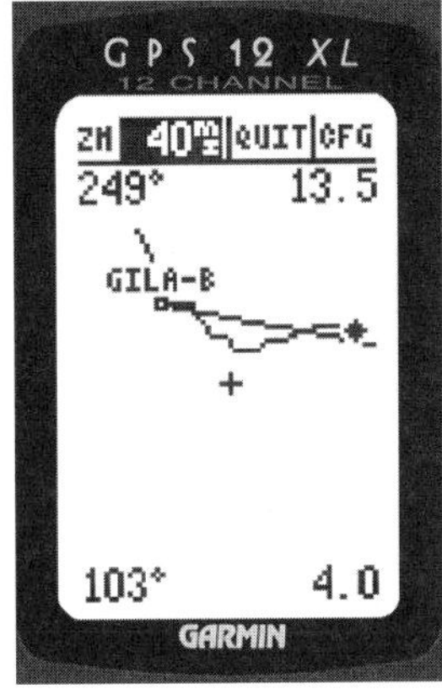

You activate the route and ignore the receiver until you get through Gila Bend and onto Highway 8. When the highway curves, the arrow on the navigation screen does not point straight ahead because you are off the direct line course. After traveling several miles you switch to the moving map screen to see how your path compares with the straight line between Gila Bend and Exit 161. The straight line is the course the receiver plots directly between waypoints. The curving line is the actual course you have traveled on the highway.

You leave the receiver on the map display in the "track up" mode and watch as your position, represented by the diamond shape, approaches EX-161. Soon the receiver indicates that you are approaching the turn-off. Just as you reach the exit, the receiver begins pointing to the next waypoint in the route, KOHATK. You switch the receiver to the navigation screen and notice the direction arrow is also pointing to the right, which is the direction you need to exit. You turn off and continue south on Highway 42.

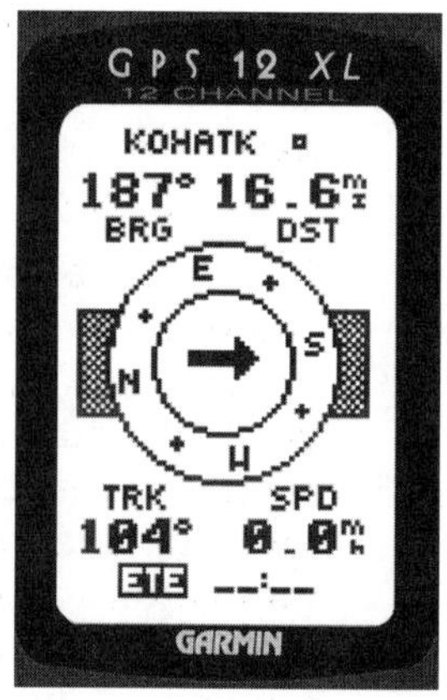

As you travel toward the KOHATK waypoint, you watch the receiver's map and notice that your path on the screen looks like the shape of the highway on the map. This makes sense because the receiver is tracking your movements.

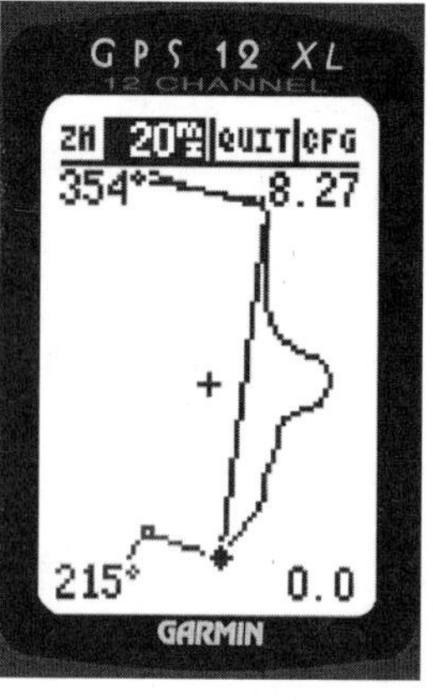

When the receiver indicates that you are close to KOHATK, you slow down and look for the turn-off on the right side of the road. The arrow on the navigation screen also points to the right. You find the dirt road and turn right to head toward the mines at Sif Vaya.When the road to the left appears at the intersection, just before the mines, the arrow points straight ahead because you chose a waypoint beyond the intersection. You follow the arrow straight and soon find the signs marking the mine entrances.

When you get back to your truck, the navigation arrow points straight ahead toward the S-VAYA waypoint, which you still have not reached.

Once past S-VAYA, you simply follow the road until it comes to the T-intersection. You already know you need to turn right, but because the last waypoint, VEKOL, also lies to the right, the navigation arrow points the same direction you need to turn. As you make the right turn, you know that the receiver has completed its job of warning you when important intersections were getting close.

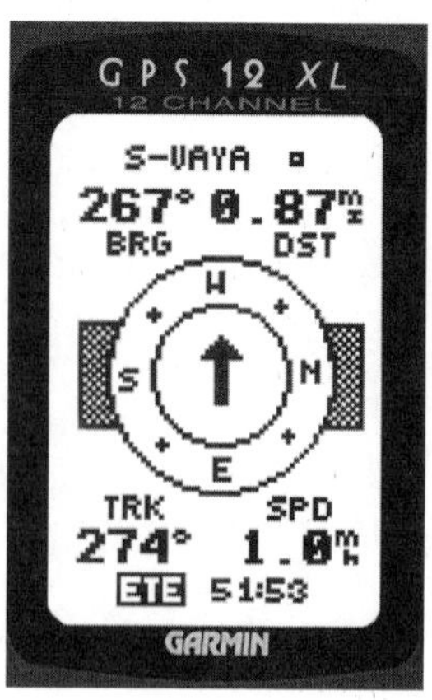

A Metric Map for Road Trips

Other maps that are good for extended road trips are the USGS 1:100,000 metric maps because they show enough detail to easily get the coordinates of freeway intersections and major back roads while still covering a large area. The UTM grid is printed on the USGS metric maps, but instead of using a 1 km (0.621 mi.) square as demonstrated in Chapters 5, 6 and 7; it uses a 10 km (6.21 mi.) square. The northing and easting numbers of the southeast corner of the USGS Norfolk map are shown in the figure.

On this map the abbreviations are different than previously described and stand for the following:

3**9** means 3**90**000m.E.
40**5** means 40**50**000m.N.

The lines of the grid are too far apart to measure the coordinates of a location with the eye alone, so accurate measurements can be made by either subdividing the printed grid lines or by using a special ruler. Once again, using a ruler requires far less work than subdividing by drawing additional lines by hand. The USGS metric maps also make it easy to use a ruler because the grid is already printed on the map, so no advance

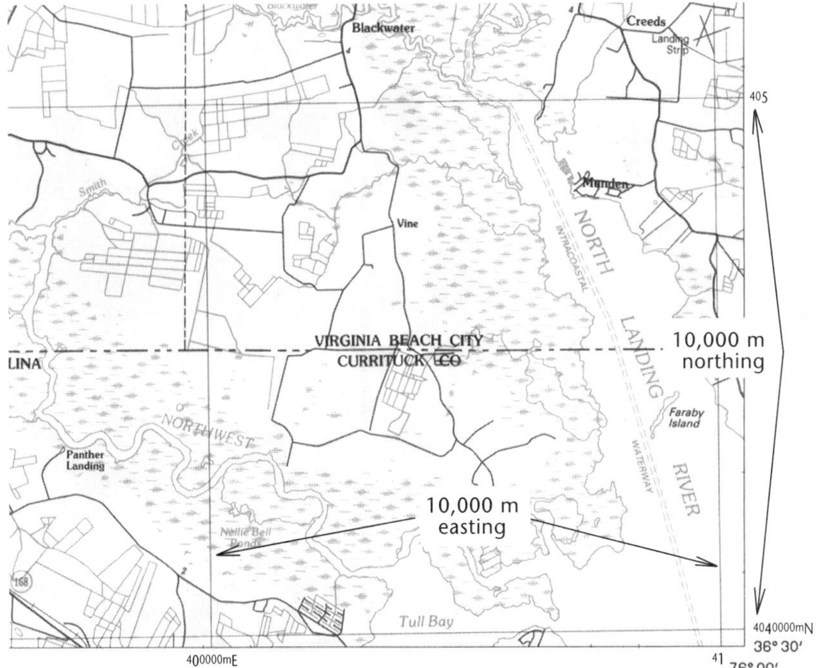

preparation is needed. A good ruler that provides the correct scale is the UTM Grid Reader shown in the picture.

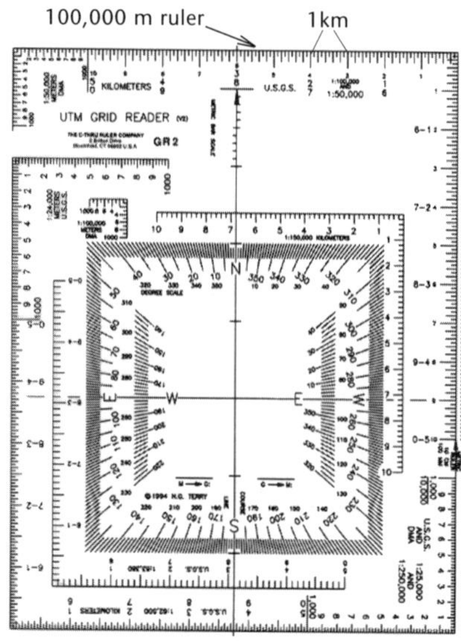

There are numerous grids available, but the 1:100,000 scale ruler is along the top and right-hand side. The entire length of the ruler is 10,000 m to match the 10 km (6.21 mi.) grid. There are numbers to indicate the 1, 2, 3, etc., kilometer marks. Each kilometer is further subdivided into 10 units, each of which is equivalent to 100 m (328.1 ft.) and means the coordinate of a location can be measured to an accuracy of about half of a mark, which is 50 m (164 ft.).

A coordinate is measured by placing the corner of the ruler on the location, then noting where the easting grid line crosses the horizontal scale and the northing grid line crosses the vertical scale. Final easting and northing coordinates are determined by adding the numbers noted above, in thousands of meters, to the easting and northing values of the grid lines that intersect the scales.

The map on the next page shows a ruler placed at the intersection near Back Bay. The ruler indicates that the 4**00**000m.E. grid line intersects the horizontal scale at 7,700, making the easting coordinate:

4**00**000m.E. + 7,700 = 4**07**700m.E.

The 40**50**000m.N. grid line crosses the vertical scale at 6,750 resulting in a northing coordinate of:

40**50**000m.N. + 6,750 = 40**56**750m.N.

The final coordinate is determined by finding the zone on the map and the latitude band letter from the diagram in Chapter 6 to get:

18 S 40**7**700m.E.   40**56**750m.N.

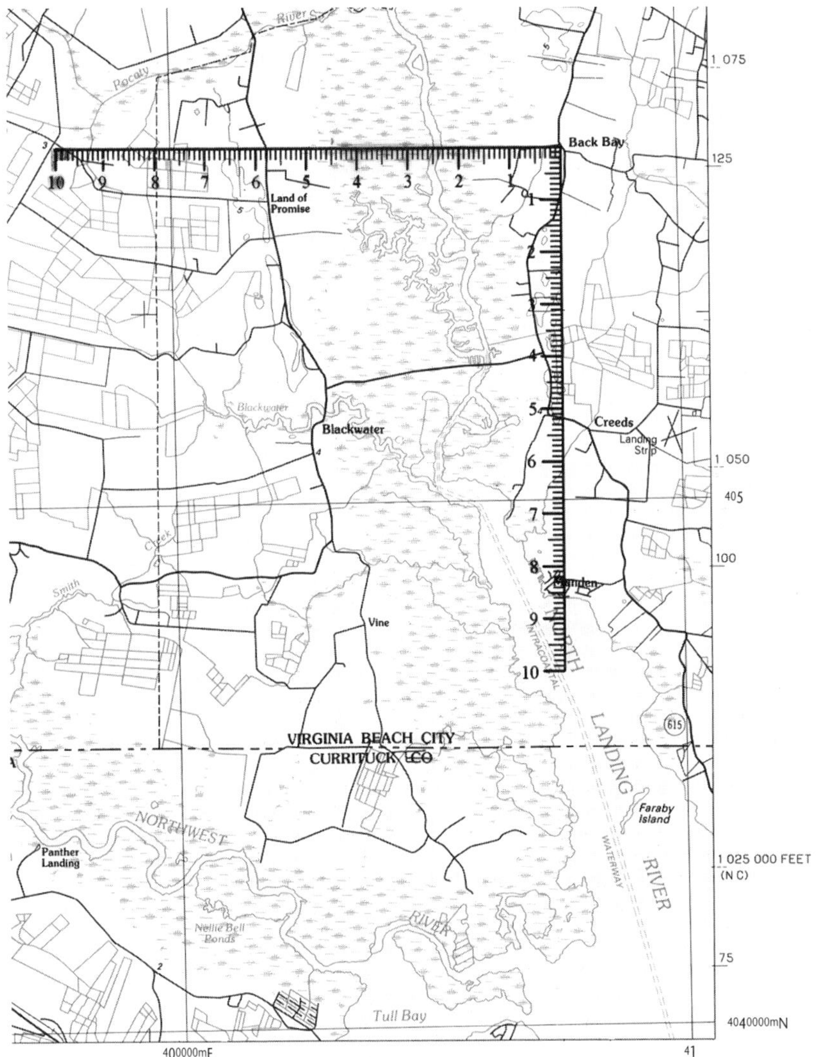

NORFOLK, VIRGINIA – NORTH CAROLINA
36076-E1-TM-100

When using metric maps, road trips would be planned and traveled in the manner described in the previous example of this chapter. The only difference is that the first example uses the latitude/longitude grid on a 1:250,000 scale map, while the USGS metric maps such as the one reproduced above offer the UTM grid on a larger scale of 1:100,000.

11 Recovering from Disaster

In all the previous examples, the GPS receiver performed flawlessly. It provided sure knowledge of your current position and guided you, with the Goto and route functions, to where you wanted to go. The results described in the previous chapters are completely achievable, but you still need to be prepared to cope with poor signal reception and possibly the entire loss of the receiver. This chapter stresses manual navigation techniques. Refer also to the books listed on page 201 if you would like to be more proficient with a map and compass. Read also Chapter 3, which describes the importance of field notes to track your path. A GPS receiver can also help you become more proficient in manual navigation skills as described in Chapter 4, under the heading Point-to-Point Calculations.

The Lava Flows

Your neighbor owns a cabin in Duck Creek Village, and at the yearly block party he tells you about the lava flows in the middle of the forest. It does not seem too interesting until he tells you that there are supposed to be huge underground tunnels that stretch for hundreds of miles. He has not seen them himself, but claims the locals know all about them. You had read about a lava tube, in an excellent Arizona guidebook, that is like a railway tunnel snaking under the forest floor. It sounded fascinating, so you decided to look for the tunnels near Duck Creek. You buy the USGS Henrie Knolls map of southern Utah.

Your neighbor said there were openings near Anderson Spring and near the two peaks east-southeast of the spring. As you can only spare one weekend, you and a friend will drive to Duck Creek on Friday after work, search for the tubes on Saturday, fish in the lake on Sunday, then return home.

You have owned a GPS receiver for quite a while. It has always worked and you have come to rely on it. You generally use a map, but take a compass only out of habit. You will take the trip in late September when the cooler weather has killed all the mosquitoes. The receiver calculates the sunrise and sunset to be 6:17 am and 6:30 pm respectively. You will leave from Duck Lake and hike up a dry creekbed to the point labeled #1. The receiver's map screen will be used to guide you over the large lava flow to the two small hills labeled TWOPKS. From there it will be onto Anderson Spring. The return trip will be across the lava flow to the south to a point labeled #2, then back to #1 and down the creekbed. The total trip is about 7.5 mi. (12.1 km). It is light for only 12 hours, which is not a long day, but if you leave camp at 6:00 am there will be enough time to make the trip and do some exploring.

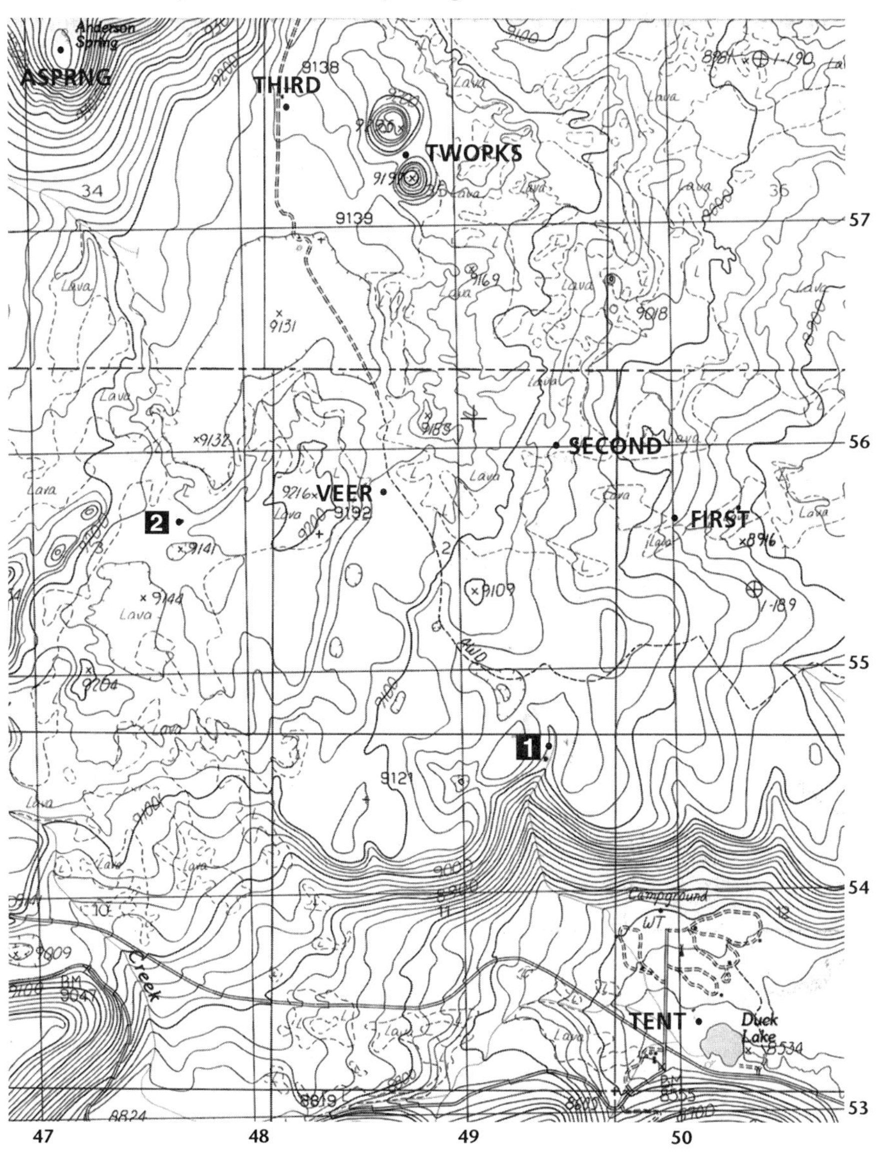

The Trip

The Friday for the trip finally arrives. The second work ends, you rush to pick up your friend and you're off. It is dark by the time you arrive at Duck Lake, but because it is late in the camping season there are only a few other campers and it is easy to find a deluxe spot for your tent right on the shore.

In the morning, you are up before sunrise and right at 5:45 am you turn the receiver on to mark the camp's position:

12 S 3**50**207m.E. 41**53**453m.N. TENT

You jot the coordinate down in your notebook along with the time. The mouth of the dry creek is not as easy to find as you thought it would be and it is not until 7:00 am that the ground levels off at what should be the end of the creek. You pull out your receiver just to verify your position, but after five minutes it still has not locked onto the satellite signals. The satellite status screen shows there are six satellites in the area, but only two have strong signals. You know foliage will block the signals, so you walk around trying to see if they get stronger at different positions. Nothing seems to work, which is strange because you have hiked and biked all over and your receiver has always been able to pick up enough satellites to lock. The growth in this forest does not seem more dense than any of the others where the receiver worked flawlessly. You wish you had brought your remote antenna because its higher performance and increased sensitivity would help in a situation like this. You look at the map and find a four-wheel drive road due north. Maybe it will provide enough of an opening to allow the receiver to lock, so you head north. You make a note that it is 7:10 am.

As you walk, you notice the beauty of the forest. The sunlight filters through the trees, a slight breeze stirs the quaking aspens and birds sing as they flutter and chase each other. Forty minutes later, you still have not found the road. The map must be out-of-date, but it does not pose a problem because soon you will reach a lava flow where it will certainly be clear enough for the receiver to lock. Sure enough, at 8:10 am you step out of the forest onto a rough and broken lava flow. When you reach the edge of the flow, your receiver locks and you store your position as FIRST.

12 S 3**50**018m.E. 41**55**622m.N. FIRST

When you look at the map, you discover you are way off course. The plan was to go directly from the creekbed to TWOPKS shown at the top of the map. You could kick yourself for not using your compass because you now have a lot of extra walking ahead of you.

The map shows you need to cross through a stretch of forest before you hit the flow that leads to TWOPKS. The receiver will work on the flow, but not in the thick forest, so from now on you will use your compass to stay on course when the receiver cannot lock. You enter the coordinate for TWOPKS into the receiver:

12 S 3**48**700m.E. 41**57**400m.N. TWOPKS

You set the receiver to report magnetic coordinates, then use the point-to-point calculation to determine that the bearing between FIRST and TWOPKS is 303°. Once you enter the forest and try to sight a bearing, you discover how dense it really is because you can only sight a short distance ahead. Walking the bearing with absolute precision is not vital because as soon as you get onto the next flow the receiver will determine your position, but staying on course will save time. Using your compass and a bit of care, you work your way to the next lava flow.

It is 9:10 am before you are far enough out on the second flow to get a lock with the receiver. You mark the position as SECOND.

12 S 3**49**567m.E. 41**56**021m.N. SECOND

Just to see how well you stayed on course, you have the receiver calculate the bearing from FIRST to SECOND. When the receiver reports the bearing as 278°, you know you were not very careful because you were off by 25°. The receiver works fine as long as you are on the flow and you use it to continue your journey. After almost two hours of climbing over the lava boulders that litter the uneven flow, you arrive at TWOPKS where you search for lava tubes with no luck until noon. After lunch, you head in a general westerly direction until you reach another flow where the receiver locks and you mark your position as THIRD.

12 S 3**48**257m.E. 41**57**602m.N. THIRD

You will have to use your compass to get through the forest to Anderson Spring and you want the receiver to tell you the bearing, so you enter Anderson Spring's coordinate into the receiver:

12 S 3**47**200m.E. 41**57**800m.N. ASPNG

The bearing between the two points is reported as 272°. Exercising more care, you use your compass to walk the bearing and arrive at the spring at 1:15 pm. During the hike to the spring, you have written times, positions and bearings in your notebook as follows:

- 5:45 am TENT: 3**50**207 41**53**453
Nobody else up. Very quiet.
- 7:10 am Receiver no lock. North to 4WD road.
- 8:35 am FIRST: 3**50**018 41**55**622
TWOPKS: 3**48**700 41**57**400
FIRST to TWOPKS 303°.
- 9:10 am SECOND: 3**49**567 41**56**021
FIRST to SECOND 278°.
- 10:58 am Arrive at TWOPKS.
- 12:00 pm Lunch. No tubes at TWOPKS.
- 12:20 pm Start for Anderson.
- 12:36 pm THIRD: 3**48**257 41**57**602
Close to road.
ASPNG: 3**47**200 41**57**800
THIRD to ASPNG 272°.
- 1:15 pm Arrive at Anderson Spring.

You use the information and estimate that it will take about 3.5 hours to get back to camp. You do not want to get caught by darkness, which means you have until 3:00 pm to search for tubes. When the time to return arrives, you have not found anything that even remotely resembles a lava tube. Disappointed, you prepare for the trip back by entering the coordinate for point #2 and calculate a bearing of 152° to get there. Using the compass, you start back.

The Disaster

Only 15 minutes later, you slip while climbing over a huge log. Fortunately, your fall is broken. Unfortunately, your fall is broken by your receiver. It is dented and you know it is inoperable because nothing appears on the screen when you turn it on. Slight panic sets in. You depended on the receiver to give you precise knowledge of your position. Navigating with map and compass alone is nothing new, but GPS technology has changed your mode of navigation. You no longer confine your movements to take you from one recognizable landform to the next. You just hike without much thought of where you are and occasionally use the receiver to find your position.

Your first concern is getting back to camp before dark. You do have a flashlight, but no extra batteries. You could survive a night outside, but it does get rather cold and you prefer to sleep in your tent. You open your notebook to study the times and locations you recorded. Dead reckoning tells you that you are about 0.25 mi. (0.4 km) south of Anderson Spring. It dawns on you that the confidence the receiver provided is gone. You are back to the days of "I think we're about here." Your notebook convinces you that crossing the lava flows is much slower than going through the forest. It also reminds you of the road you saw near THIRD. It will be a lot faster to go directly to the road and take it south. You hope it goes as far as the map shows, as the four-wheel drive road is also shown, and it no longer exists. You will just have to take it as far as it goes.

Your new plan quickly jells. Head due east until you hit the road. Follow the road until it either ends or turns into a trail. It should end by a flow. From the end of the road, walk a bearing of 160° for 0.25 mi. (0.4 km), to get clear of any lava flows. From that point you will veer to a bearing of 134° until you run into the camp, the lake or the highway. Then you will return to your tent.

Due east is 90° on the map, but you need to account for the east 14° declination. You repeat the phrase "East is least, West is best" to remind yourself that true north bearings are converted to magnetic bearings by subtracting east or adding west declinations. You subtract 14° from 90°, dial in 76° into your compass and start moving. Much to your relief, at 4:45 pm you arrive at the road. You are not quite sure where you are, but at 5:50 pm the road ends. There is one more hour of daylight with just over 2 mi. (3.2 km) to go. You count paces until you have gone approximately 0.25 mi. (0.4 km) from the end of the road on a bearing of 160°. You think you are around the point labeled VEER on the map. You set the compass for 134° and carefully walk the bearing.

The sun sets while you are still walking, but you have started a sharp descent. Within minutes, you see the light of a fire. Someone is just ahead. When the people around the campfire tell you that you are in the Duck Lake campground, you suppress a small leap of joy. You will soon be back at your tent to spend a warm night. The batteries in your flashlight go dead before you can find your tent. It is like amnesia has struck. You cannot find your tent and you cannot seem to remember where you saw it last. You ask a passing Forest Ranger for help. "Oh, we confiscated the tent this morning. You should have read the signs: no camping on the shore."

12 GPS Receivers and Personal Computers

A GPS receiver is an electronic calculator of navigational data. It is only natural that it connects to a personal computer to provide extended capabilities and conveniences. The two most common and useful applications for computers in relation to GPS receivers are:

- Map Databases
- Moving Maps

Both concepts are described below and manufacturers of map software for computers are listed in the Resources section at the back of the book.

Map Databases

A map database is an electronic map, usually stored on CDROMs, that is accessible by a computer. The computer can not only display the maps on the screen, but it can also print paper copies at user-selected scales with varying amounts of detail. The computer also allows the user to make custom maps by adding information to the basic maps in the database. Imagine you had to track the locations of all the automobile accidents in a large metropolitan area. Electronic maps allow you to store the information of each incident right on the map, so it can be displayed and analyzed. Some map databases concentrate on streets, others on topographical maps and some on marine charts.

Map databases are the coming trend in map management. Electronic maps will not make paper maps obsolete—at least not for several years, but they will affect the way you purchase and use maps. Soon it will be more economical to buy the database of a large area, possibly the entire country, and produce any paper maps you may need of a specific area on your own printer. The computer and electronic maps also make it easier to store and display custom data such as campsites, good fishing areas, boat ramps, telephone poles, cable networks, easements or any other information important to you personally or professionally. Maps on CDROMs also make map storage much simpler in far less space.

Paper maps will be entirely replaced when a lightweight display unit is developed that can withstand the rigors of the outdoors. The unit will probably be combined with a GPS receiver and a backup map in case of equipment failure. It will be a while until all the technology comes together, so do not hold your breath.

All map programs and databases provide some, if not all, of the following features:

Coordinate Identification

Simply place the cursor on any location and the map program instantly provides its coordinate. Databases of topographical maps also provide the altitude. Virtually all map databases provide coordinates using the latitude/longitude grid system, but some allow the user to select other grids such as UTM or MGRS. It does not really matter which grid is used because you can enter the data into the receiver in one format and then switch to another when necessary and the receiver will make all the conversions.

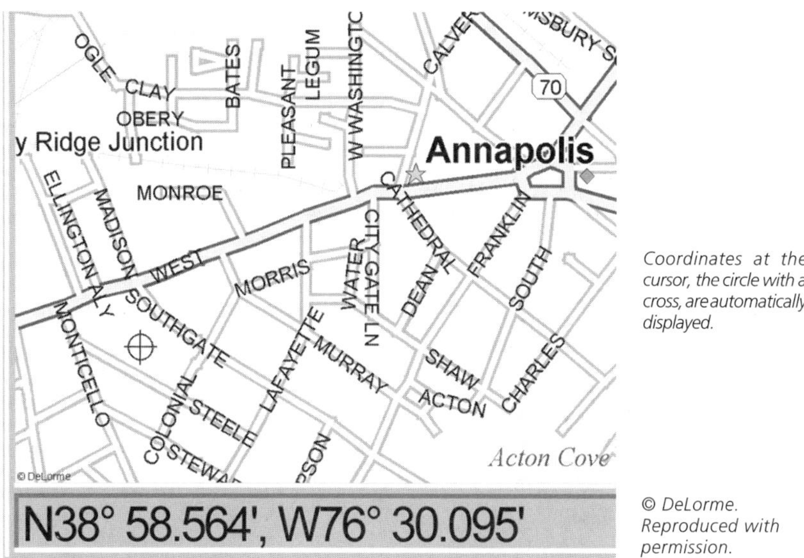

Coordinates at the cursor, the circle with a cross, are automatically displayed.

© DeLorme. Reproduced with permission.

A lot of time is spent in this book showing how to measure coordinates from a map. An electronic map makes all the manual labor unnecessary. However, do not get rid of your map rulers quite yet or forget everything you learned in the previous chapters, because unless you plan on lugging your portable computer with you on your next hike, you may still need the manual techniques in the field.

A good strategy is to use the computer and the map database program to provide the coordinates of all waypoints that can be identified before the trip and carry a map with an appropriate grid into the field for everything else.

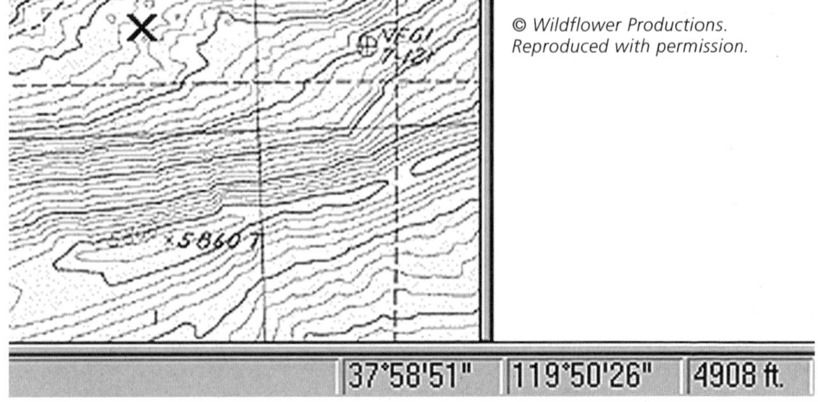

Topographical map databases provide altitude along with the coordinate.

Search Engine

A search engine accepts key words, zip codes, area codes, coordinates, etc., and finds locations or objects that match the specification. The matches are either highlighted or shown on a list. Selecting an object from the match list causes the program to display the object's location on the screen. The capability to search is important because map databases are usually very large and cover a lot of area. Instead of panning around the map trying to find a location, simply type in anything you remember about it and let the computer do the rest. If you are trying to find Lake Hiawatha, you would type in Hiawatha and the program would list all potential locations:

- Hiawatha Creek
- Hiawatha Falls
- Hiawatha Gulch
- Hiawatha Mountain
- Hiawatha Trail
- Lower Hiawatha Lake
- Mount Hiawatha
- Upper Hiawatha Lake

The computer did not find Lake Hiawatha, so you have to look at both Upper and Lower Hiawatha Lake to see if they are what you really want.

Searching works on user-specified data also. If you were setting up a cellular telephone network, you would use your DGPS receiver to accurately position each transmission tower in the field. Back in the office, you would transfer all the locations to the map using a naming convention to indicate the towers' kilowatt (KW) output as shown below.

1 KW Towers: T0001_1, T0002_1, T0003_1
2 KW Towers: T0001_2, T0002_2, T0003_2, T0004_2
5 KW Towers: T0001_5, T0002_5

The search engine can easily distinguish between the different types of towers, making it easy to instantly locate towers of a given power output on the map.

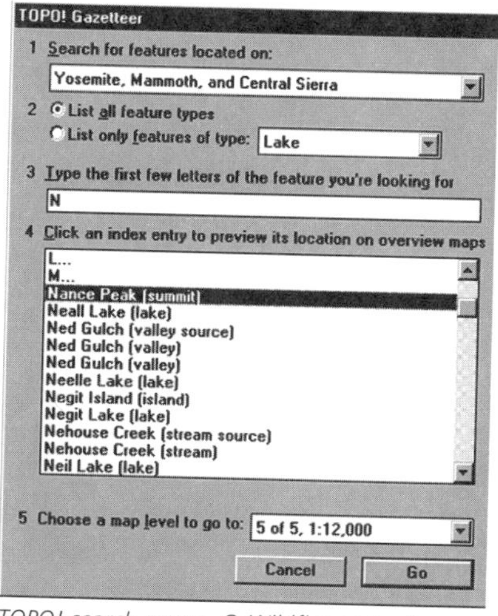

TOPO! search screen. © Wildflower Productions. Reproduced with permission.

Marking Locations

Marking a location is another easy way to find a specific place in the future. You can mark and label campsites, river rapids, bird sighting areas, telephone poles, old growth timber stands or anything else. Displaying a marked location on the screen is as simple as choosing its name from a list with the mouse.

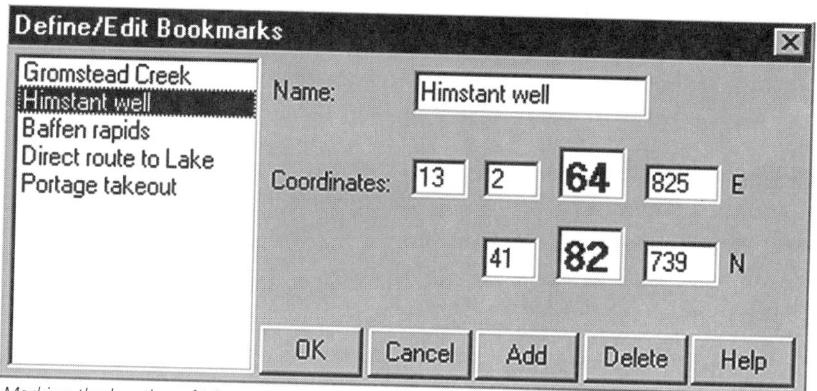

Marking the location of Himstant well. *© Maptech. Reproduced with permission.*

Marking Routes

Much like a route on a GPS receiver, lists of successive locations can be organized in the map database to show the start, end and all the important points in between. The routes, as formed on the computer, can be transferred to the receiver that guides you in the field. Most programs will provide distance and bearing between each point and total distance just like a GPS receiver.

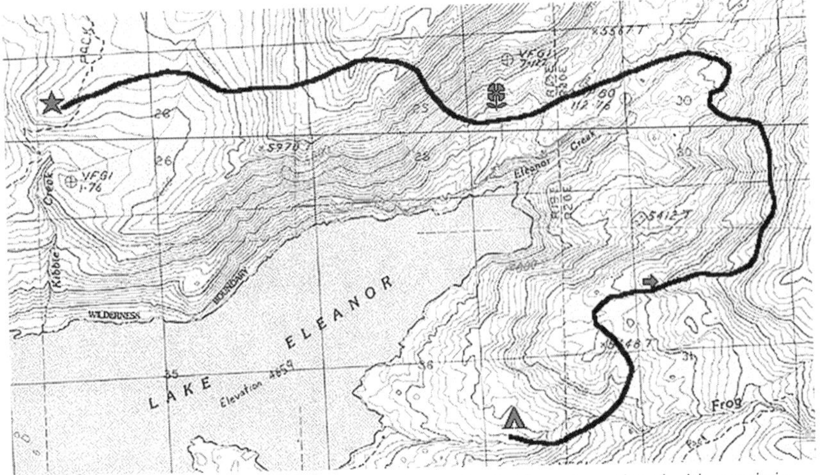

Routes are easily marked for future use. © Wildflower Productions. Reproduced with permission.

The power of the computer makes it possible to store hundreds of routes. When combined with a GPS receiver, the computer overcomes the receiver's limited memory and annotation capabilities. The map database program can become the route management tool for personal and business use. You can store the routes of every hike you have ever made on the computer to maintain a lifetime record and return to any location whenever you like. A uniform laundry business could store its pick-up routes on the database and transfer them to the GPS receiver in the vehicles of new, replacement or temporary drivers.

Distance, Bearing and Area Calculations

Calculating the distance and bearing between two points is easy with a GPS receiver, and of course mapping programs can do much more. A map program can find the length of any path no matter how much it twists or winds. You can draw the path you intend on taking and find the distance before you leave, or you can record waypoints in the field, then transfer them to the computer afterwards to find out how far you went.

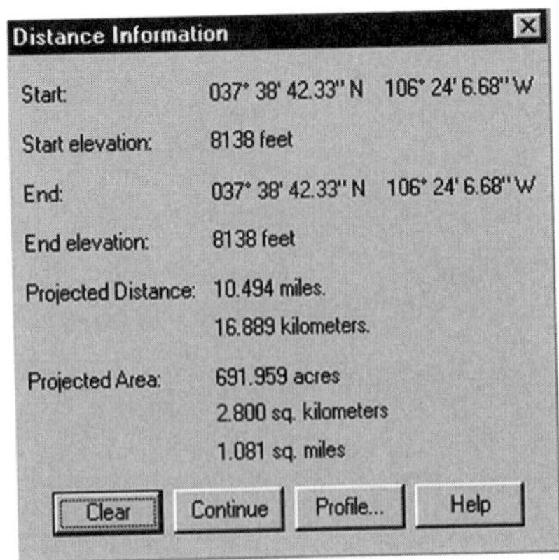

The distance from Start to End is 10.494 miles. An area of 691.959 acres is enclosed by the route. © Maptech. Reproduced with permission.

Area calculation is a powerful tool that may not be used by most outdoor enthusiasts, but it can be invaluable to professionals. The size of a forest fire can easily be calculated even when fighting the blaze if coordinates from a few of its edges are reported to the central command. The points can be connected using the database program and the area immediately quantified. The size of oil spills, water coverage, mountain acreage or a search area can all easily be measured by taking a few coordinates from the area and feeding them to the computer.

Altitude Profiling

One of the best features of topographical databases is altitude profiling. After the user draws a route on the map, the computer instantly produces a cross-section showing all the changes in altitude along the path. Try profiling a trail on a paper map and you will see the power of this feature. Profiling allows you to see in advance which sections of the trail will be challenging and which will be easy. Most map programs can only generate a two-dimensional profile of a path that is useful to professionals who design trails, plan evacuation routes, etc. If the programs were improved to produce three-dimensional profiles of an area, they would give a picture of the lay of the land and would help develop watersheds, reforestation plans and more. Guidebook writers can use a GPS receiver in the field to accurately mark the trail, then transfer the waypoints to the map database to calculate its length and profile, thereby making their maps accurate and informative.

Some map programs will show named points along the trail on the profile, which correlates the profile to places that are easily identifiable in the field.

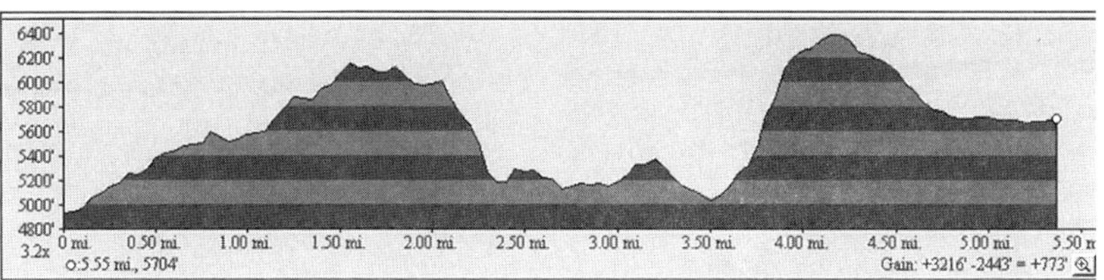

Generating a profile of a trail is one of the most useful and powerful features of a topographical map database. © Wildflower Productions. Reproduced with permission.

Printing

There is no need to buy separate paper maps in addition to a map database program because maps can easily be printed from the database for use in the field. The user specifies the area to be printed, the scale, the amount of detail and if a grid is to appear on the print. User information added to the database can also appear on the printed version, so when you need to see the towers of the cellular phone network, the accidents in the metro area or a watershed's boundaries, the information is superimposed on the map. Even if you are in a situation where you can take a portable computer on your trip, printing out hard copies of the route is still important because in the case of computer failure, a backup plan is always important.

Presently map database programs can put a grid on the map. However, many times the grid is not directly usable for finding coordinates without additional preparation. All the techniques taught in the previous chapters will help you deal with whatever grid the database program produces. If you always print maps at the same scale, you can even make a ruler as described in Chapter 10 to quickly find coordinates. Fortunately, the map programs are improving daily and soon the grid on the map from your database program will be useful just as it is printed.

Upload, Download

Another powerful feature of map database programs is to transfer waypoints from the GPS receiver to the database and from the database to the GPS receiver. Electronic transfers between a computer and a GPS receiver saves manual copying of waypoints between the two machines. Electronic transfer saves lots of time and potential error. Not all programs can presently transfer to and from a receiver, but in the future they all will. Be sure the program you choose interfaces to your receiver.

Transferring to a receiver is important if you have marked a route on the computer and want the waypoints sent to the receiver for use in the field. Planning a trip with a map program and transferring the information to the receiver saves a lot of time and button pressing. Choose a program that allows the waypoint name to be transferred with the coordinate.

Transferring waypoints from a GPS receiver to the database allows the user to record a trip in the field and produce an overlay of the route on the computer's map. Electronically documenting your trip allows you to see how far you went, produce a profile and store the information for future reference. Documentation is even more useful to professionals. Search and Rescue teams can each transfer an electronic record of the area they search into the central command computer to provide a comprehensive record of the areas covered.

Moving Map

A moving map is a logical extension to a map database program. It requires the receiver be connected via a cable to the computer running the map program.

The receiver determines its position and sends coordinates to the portable computer. The computer takes the information and displays your current position on the map. As you move, the map also moves to show your present position and direction of travel on the screen.

Not all map database programs currently provide a moving map, but in the future all will provide the capability. One program, Street Atlas USA from DeLorme, offers a moving map on a database of all the streets in the entire United States. It can be used with a portable computer as a moving map during the trip or on your computer at home as a planning tool for a trip where only the receiver will be used.

The use of small scale maps for road trips was discussed in Chapter 10. Small scale maps, for road travel, are advantageous because they cover a large area with enough detail to find major freeway and back road turn-offs, but they do not have enough detail to allow accurate navigation of city streets. Street Atlas USA overcomes all the disadvantages of paper maps because, with the touch of a button, it adjusts from a minuscule scale of 1:31,680,000, which covers the entire United States, to a very large scale of 1:6,336 that allows individual intersections to be located.

Street Atlas USA 5.0 at its smallest scale covers the entire USA, but shows only interstate highways. © DeLorme. Reproduced with permission.

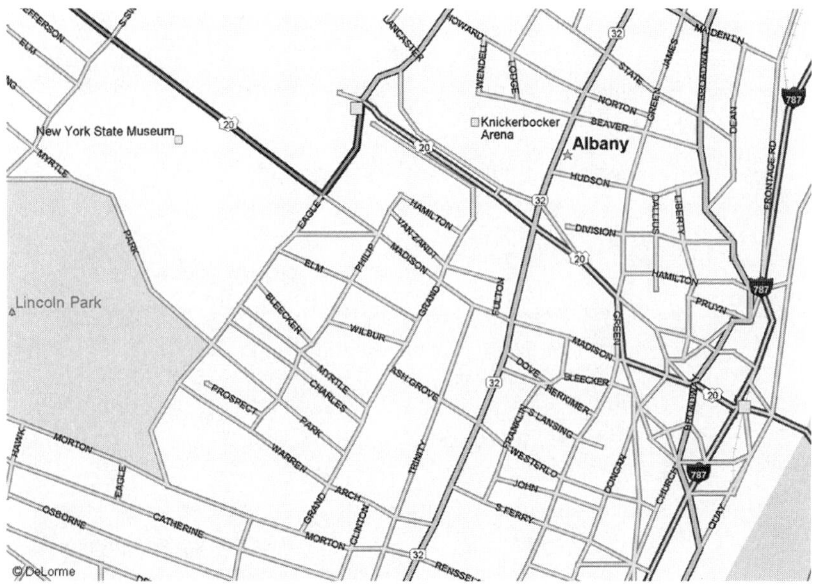

Street Atlas USA 5.0 at its largest scale showing individual surface streets.

The program can be used as a moving map only if you have a portable computer in the vehicle with you and it is connected to your GPS receiver with the data cable available from the manufacturer. As you move, the program shows your position and direction of travel with an arrow. The map scale can be adjusted to show the individual street with its name or your overall location in a large city. Selective Availability does affect the receiver, so when the map is at the very

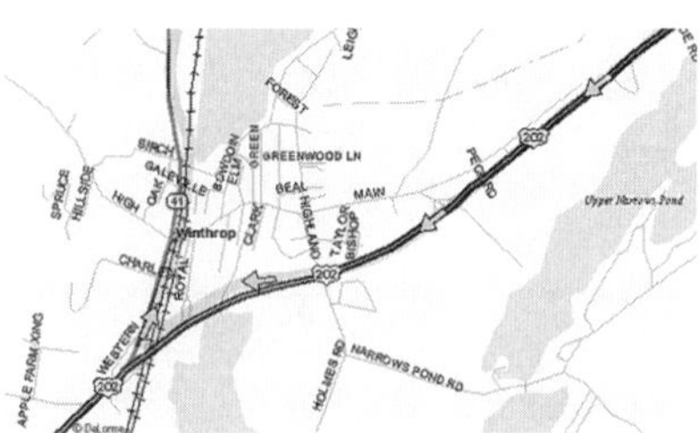

A medium scale shows major highways. Direction of travel is indicated by arrows.

GPS receiver status screen.

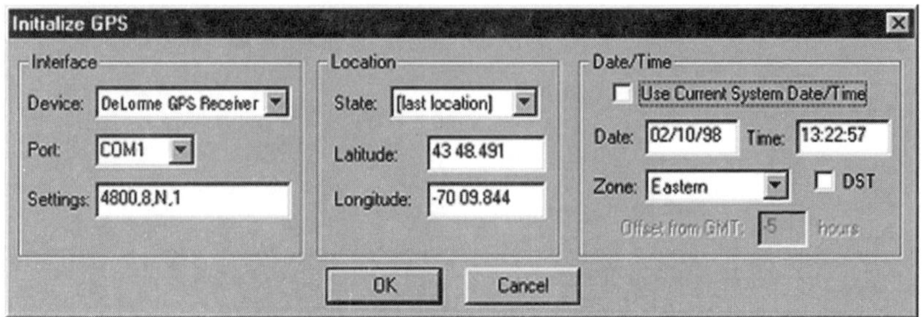

largest scale, the arrow may not be exactly on the road or at the intersection, but it will be close. When Selective Availability is removed, your position will be indicated to an accuracy of approximately 15 m (49.2), which is about the width of most roads.

The program also displays the receiver's status information, which includes if it has locked the time and speed. Street names and highway numbers are displayed simply by placing the mouse over the object and reading the screen.

If you do not have a portable computer to use the program as a moving map on the trip, it can still be used before the trip to plan the route because like any good map database, Street Atlas USA displays coordinates, in latitude/longitude, of any point. The coordinates of every important inter-

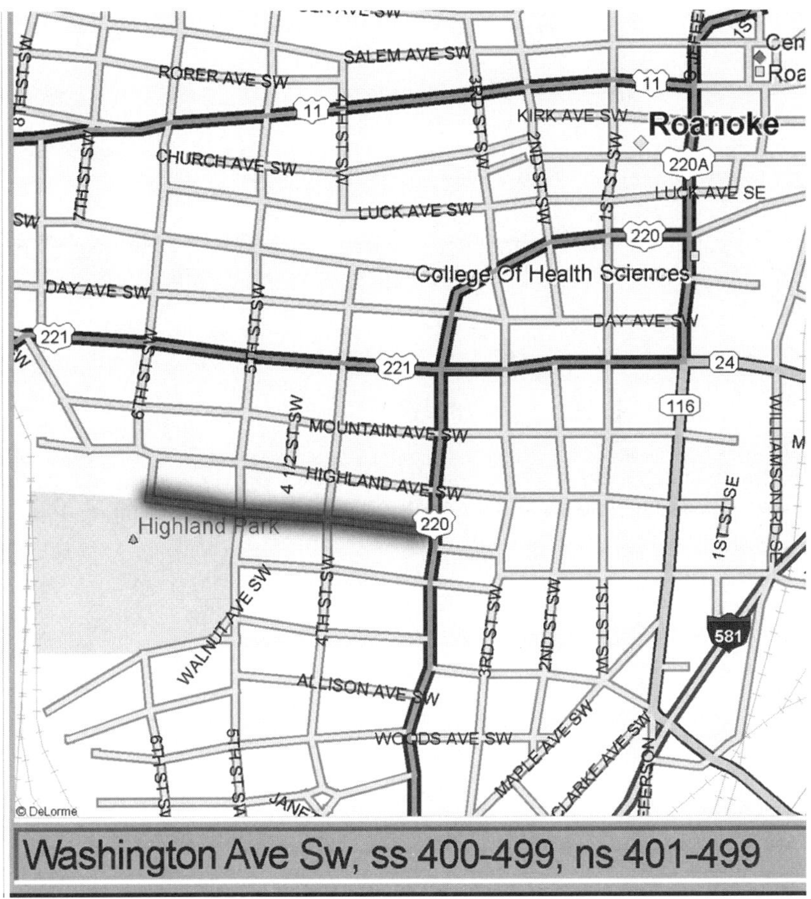

Street names are reported when the street is selected or highlighted.
© DeLorme. Reproduced with permission.

section can easily be found, transferred to the receiver and the receiver alone can be used in the car. If you are traveling on the road and you do not think you will need to put any additional waypoints into the receiver, Street Atlas USA can remove all the drudgery and possible inaccuracies of measuring coordinates by hand.

Built-in Maps

Some handheld receivers actually have road maps permanently stored in their memory. If you want a receiver to use on the road, but cannot afford or do not want to carry a portable PC on the trip, a handheld receiver with a map database is the answer. The maps contain all the major interstate and state highways along with many of the major surface streets in large cities. Soon some receivers will accept a plug-in cartridge that contains all the streets of select major cities.

Small scales show only major highways.

The maps on handheld receivers are not as complete as programs that run on computers such as Street Atlas USA discussed above. The small receiver screen cannot compare to the relatively enormous portable computer screen, nor do the handheld receivers have topographical data like the map databases described earlier. But if you want a receiver that provides some indication of your position relative to known streets and still use it in the wilderness on the weekend, get a receiver with a map database.

Smaller state highways appear at a medium scale.

The amount of detail changes with the scale. Small scales display only highways. Medium scales include the state highways while the smallest scales display whatever surface streets are stored in the database. It does not take very much foresight to predict that complete maps of street and wilderness terrain will be available on handheld receivers in the future. However, it is still several years away.

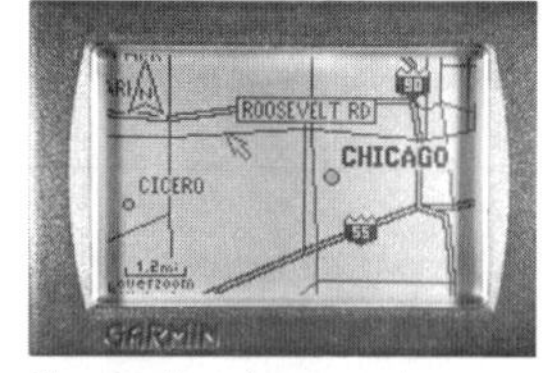

The small scale maps show everything stored in memory including some surface streets.

13 Another Input Device

The most labor intensive aspect of using a GPS receiver is getting coordinates from a map and typing them into the receiver. The use of maps on a computer to instantly find coordinates and automatically transfer them to the receiver was discussed in Chapter 12. For those who cannot carry a computer on their trip, there is another device that makes waypoint extraction and navigation simple. The device is produced by Yeoman. Presently the only version available on the market is called the Navimap, which works with the Brunton GPS XL1000 and GPS XL1000 Forest receivers. Yeoman plans to release a different version soon that works with most receivers on the market.

The Navimap is like a small clipboard that holds a map and a mouse or puck. The Navimap is capable of doing the following:

- Show your present location
- Transfer coordinates to the receiver
- Report range and bearing from current position
- Work with any map regardless of grid or scale
- Calculating an enclosed area if used with XL1000 Forest

The Navimap in conjunction with Brunton XL 1000 Forest provides fast manipulation of waypoint coordinates.

The Navimap mouse is also called a puck.

The Navimap is most useful in situations where you need to mark a lot of waypoints in the field, where you need to concentrate on your work more than manually extracting coordinates, when a map does not have a grid supported by the receiver or where a mistake in reading a coordinate would be disastrous. It is possible, with the Navimap, to successfully use a GPS receiver without understanding anything about grids or coordinates because it will always explicitly show you where you are on the map. However, it is not wise to rely on just one tool for navigation. If the Navimap failed to work, but the receiver still functioned, you would need to understand the map's grid to continue navigation. If it is used in a situation where there is no danger of getting lost, but there is a need to mark the coordinates of locations, it is the perfect tool for those who do not really want to learn anything about maps. The cost of using the Navimap is increased weight and battery consumption, so its capabilities are described below to help you determine if it is appropriate for your situation.

Calibration

Before it can function properly, the Navimap must be calibrated to the map. There are two methods: single point and dual point. Calibration using a single point requires you to know:

- Your current position on the map.
- Location of two points on a north-south line.
- The map's scale.

When the receiver locks onto the satellites, it knows the coordinate of your current position. When you mark your position on the map using the puck, the receiver knows that the position it calculated from the satellite signals is the exact same place you just indicated on the map. Next you select any point on the map as a north reference, then you move the puck due south and mark a point as the south reference. The receiver can now relate the puck's position to direction. If you want the receiver to report true north bearings, choose reference points along a true north-south line. Magnetic bearings are reported if reference points are chosen along magnetic lines. Once the map's scale is given to the receiver, any change in the puck's position can be directly correlated to the correct map coordinate. If you move the puck 3 inches in the southwest direction, the receiver uses the north-south reference to determine direction, the scale to determine the distance and the first point's coordinate to calculate the new coordinate.

Calibration using two known points means you do not have to know the map's scale or which direction is north-south because the receiver can deduce all that from the two points. The two points can be:

- **Present position and another point of known coordinate.**
- **Two points of known coordinates.**

The coordinates of the two points can be found by knowing where you were on the map when you marked the locations as waypoints or you can use the map grid to find the coordinates. The easiest coordinates to read from a map are where the grid lines cross, but the two points must be more than 1 km (0.62 mi.) apart to calibrate the map properly. Both points must be stored as waypoints in the receiver's memory before starting. To calibrate, place the puck over the first point and press the button, so the receiver knows that the coordinate of the first waypoint corresponds with that spot on the map. Place the puck over the second location and press the button to tell the receiver that the coordinate of the second waypoint corresponds to that physical position on the map. The receiver uses the two points' coordinates and their physical locations on the map to calculate the scale and direction.

Navimap is well suited for use with the Thomas Brother maps, which have a specialized grid that is not supported by all receivers. It is easy to know exactly where you are on the map when you mark a location because you just need to look at the street signs. Two points on any map page can be stored to make calibrating the map simple. A power company could download the locations of power poles that need repair into the receiver; the user would calibrate the map on the Navimap and use it to easily find where the work needed to be done.

Finding Your Location On the Map

As you move around, the receiver knows your present position. If you want to see where you are on the map, lights on the puck tell you where to move it. If you move the puck past your position on the map, the lights change to tell you to go the opposite direction. When the puck's position on the map matches the position reported by the receiver, the lights go off and you know your exact position.

Transferring Coordinates to the Receiver

Once the map is calibrated, a simple press of the button on the puck transfers the coordinate from the map to the receiver as a waypoint. You do not have to even look at the map grid to find a coordinate because the Navimap already knows the coordinate of any location where you place the puck. Imagine you manage a forest and need to mark the locations of sick trees in a stand. As you walk through the trees, the Navimap shows your present position on the map and when you find a sick tree, you mark the location with the puck and the coordinate would instantly be transferred to the receiver as a waypoint.

The ease of finding coordinates on the map also makes it easy to plan a route of travel. As you look at the map, decide the best path to go, then mark the waypoints along the way. Each point is sent to the receiver where the Goto function leads you to the destination.

Distance and Area

The Navimap makes it simple to find the range and bearing from your present position to any point on the map. It can also easily calculate the distance between points. The XL1000 Forest model can also calculate the area enclosed by waypoints. Imagine you are with the Coast Guard and need to report the exact size of an oil spill. Sailing the perimeter, you would use the Navimap to mark waypoints as you go, then tell the receiver to calculate the area inside the waypoints.

14 Other Grids

There are innumerable grids in addition to UTM and latitude/longitude. Some are limited to a single country or area like Universal Polar Stereographic or Ordnance Survey Great Britain. Even though most maps have latitude/longitude, it may be the secondary grid and the primary grid may be more convenient to use. If you think you will need a grid that is not UTM or latitude/longitude, be sure the receiver supports it before you buy. This chapter describes the basics of the following grids:

- Universal Polar Stereographic (UPS)
- Ordnance Survey Great Britain (OSGB)
- Military Grid Reference System (MGRS)
- Maidenhead
- Trimble Over and Up
- Thomas Brothers Page and Grid and Trimble Atlas

Universal Polar Stereographic (UPS)

The Universal Polar Stereographic (UPS) grid was developed to provide the Arctic and Antarctic regions with a uniform grid. The UTM grid can extend to cover the entire earth, but it can be confusing near the poles because the zones would be very narrow. Like UTM, the UPS grid has eastings and northings that form 1 km (0.62 mi.) squares. The UPS coordinates for both the north and south poles are given in the tables. Most receivers display the zone as 0. The Greenwich Meridian (0° longitude) and the International Date Line (W 180° longitude) form the zone meridian that references all easting measurements. The longitude lines W 90° and E 90° form the meridian for measuring northing coordinates. Some receivers use the MGRS letters Y and Z for the north pole and A and B for the south pole to label west and east of the easting meridian respectively. The number of points in the figure correspond to the coordinates listed below. There is a direct correspondence between the latitude/longitude grid and the UPS grid only at the meridians, but the tables include latitude/longitude for all the points to help you relate the UPS coordinate to a grid you already know.

Arctic UPS Coordinates

Point	lat/long	UPS Coordinate		
#1	N 84°, W 180°	0 Y	20**00**000m.E.	26**66**760m.N.
#2	N 88°, W 135°	0 Y	18**42**965m.E.	21**57**035m.N.
#3	N 84°, W 90°	0 Y	13**33**237m.E.	20**00**000m.N.
#4	N 88°, W 45°	0 Y	18**42**965m.E.	18**42**965m.N.
#5	N 84°, E 0°	0 Z	20**00**000m.E.	13**33**237m.N.
#6	N 88°, E 45°	0 Z	21**57**035m.E.	18**42**965m.N.
#7	N 84°, E 90°	0 Z	26**66**764m.E.	20**00**000m.N.
#8	N 88°, E 135°	0 Z	21**57**035m.E.	21**57**035m.N.
North Pole	N 90°	0 Z	20**00**000m.E.	20**00**000m.N.

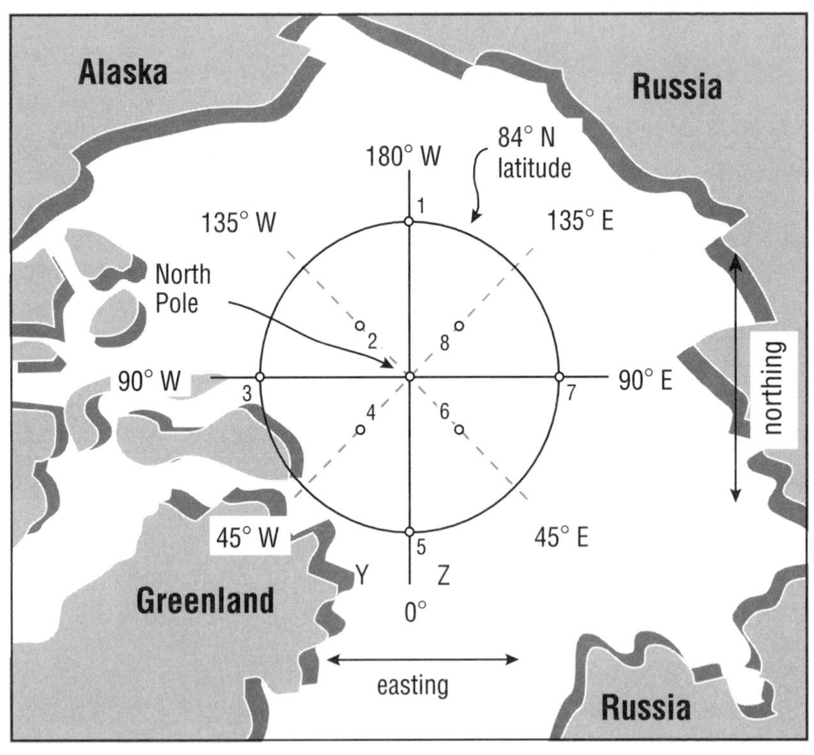

The Antarctic region is similar to the Arctic except the outer circle is S 80°. The figure shows how the UPS grid is laid out for the south pole and also gives the coordinates of some points.

Antarctic UPS Coordinates

Point	lat/long	UPS Coordinate		
#1	S 80°, W 180°	0 A	2000000m.E.	886989m.N.
#2	S 85°, W 135°	0 A	1607211m.E.	1607211m.N.
#3	S 80°, W 90°	0 A	886989m.E.	2000000m.N.
#4	S 85°, W 45°	0 A	1607211m.E.	2392789m.N.
#5	S 80°, E 0°	0 B	2000000m.E.	3113011m.N.
#6	S 85°, E 45°	0 B	2392789m.E.	2392789m.N.
#7	S 80°, E 90°	0 B	3113011m.E.	2000000m.N.
#8	S 85°, E 135°	0 B	2392789m.E.	1607311m.N.
South Pole	S 90°	0 B	2000000m.E.	2000000m.N.

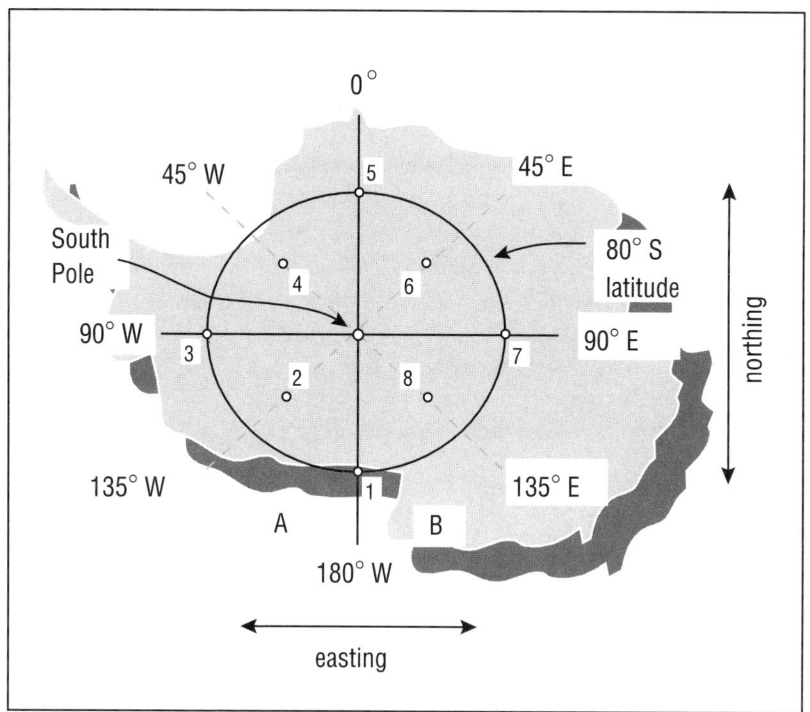

Ordnance Survey Great Britain (OSGB)

The Ordnance Survey Great Britain is a national grid that covers only Great Britain. The country is divided into 100 km (62.1 mi.) square sections (100 km x 100 km) that are lettered with two letters as shown in the figure. Each section is divided into 1 km squares. The grid uses easting and northing numbers to describe location like the UTM grid. A large scale map (1:25,000 or 1:50:000) covers only a portion of the 100 km section.

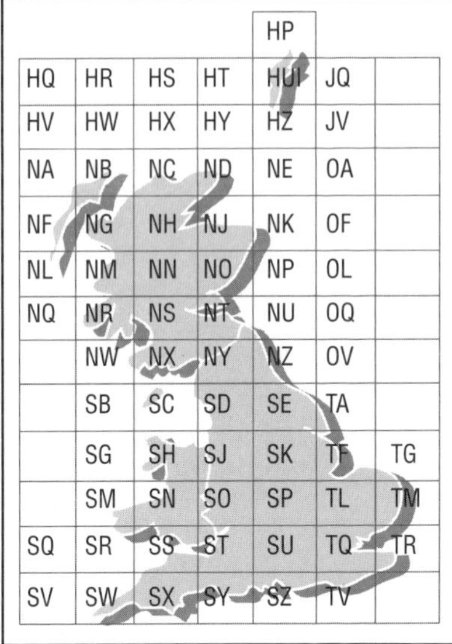

Eastings and Northings

OSGB easting and northing coordinates are much like UTM:

- Increasing easting numbers means you are going east.
- Increasing northing numbers means you are going north.
- Full coordinate is 4**40**000m, 4**57**000m.
- The large numbers shown on a map are an abbreviation.
- For example: 40 means 4**40**000m and 57 means 4**57**000m.
- Distance between **40** and **41** is 1000 m (1 km).
- The last three numbers stand for meters.
- Distance between 3**39**000m and 3**39**541m is 541 m.

OSGB Coordinates

- An OSGB coordinate is section letters, easting and northing.
- The section is printed on the map. A typical value is SE.
- When the section is specified, omit the small number in front.
- An OSGB coordinate would be written as:
  SE **38**000m, **57**900m.
- It may also be shown abbreviated as: SE **38**0 **57**9
- Eastings and northings are not marked m.E. and m.N.
- When using a GPS receiver, the full coordinate: section letters, easting and northing, must be used. Abbreviations are too map specific.

If you travel in Great Britain and use your GPS receiver, you will find the OSGB grid is much easier to use than the latitude/longitude grid because the 1 km (0.62 mi.) squares are printed on the map. On large scale maps, it is possible to read coordinates directly from the grid. However, if you prefer to use a ruler, you can use any of those introduced in the UTM grid chapters if you have the correct scale.

Military Grid Reference System (MGRS)

Most outdoor enthusiasts do not use the MGRS grid because USGS topographical maps do not provide it. However, if you prefer the MGRS grid, see Chapter 12. Electronic map databases will print a map with the MGRS grid. MGRS is simply a modified form of the UTM grid where the first two numbers of the easting and northing are replaced with letters. It is a lot like the OSGB grid because the letters are assigned to 100 km x 100 km squares.

The UTM and MGRS coordinates for the same location are shown below. The first two numbers of the easting and northing were converted to the letters "WB." The 05 from the easting became the "W" while the 36 from the northing became "B." The m.E. and m.N. were removed. All the other numbers remain the same. Sometimes MGRS coordinates are written as a continuous string of numbers and letters as shown on the last line, but most GPS receivers keep the zone designator, the easting and northing separate, so everything is legible.

UTM:	12 S	05**01**788m.E. 36**90**619m.N.
MGRS:	12 S	WB 01788, 90619
	12 SWB 0178890619	

Much like any other grid, GPS receivers require you to enter all the numbers of each coordinate, which means a position is specified down to 1 m. The two tables below can be used to convert from UTM to MGRS, but if you ever have a full UTM coordinate and need to convert it to MGRS, simply enter the UTM coordinate into the receiver and let it do the conversion.

Converting the Easting Number

Some receivers do not show the easting coordinate with a leading zero. The table below assumes a leading zero. To use the table, find the zone to the right and the first digits of the easting at the top and where they intersect is the letter that replaces the easting digits. For example, if you were in zone 47 and the first two numbers of the easting is 03, the numbers 03 would be replaced by the letter "L."

Easting	01	02	03	04	05	06	07	08	Zone
	S	T	U	V	W	X	Y	Z	3, 6, 9, 12, 15, 18, 21, 24, 27, 30, 33, 36, 39, 42, 45, 48, 51, 54, 57, 60
	J	K	L	M	N	P	Q	R	2, 5, 8, 11, 14, 17, 20, 23, 26, 29, 32, 35, 38, 41, 44, 47, 50, 53, 56, 59
	A	B	C	D	E	F	G	H	1, 4, 7, 10, 13, 16, 19, 22, 25, 28, 31, 34, 37, 40, 43, 46, 49, 52, 55, 58

Converting the Northing Number

The first two digits of the northing number are converted to a letter by finding the leading two digits at the bottom of the table and the zone number to the right and where they intersect is the letter that replaces the northing digits. If the zone were 34 and the first digits of the northing 03, the northing numbers would be converted to a letter as follows: The first digit of the northing number is 0, which is even, so you would look at the left half of the table in the section "Even first northing digit." The second northing digit is 3, so you would select the column in the even section that has a 3, which is the fourth column over from the left side of the table. The zone, 34, is even, so you would select the upper row of letters to get the letter "J" to replace the first two digits of the northing number. A few examples are given below to help learn to use the tables if you want to convert from UTM to MGRS or vice versa by hand.

																				Zone
F	G	H	J	K	L	M	N	P	Q	R	S	T	U	V	A	B	C	D	E	Even
A	B	C	D	E	F	G	H	J	K	L	M	N	P	Q	R	S	T	U	V	Odd
0	1	2	3	4	5	6	7	8	9	0	1	2	3	4	5	6	7	8	9	
Even first northing digit										**Odd first northing digit**										

UTM:	56 S	03**46**629m.E.	37**84**395m.N.
MGRS:	56 S	LC 46629	84395
UTM:	19 V	05**13**897m.E.	66**36**786m.N.
MGRS:	19 V	EG 13897	36786
UTM:	42 N	07**84**368m.E.	01**47**169m.N.
MGRS:	42 N	YG 84368	47169

Maidenhead and Trimble Grid Locator

The Maidenhead grid was developed and is used by amateur radio operators. It divides the world into grids with dimensions 20° of longitude by 10° of latitude, which are identified by two letters, AA-RR. The grids are subdivided into areas 2° X 1° and labeled with two numbers 00-99. The areas are further subdivided into sub-areas that are 5' of

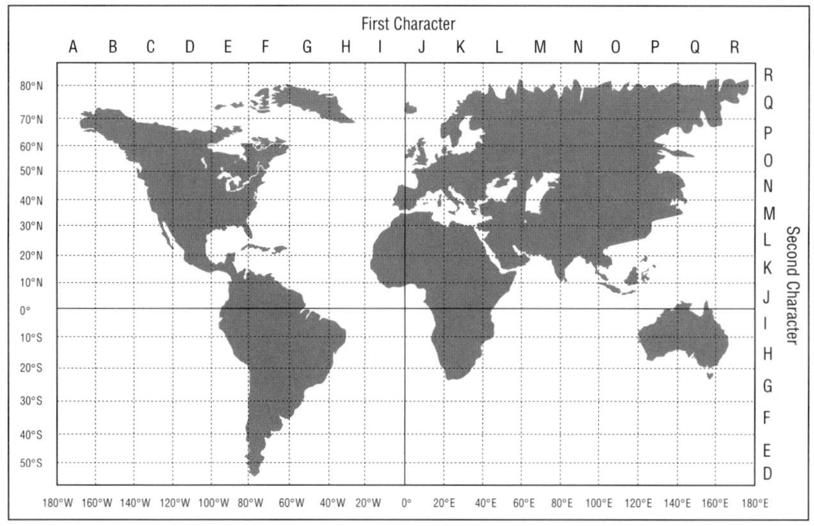

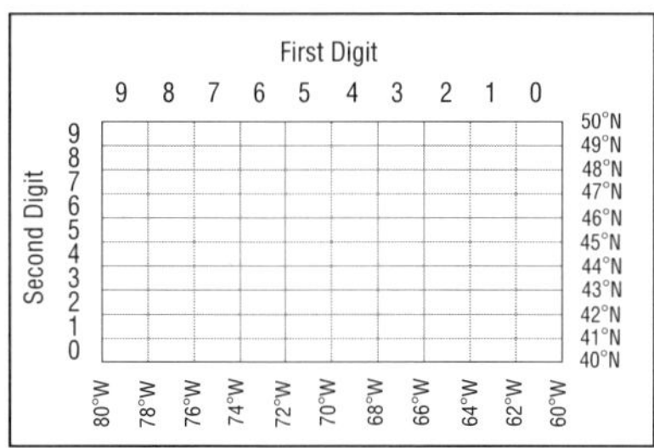

Maidenhead area subdivisions.

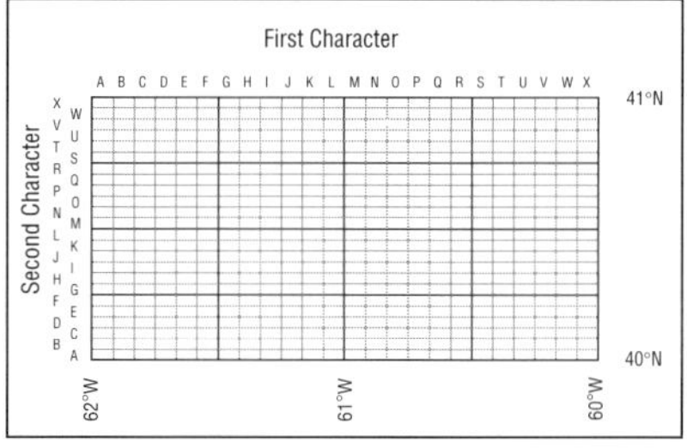

Maidenhead sub-areas.

Garmin receiver showing Maidenhead coordinate.

longitude by 2.5' of latitude and labeled with letters AA-XX. A Maidenhead coordinate looks like this: EM18BX.

Trimble Grid Locator is an extension to the Maidenhead grid that makes it more accurate and suitable for GPS receivers. A Maidenhead sub-area can cover up to 8.9 km x 4.8 km (5.5 mi. x 3 mi.). A receiver can pinpoint an area much smaller than that, so Trimble Navigation receivers subdivide the sub-area even further. The Trimble Grid Locator extension appends a pair of numbers (00-99) and letters (AA-YY) to the Maidenhead coordinate. A Maidenhead coordinate with the Trimble extension would be AQ57DK 23SU.

Many receivers provide the Maidenhead grid, but only Trimble receivers provide the extended format. Trimble Grid Locator is a trademark of Trimble Navigation, Ltd.

Trimble Over and Up

The Over and Up grid reports position by the number of inches over and up from the bottom right-hand corner of the map. It can be used with any map. You need to tell the receiver the coordinate of the southeast corner of the map and the map's scale. It works with most map scales from 1:10,000 up to 1:500,000, and even one custom scale. You can also enter waypoint coordinates in the inches over and up from the southeast reference point.

The Over and Up concept intends to aid outdoor enthusiasts who do not know very much about maps. As novel as it sounds, it is not a very useful grid. It might come in handy if you occasionally want to use maps, but it is not meant for serious navigation. Coordinates in inches do not offer the advantages of the UTM grid. The UTM grid is a visual grid. You can determine coordinates by eyeball alone and it gives an indication of distance. UTM can be used in the field without any additional tools, not even a ruler. Over and Up inches for a certain scale do not directly relate to maps of other scales; the inches must be converted to UTM or latitude/longitude for use with other maps. Your time is better spent reading Chapters 5 through 7 of this book to learn the UTM grid. The Over and Up grid is a trademark of Trimble Navigation, Ltd.

Thomas Brothers Page and Grid and Trimble Atlas

Thomas Bros. Maps produces small-scale road maps for the continental United States and large-scale maps of select metropolitan areas in Washington, Oregon and California. Thomas Bros. do not print a secondary grid, like latitude/longitude or UTM, on their maps, so there are only two ways to use a receiver with their maps: buy a Trimble receiver that supports the Thomas Bros. grid or use the Navimap described in Chapter 13.

Navigation with a Trimble GPS receiver and Thomas Bros. maps requires a combination of the Trimble Atlas and Thomas Guides. Trimble Atlas, produced by Thomas Bros. Maps for Trimble Navigation, divides the U.S. into nine regions at a scale of 1:1,900,800. Portions of a region may be subdivided into an area map with a 1:316,800 scale. Area maps of selected metropolitan areas are further divided in Thomas Guides Detail pages that have a scale of 1:28,800.

The Thomas Bros. grid system is called Page and Grid. Maps are bound in an atlas where each page has a grid of numbers and letters. A location is specified by its page and the grid location. For example, 256 G5 means page 256 grid square G5. The grid system provides a unique page and grid for any location. The entire continental U.S. is covered by a combination of Trimble Atlas and Thomas Guide, but the area you may want to travel may not have a map at a large enough scale to be useful.

Trimble Navigation has extended the Page and Grid system to increase accuracy. Trimble divides the grid of any page into nine squares:

UL	UC	UR
ML	MC	MR
LL	LC	LR

The letters correspond to Upper Left (UL), Middle Left (ML), Lower Left (LL), etc. The Trimble extension is added to region, area and detail coordinates to increase precision and ease of use. For example, the Thomas Guide Detail coordinate of Perraud Drive in Folsom, California is 262 D5. The road stretches the length of the grid. If you needed to get to a certain house, you would find the road without the Trimble extension, but you would still have to do some searching to find the house. If you needed to go to a house at the south end of the road, the coordinate with the Trimble extension would be 262 D5 MR. The extension enables your receiver to take you to within two or three houses of your destination.

The full Thomas Bros. coordinate with the Trimble extension for the south end of Perraud Drive is:

	region	page	grid	Trimble
region:	R6	9	D2	UC
area:		204	H1	LR
detail:		262	D5	MR

In the metropolitan areas that are covered by Thomas Guide, you will be able to get to any location with surety. If the city you want to explore is not included in a Thomas Guide, you may have to use a different map and grid system. If you are traveling on major freeways in the U.S. and want to use your GPS receiver to mark freeway exits, the scale of the Trimble Atlas Area pages is large enough to provide the accuracy you need if the area is covered. The receiver will always report the Page and Grid coordinate for Area and Detail pages even if the map does not exist.

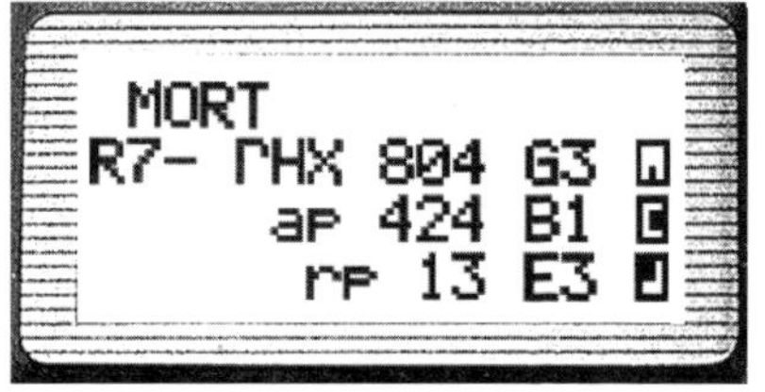

On this screen, the Trimble extension is indicated by the graphic on the right.

15 Differential GPS

The largest source of error in a civilian receiver is Selective Availability, which limits accuracy to 100 m (328 ft.). For most people, 100 m accuracy is good enough. When Selective Availability is eliminated and receivers' accuracy improves to 15 m (49.2), the system will provide enough accuracy for the vast majority of users. However, there will always be some who need more accuracy like pilots, ship navigators, utility companies, trucking companies, etc. Fortunately, a solution is available with Differential GPS (DGPS), which improves the accuracy of a civilian receiver to between 2 cm to 15 m (0.79 in. to 49.2 ft.). DGPS equipment costs more than regular civilian receivers, but if you need the accuracy, at least the precision is available.

DGPS uses two methods to correct position errors. They are called:

- Real-time corrections
- Post-processed corrections

Real-Time Corrections

Real-time corrections are used in the field for navigation. The figure illustrates how DGPS real-time works. The captain of a ship has entered an unknown port. His chart shows there is a large underwater rock some place in the lane that he needs to avoid, but try as he might he cannot see any marking buoys. The water is crowded, so there is not much room to maneuver and the captain desperately needs to know his exact position in relationship to the rock. Both the ship and the DGPS site have GPS receivers to determine their position. The DGPS site was built on an accurately surveyed spot, so its equipment independently knows its exact position. When its receiver reports a position of (x+3, y-5), the site computer knows that its true position, via the survey, is (x, y). This means the computer knows the amount of error introduced by Selective Availability. In this example, the error is +3 units in the x direction and -5 units in the y direction. The DGPS site is also equipped with a radio transmitter, so as soon as it determines the direction and amount of error, it broadcasts the information on the Loran-C frequency. The ship has a DGPS converter box with a Loran-C antenna, which receives the correction information and sends it to the GPS receiver. The receiver applies the correction information to the position it reports and for this example, the ship's receiver changes its position from (x+34, y+60) to (x+31, y+65). The captain now accurately knows his position, so he steers to miss the rock.

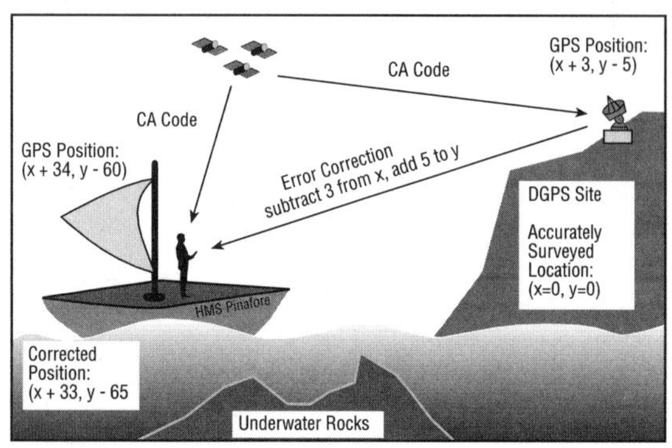

DGPS, available in most U.S. ports, defeats Selective Availability and increases civilian receiver accuracy.

If the DGPS site sent position correction information, like in this example, the ship and the site must use the same satellites to calculate position. Position correction data is valid up to a maximum of 274 km (170 mi.), which requires that many stations be built to adequately cover an area.

Another method of correction is for the site to determine the timing inaccuracies introduced by Selective Availability. If the site knows that one satellite is broadcasting 900 nanoseconds too early and another 200 nanoseconds too late, it can tell the receiver the timing errors and the receiver can apply the corrections before it makes a position calculation. Timing corrections are more accurate and can be broadcast over a larger area than position-only corrections. When correction information is broadcast over a wide area by satellites, it is called Wide Area DGPS (WADGPS).

DGPS is already available to the public for navigation in many areas. The U.S. Coast Guard constructed 48 DGPS sites along both U.S. coasts, the Mississippi River, Hawaii, Costa Rica and the southern coast of Alaska. The U.S. Coast Guard DGPS sites are shown in the figure. The system started broadcasting in January of 1996, but it has not yet been declared fully operational. If you want to use the

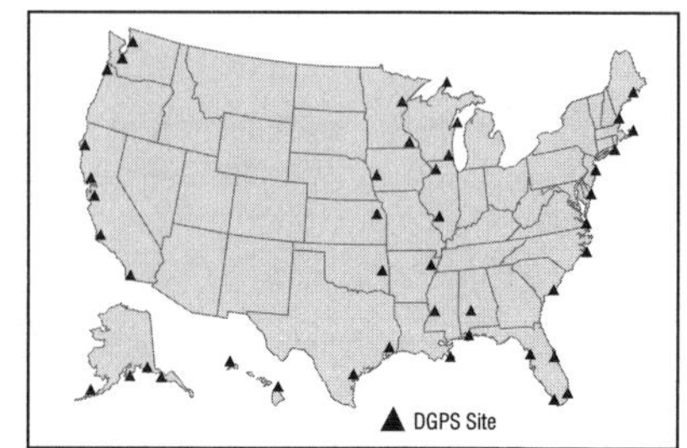

DGPS correction information from these sites, you need a receiver capable of understanding information in the RTCM format, a converter box to translate the correction radio signal to RTCM and a Loran-C antenna to pick up the radio signal. The goal of the U.S. system is to provide 10 m (32.8 ft.) accuracy or better.

Several other countries like Norway, Sweden, Finland and the Netherlands have established DGPS sites that broadcast corrections using the RTCM format and still more countries are planning to install systems. Because they use the same data format, your receiver will accept data from their sites if your antenna picks up their broadcast frequencies.

DGPS is not limited to coastal areas. Private companies broadcast correction data in many parts of the U.S. and Canada. However, there is a yearly fee for a receiver capable of receiving the correction data. A few of these subscription DGPS companies are listed in the back of the book in the section labeled Resources. The correction data can be broadcast over a local area or over a wide area. Local broadcasts are usually done over existing FM radio stations and provide a radius of coverage of 30 to 60 mi. (48 to 96 km). Some services provide data in the RTCM format so it will work with your existing receiver, while others require you to buy a special receiver.

It is also possible to set up temporary DGPS sites for infrequent use. With today's satellite technology, it is possible for a farmer to get an infrared photo of his fields that reveals the plant growth at every point. Where the plant growth is good, there is no need to use as much fertilizer as is needed where there is less plant growth. The information from the photo is programed into the airplane's computer and a DGPS site is set up to broadcast correction information over the entire field. As the plane spreads the fertilizer, the DGPS equipment provides exact position information, so the fertilizing equipment can automatically change the chemical mix depending on where it is in the field and what the plants need. It may sound expensive to use such advanced equipment, but overall the cost savings can be tremendous.

Other areas where DGPS will be used is at airports, because it reduces the cost of the equipment required for instrument-only landings. DGPS will also provide information to manage plane traffic to and from the runway along with service vehicles.

One unsuspecting place that uses DGPS equipment is hydrological dams. One wonders why the exact position of something so large and immobile would have to be tracked, but extremely accurate DGPS equipment monitors the dam as it flexes and expands when the reservoir fills with water. DGPS provides a very accurate way to safely manage the water levels to keep the dam from breaking.

Post-Processed Corrections

Just as the name implies, post-processing corrections are not applied in the field, but in the office after the trip is over. Post-processing is an inexpensive way to achieve DGPS accuracy without all the associated cost of real-time corrections, but it does require a receiver that records more information than most handheld units presently store. Government agencies monitor the GPS satellites and provide correction data that details the amount of error introduced by any given satellite at any given time. In the field, your receiver's accuracy is limited by Selective Availability. However, each time you recorded a coordinate, the receiver remembers the exact time it was recorded and the satellites it used to make the measurement. As you make your trip you store as many points as you need to document your path.

Once you are back in the office, you transfer the information about each point from the receiver into the computer. The correction software looks at each coordinate, the time and the satellites, then looks up the correction data. It recalculates the coordinate and makes it as accurate as the correction data allows. Post-processing is a viable option for guidebook writers, forest personnel or any other person who needs to accurately document the trail they traveled.

Professionals who must accurately mark locations in the backcountry will profit from a DGPS subscription service or very expensive and highly accurate receivers. For most outdoor enthusiasts, DGPS simply is not worth the increased expense. The equipment is heavier, it uses more power and it costs more to purchase and operate. Although you may never use DGPS, you may want to buy a receiver that is DGPS ready solely because any receiver that has IO capabilities usually can accept DGPS corrections on the RTCM format. Many adventurers will want to use their receivers with a computer, which means it will most likely be DGPS ready.

16 Degrees, Minutes, Seconds and Mils

The circle is an important part of navigation because once the circle on the compass is oriented correctly, you can orient yourself and travel in the right direction. How the circle is subdivided into degrees, minutes, seconds and mils is described below. How to do arithmetic on degrees, etc., is also demonstrated.

Relating Degrees, Minutes and Seconds to Each Other

In order to understand latitude/longitude or bearings, you need to understand how degrees, minutes, seconds and mils are related. The equator wraps around the entire earth and forms a circle that is the basis of degrees, minutes, seconds and mils. If you want to talk about only part of the circle, it must be subdivided. The most common subdivision of a circle is called the degree. The unit of mils is another way to subdivide the circle, but it will be discussed after degrees, minutes and seconds are explained. There are 360° (the small circle next to the zero is the symbol for degrees) in a circle as shown in the figure. A part of a circle can be expressed as degrees. A quarter is 90°, an eighth of a circle 45°, and so forth as shown.

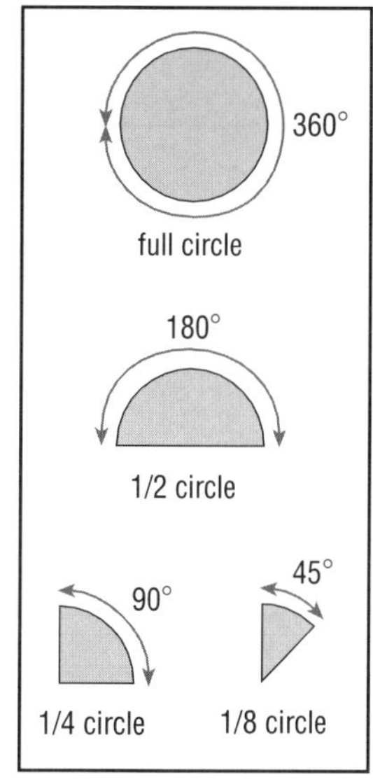

The degree is subdivided into minutes. There are 60' (the single tick mark is the symbol for minutes) in a degree. Minutes are also subdivided into seconds and following a familiar pattern, there are 60" (the symbol for seconds is two tick marks) in a minute. The relationships between degrees, minutes and seconds are as follows:

1 full circle = 360°
1° = 60' = 3,600"
1' = 60"

When adding degrees, remember to wrap around from 359° to 0° and when subtracting, 0° is followed by 359°. It is possible to have more than 360°, but it just means you have turned full circle and then some more. For example, 526° is simply a full circle of 360° plus an additional 166° as shown in the figure.

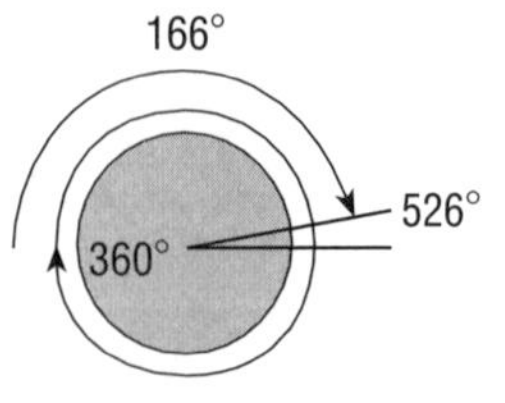

When a bearing is greater than 360°, simply subtract 360 until the result is less than 360° and that is the direction you should go. For example, if you are told to walk a bearing of 810°, you would do the following math:

810° - 360° = 450°

450° - 360° = 90°

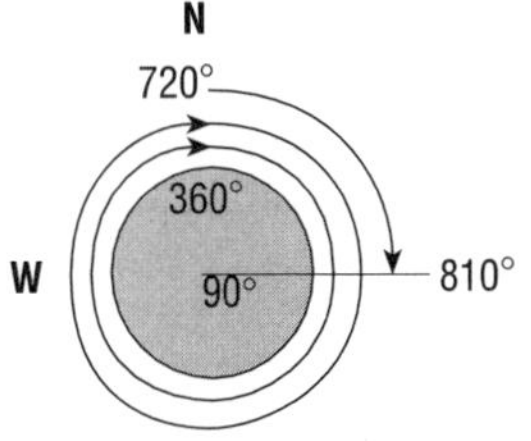

The result shows that the bearing 810° is really just 90°, which is due east as shown in the figure opposite.

Adding and Subtracting Minutes and Seconds

When working with minutes and seconds, the value wraps from 59 to 0 and 0 to 59 when adding and subtracting respectively, but in these cases, either the degrees or minutes is also affected, so you have to keep track of them. Here are a few examples:

45" + 20" = 65" = 60" + 5" = 1' 5"

23' + 58' = 81' = 60' + 21' = 1° 21'

5' 19" – 20" = 4' (60" + 19") – 20" = 4' 79" – 20" = 4' 59"

56° 25' – 47' = 55° (60' + 25') – 47' = 55° 85' – 47' = 55° 38'

82° 45' 23" – 56' 43"
= 82° 44' (60" + 23") - 56' 43"
= 82° 44' 83" – 56' 43"
= 81° (60' + 44') 83" – 56' 43"
= 81° 104' 83" – 56' 43"
= 81° (104' – 56') (83" – 43")
= 81° 48' 40"

Adding/Subtracting Degrees and Minutes

The same care with minutes must be taken when the format is degrees and minutes as demonstrated in the examples below:

219° 19.42' + 36.81'
= 219° (19.42' + 36.81')
= 219° 56.23'

61° 27.46' – 53.41'
= 60° (60' + 27.46') – 53.41'
= 60° 87.46' – 53.41'
= 60° 34.05'

The use of degrees only eliminates all the work required to keep track of minutes and seconds, but you still need to remember there are 360° in a circle.

46.492° - 21.613° = 24.879°

105.386° - 283.426°
= (360° + 105.386°) - 283.426°
= 465.386° - 283.426°
= 181.96°

315.395° + 284.305° = 599.7°
= 599.7° - 360°
= 239.7°

Converting Degrees to Degrees and Minutes

Another requirement to become proficient is the ability to convert from degrees to degrees and minutes. The transformation is done as follows.

57.146° = 57° (0.146 x 60')
= 57° 8.76'

357.963° = 357° (0.963 x 60')
= 357° 57.78'

Converting Degrees to Degrees, Minutes and Seconds

Conversion from degrees to degrees, minutes and seconds is similar to the above translation with one additional step.

295.248° = 295° (0.248 x 60')
= 295° 14.88'
= 295° 14' (0.88 x 60")
= 295° 14' 52.8"

136.389° = 136° (0.389 x 60')
= 136° 23.34'
= 136° 23' (0.34 x 60")
= 136° 23' 20.4"

Converting Seconds to Minutes

The conversion of degrees, minutes and seconds to degrees and minutes is also important. Seconds are converted to minutes by multiplying by 1'/60". Remember from above that 1' is equal to 60", so the term 1'/60" is really just equal to one. This means you are multiplying the seconds by a number with a value of 1, so its value does not change, but it allows the units to convert from seconds to minutes. The example below explicitly shows the number's units.

$$39'' \times [1'/60''] = \frac{39'' \times 1'}{60''}$$

The seconds unit of the 39" on top cancel out with the seconds unit of the 60" on the bottom. The equation becomes:

$\frac{39 \times 1'}{60}$ The final value becomes $\frac{39}{60} \times 1' = (0.65) \times 1' = 0.65'$

The examples below demonstrate conversion from degrees, minutes and seconds to degrees and minutes. The units are not explicitly shown, but just remember that when seconds are divided by 60, they become minutes.

105° 47' 51" = 105° (47 + [51/60])'
= 105° (47 + 0.85)'
= 105° 47.85'

$326° 9' 32.4" = 326° (9 + [32.4/60])'$
$= 326° (9 + 0.54)'$
$= 326° 9.54'$

Converting Minutes to Degrees

The conversion from degrees and minutes to degrees requires minutes to be converted to degrees. Minutes are converted to degrees by multiplying by 1°/60'. As with the previous case, 1° is equal to 60', so multiplying by the term 1°/60' does not change the value of the minutes, it simply converts the unit from minutes to degrees. The units are explicitly shown below:

$$46' \times [1°/60'] = \frac{46' \times 1°}{60'}$$

The minutes unit of the 46' on top cancel out with the minutes unit of the 60' on the bottom and the equation becomes:

$\frac{46 \times 1°}{60}$ The final value becomes $\frac{46}{60} \times 1° = (0.767) \times 1° = 0.767°$

The examples below demonstrate conversion from degrees and minutes to degrees. The units are not explicitly shown, but just as it was shown above, when minutes are divided by 60, they become degrees.

$261° 36' = (261 + [36/60])°$
$= (261 + 0.6)°$
$= 261.6°$

$57° 41.475' = (57 + [41.475/60])°$
$= (57 + 0.691)°$
$= 57.691°$

Converting Degrees, Minutes and Seconds to Degrees

Take all the conversion knowledge acquired and convert degrees, minutes and seconds to degrees.

269° 42' 35" = 269° (42 + [35/60])'

= 269° 42.583'

= (269 + [42.583/60])°

= 269.71°

48° 37' 3.4" = 48° (37 + [3.4/60])'

= 48° 37.057'

= (48 + [37.057/60])°

= 48.618°

Finding the Opposite Direction

The opposite direction to any bearing can be found by simply adding or subtracting 180°. Obvious opposites are E at 90° and W at 270°, which have a difference between them of 180°. The other examples shown below reiterate what to do when addition results in a bearing over 360° or less than 0°. Just remember that adding or subtracting 180° provides the same result, so do whichever results in the easiest math.

271° 15' 39" + 180° = (271 + 180)° 15' 39"

= 451° 15' 39"

= (451 - 360)° 15' 39"

= 91° 15' 39"

271° 15' 39" - 180° = (271 - 180)° 15' 39"

= 91° 15' 39"

23° 43' 9" - 180 = (23 - 180)° 43' 9"

= ([23 + 360] - 180)° 43' 9"

= (383 - 180)° 43' 9"

= 203° 43' 9"

23° 43' 9" + 180 = (23 + 180)° 43' 9"

= 203° 43' 9"

How Mils Relate to Degrees

There is more than one way to subdivide a circle. The degrees subdivision is the most common unit on maps, but mils are also used and should be understood. A mil is one sixty-four hundredth (1/6400) of a circle. The mil has the advantage that there are no conversions between units like minutes and seconds and it is also a finer division of the circle as there are only 3600" in a circle. For most navigators, the best use of the mil is to know how the mil relates to the degree. That relationship is listed below:

$$1\text{mil} = \frac{360^\circ}{6400} = 0.05625^\circ$$

$$1^\circ = \frac{6400 \text{ mils}}{360} = 17.778 \text{ mils}$$

To convert from degrees to mils, multiply the number of degrees by 17.778. To convert from mils to degrees, multiply the number of mils by 0.05625.

A few examples of equivalent mils and degrees are given below.

0° = 0 mils
90° = 1,600 mils
180° = 3,200 mils
270° = 4,800 mils

Glossary

2D Mode. Position calculations in two dimensions. In terms of a GPS receiver, it means the receiver can lock on to only 3 satellites, so it cannot provide altitude. There may be substantial error in the horizontal coordinate it does provide.

3D Mode. Position calculations in three dimensions. The GPS receiver has locked on to 4 satellites. It provides an altitude in addition to a horizontal coordinate.

Almanac Data. Satellite position information. Each satellite broadcasts the position information for all the satellites. The receiver stores the information, so it can determine its own position. It takes about 12.5 minutes for the satellites to transfer the position data to the receiver.

Altimeter. A device that measures distance above sea level. Atmospheric pressure decreases as you rise in altitude, so most altimeters measure atmospheric pressure and relate it to height above sea level.

Antenna. A receiver needs an antenna to pick up the satellite signals beamed down from space. There are two common types for handheld receivers: patch (microstrip) and quadrifilar helix. The antenna is one of the most important components of a receiver. A remote antenna is separate from the antenna built into the receiver and is usually connected to the receiver by a cable. An active remote antenna is one that amplifies the satellite signals before sending them through the cable to the receiver.

Anti-Spoofing. It is possible to confuse GPS receivers by transmitting signals that look similar to the real satellite signals. Such an attack is known as spoofing. The military countermeasure is to encrypt the P-code so only authorized users can recognize it and can detect and reject faked signals.

Azimuth. The direction of travel or the direction between two points in reference to true or magnetic north. When expressed in degrees, its value ranges from 0° to 360°. A compass heading is an azimuth. In most places, the word bearing has grown to mean the same thing as azimuth. See bearing.

Bearing. A bearing is your direction of travel or the direction between two points. Like an azimuth, a bearing is measured in reference to true or magnetic north, but its value never goes over 90°. A bearing is always measured from the cardinal directions north or south. A typical bearing would be N45°E, which is the same as an azimuth of 45°. The bearing S45°W is an azimuth of 225°. The use of the word bearing has changed over the years and now means the same thing as azimuth.

Channel. The part of the GPS receiver's electronics that tunes in on a satellite's signal and sends the resulting information to the receiver's processor for position calculation.

Chart. A map of waterways or airways.

Coarse Acquisition Codes. The GPS satellites send two distinct signals: precision codes (P codes) and coarse acquisition codes (CA codes). Civilian receivers use the CA codes to determine position. Military receivers use the CA codes to synchronize to the P codes before switching to using the P code exclusively. Selective Availability affects the CA codes and thereby the accuracy of civilian receivers. The CA codes are transmitted on only one radio frequency, so it is impossible for a civilian receiver to detect the delay through the ionosphere. The accuracy provided by the CA codes is called the Standard Positioning Service (SPS).

Codeless Receivers. A class of GPS receivers that do not use the P codes or the CA codes to determine position. Codeless receivers measure the change in modulation in the satellite radio waves. They use sophisticated signal processing techniques to make position measurements accurate to centimeters. It can take days to make a single measurement.

Cold Start. A receiver experiences a cold start when it has to download the almanac information from the satellites before it can begin to calculate its own position. Refer to Time to First Fix.

Coordinate. The numbers and letters that describe a position. Every position on earth has a unique coordinate. The coordinate system determines the grid and how the coordinate is written.

Course. The path between two points. GPS receivers always indicate the straight line between the two points.

Course Deviation Indicator (CDI). A method for displaying the amount and direction of CrossTrack error (XTE).

Course Made Good (CMG). The bearing from your starting point to your present position.

Course Over Ground (COG). Same as Course Made Good (CMG).

CrossTrack Error (XTE). The distance between your present position and the straight-line course between two points. It is the amount you are off the desired track (DTK).

Declination. The difference, in degrees or mils, between the north pole and the magnetic pole from your position. Many receivers have tables in their memory that tell them the amount and direction of declination for any position on earth, which means the receiver, once locked to the satellites, can automatically convert true north bearings to magnetic bearings and vice versa.

Degree. A part of a circle. The degree divides the circle into 360 even pieces. Bearings are also expressed in degrees. Degrees are subdivided into 60 minutes, which in turn are split into 60 second intervals.

DGPS Ready. A receiver is DGPS ready if it is capable of accepting Differential GPS correction data and using it to make its own position calculation more accurate. Additional equipment must be connected to the receiver to pick up the correction radio transmissions.

Differential GPS (DGPS). A method of improving civilian receiver accuracy. Selective Availability limits the accuracy of civilian receivers to between 15 to 100 m (49.2 to 328 ft.). DGPS can be accurate to 15 m and below. DGPS corrections can be made instantaneously (real-time) as you are traveling or after the trip on stored waypoints (post-processing).

Dilution of Precision (DOP). An analysis of the satellite geometry and its impact on accuracy. Some satellite geometry's provide more accurate position calculations. The receiver measures several factors that dilute the position accuracy and add them all together to estimate how much error is present in its position calculation. Components of the DOP are horizontal, vertical, position and time dilutions of precision. A low value for a DOP means the receiver can accurately make a position calculation. A high value means there is increasingly more error in the position reported. Good DOP values range between 1 and 3. Most receivers will not even try to calculate position if the DOP values are greater than 6.

Easting. The distance east or west from the zone meridian. Easting coordinates are used in several grid systems. UTM, OSGB and MGRS are a few.

Ephemeris. The path and orbit information for a specific satellite. Selective Availability truncates the ephemeris information to limit the civilian receiver's accuracy.

Estimated Position Error (EPE). Many receivers report the potential error of a position calculation. The receiver knows the satellite geometry, and using the DOP values it estimates the amount of error that may be present in the position it calculates.

Estimated Time En Route (ETE). The amount of time remaining to arrive at the destination. ETE depends on the speed you are going directly toward the destination, which is called Velocity Made Good (VMG). If you are traveling away from the destination, the ETE cannot be calculated because you will never arrive.

Estimated Time of Arrival (ETA). The time of the day of arrival at the destination. ETA depends on the speed you are going directly toward the destination, which is called Velocity Made Good (VMG). If you are traveling away from the destination, the ETA cannot be calculated because you will never arrive.

Global Positioning System (GPS). A system of 24 satellites that allows a GPS receiver to determine its position any place in the world. There are two types of receivers: military and civilian. Military receivers are always accurate to about 1 m (3.3 ft.). Civilian receivers are made less accurate by Selective Availability. Their accuracy randomly varies between 15 to 100 m (49.2 to 328 ft.).

GLONASS. The Russian equivalent of the U.S. GPS. It does not implement Selective Availability. Its full name is Global'naya Navigatsionnaya Sputnikovaya Sistema.

Goto Function. A mode of operation where the receiver guides you to a destination. You must have previously stored the destination's coordinate in the receiver's memory. The receiver uses the satellite signals to find its present position, then it calculates the bearing and distance to the destination. In the Goto mode, the receiver usually displays a screen that points the direction you need to travel to arrive at the destination.

Greenwich Mean Time (GMT). The time as measured from Greenwich, England or 0° longitude. Refer to Universal Time Coordinated.

Grid. The horizontal and vertical lines on a map that fix your position. There are a lot of different grid systems because there are many different ways of translating a position from a sphere to a flat map. The most common grid systems are Universal Transverse Mercator (UTM) and latitude/longitude.

Grid North. The orientation of a map's grid. Cartographers try to align the vertical lines on the map with true north. However, there is usually a small difference between grid north and true north across the map, but the difference is so slight that it can usually be ignored for land navigation.

Ground Speed. Your speed across the ground regardless of direction. The speedometer in a car measures ground speed.

Heading. The direction you are traveling expressed as either a magnetic or true north bearing.

Horizontal Dilution of Precision (HDOP). See Dilution of Precision.

Ionosphere. A layer of the earth's atmosphere between 50 and 250 mi. above the surface. The GPS satellite signals are delayed as they pass through the ionosphere. If the effect of the delay is not removed or compensated, the receiver's position calculation is inaccurate.

L1 and L2. The P code is transmitted on two radio frequencies known as L1 and L2. They are 1575.42 MHz and 1227.6 MHz respectively. The CA codes are transmitted only on the L1 frequency.

Landmark. Same as a waypoint. It can also refer to a distinct landform that is easily recognizable.

Latitude/Longitude. A spherical coordinate system. The lines of latitude and longitude form a grid system used to fix position. Latitude lines run parallel to the equator and measure distance from the equator while longitude lines are drawn from pole to pole and measure distance from the prime meridian in Greenwich, England (0°). Coordinates are measured in degrees, minutes or seconds.

Lock. A receiver is locked when it can detect 3 or more satellites and it can use their signals to determine its own position.

Magnetic Declination. See Declination.

Magnetic North. The direction the compass needle points. A compass needle always points toward the magnetic pole located in northern Canada on Bathhurst Island. The magnetic pole is not the north pole.

Man-Over-Board (MOB). A GPS receiver function that allows you to quickly mark a position. It is best used in an emergency situation when you need to mark the location where you need to return, like where someone has fallen overboard.

Map Datum. All maps are drawn with respect to a reference point. The reference point is called the datum. Most map datum only cover a portion of the earth, like the North American Datum of 1927 (NAD 27), which covers only the continent of North America. The GPS makes it possible to have a worldwide datum like World Geodetic System of 1984 (WGS 84).

Map Scales. The scale of a map is usually expressed as 1:24,000 or 1:50,000, etc. The scale means that every inch on the map represents 24,000 in. or 50,000 in., etc., on the ground. A large-scale map is one that is zoomed in; whereas, a small-scale map covers a lot of area on a single page.

Meridian. A longitude line that is used as a reference. The longitude line through Greenwich, England is referred to as the prime meridian and is labeled 0°. All other longitude lines are measured in relation to the prime meridian. Each zone in the UTM system also has a zone meridian used as the reference point for all east-west measurements.

Mil. A part of a circle. A mil is one part of a circle that is divided into 6400 equal-sized pieces.

Military Grid Reference System (MGRS). The grid system used by the U.S. military. It is similar to UTM except it replaces the most significant digits of the easting and northing numbers with letters. Some mapping programs will put the MGRS grid on USGS topographical maps for use by civilians.

Multipath. When the same signal from a satellite enters a receiver's antenna from more than one direction, it is called multipath. Usually the radio waves travel straight from the satellite to the receiver, but if it happens to bounce off some hard object, then it will enter both as a direct signal and as a reflected signal.

National Maritime Electronics Association (NMEA). NMEA protocols (how data is sent and what format it uses) specify the type and order of data sent and received by navigation equipment. If two pieces of equipment use the same NMEA protocol, they will understand each other and will operate together.

Navstar. Navstar Global Positioning System was the original name for the navigation system, but the Navstar part was soon lost and it is known today as only GPS. See Global Positioning System.

Northing. The distance north or south of a fixed reference point. The UTM system uses the equator as the reference. Northing coordinates are used in several grid systems. UTM, OSGB and MGRS are a few.

Outage. An outage occurs when the satellite geometry is so poor that the receiver cannot make an accurate position calculation. Most receivers will not lock when the position dilution of precision is greater than 6.

Point-to-Point Calculation. The calculation of bearing and distance between two points.

Position Dilution of Precision (PDOP). See Dilution of Precision.

Precision Codes. The GPS satellites send two distinct signals: precision codes (P codes) and coarse acquisition codes (CA codes). Civilian receivers use the CA codes to determine position. Military receivers use the CA codes to synchronize to the P codes before switching to using the P code exclusively. Selective Availability does not affect the P codes. The P codes are transmitted from space on two different frequencies, which enable military receivers to detect and illuminate propagation delays introduced in the ionosphere. The accuracy provided by the P codes is called the Precise Positioning Service (PPS).

Ranging. Ranging is the technique used in the GPS for a receiver to measure its distance to a satellite.

Route Function. A list of sequential waypoints. The GPS receiver guides you from the first waypoint on the list to each point in order until you arrive at the destination. See Goto Function.

RS-232. A standard type of connection to a computer. It is a serial port that allows communication between a computer and a receiver. A special cable connects the computer's RS-232 port to the receiver.

Satellite Geometry. The position of the satellites in the sky relative to your position on earth. The best satellite geometry is one satellite overhead with the others spread evenly around the horizon. See Dilution of Precision.

Selective Availability (SA). The techniques used by the U.S. Department of Defense to make civilian receivers less accurate. It limits horizontal accuracy to between 15 and 100 m (49.2 and 328 ft.) and vertical accuracy to 156 m (512 ft.). It is believed that Selective Availability will someday be eliminated, which would make most receivers accurate to 15 m.

Speed of Advance (SOA). Same as VMG.

Speed Over Ground (SOG). The speed you are traveling regardless of direction. It is the same as ground speed.

Spoofing. Spoofing is a method of attacking the GPS to render it useless. The attacker transmits radio signals at the same frequency as the GPS signals so the receiver mistakes the fake signal for the real one and calculates an incorrect position. The countermeasure to spoofing is called anti-spoofing. Spoofing can be detected and foiled only by military receivers, not civilian ones.

Time to First Fix (TTFF). The amount of time (about 15 minutes) it takes a receiver to make its first position fix after it has been off for several months, lost memory or been moved more than 480 km (300 mi). Before the receiver can calculate its position, it needs to download all the position information about every satellite.

True North. The direction to the north pole. The north pole is not the magnetic pole. The difference in direction between the north pole and the magnetic pole is called declination.

Universal Polar Stereographic Grid (UPS). The grid that covers the Arctic and Antarctic regions. It is similar to UTM with eastings and northings.

Universal Time Coordinated (UTC). Essentially Greenwich Mean Time. GPS time, as maintained by the satellites, is converted to UTC inside the receiver.

Universal Transverse Mercator Grid (UTM). The grid that splits the earth into 60 zones each of which is 6° wide. Its coordinates are relative to the equator and a zone meridian and are called eastings and northings. The UTM grid is used only between North 84° and South 80° because the UPS grid already provides a uniform grid for the poles.

Velocity Made Good (VMG). Your speed toward the destination. If you are traveling directly toward the destination, VMG is the same as your ground speed. If you are not on course, the VMG is less than your ground speed. If you are headed away from the destination, VMG is zero regardless of how fast you are going.

Waterproof. A receiver is listed as waterproof if it can be completely submerged in water without being ruined.

Water Resistant. A water-resistant receiver can be used in a damp environment, but it is not designed to be submerged or get really wet.

Waypoint. The coordinates of a location. Waypoints are stored in the receiver's memory. You can store your present position, as determined by the receiver, as a waypoint or you can store the position of any place in the world by reading its coordinates from a map and typing it into the receiver.

Y Code. The encrypted version of the P code. See Anti-Spoofing.

Resources

GPS Receiver Manufacturers

- Brunton (800) 443-4871
- Eagle Electronics (800) 324-1354
- Garmin International (800) 800-1020
- Magellan Systems (909) 394-5000
- Micrologic, Inc. (818) 998-1216
- Trimble Navigation (800) 487-4662

GPS Computer Software

- DeLorme (800) 452-5931

Topographical Maps on CDROMs

- TOPO!, Wildflower Productions (415) 558-8700
- TopoScout, MapTech (800) 627-7236

Map Rulers

- Topo Companion, The Coordinator (800) 275-7526
- UTM Grid Reader (860) 243-0303
- The Card (for UTM grids) (800) 305-0036

DGPS Subscription Services

- Differential Corrections, Inc. (800) 446-0015
- OmniSTAR (888) 883-8476

Electronic Altimeters

- Avocet (650) 321-8501
- Casio (973) 361-5400

Other Books

Some basic map and compass books:

Staying Found: The Complete Map and Compass Handbook, 2nd ed., June Fleming, The Mountaineers, 1994

The Basic Essentials of Map and Compass, 2nd ed., Cliff Jacobson, ICS Books, 1997

Be Expert with Map and Compass: The Complete Orienteering Handbook, Bjorn Kjellstrom, MacMillan General Reference, 1994

Outward Bound Map and Compass Handbook, Glenn Randall, The Lyons Press, 1989

How to Read a Map (Using and Understanding Maps), Scott E. Morris, Chelsea House Publishers, 1993

An excellent book of map sources for maps all over the world is: *The Map Catalog: Every Kind of Map and Chart on Earth and Even Some Above It*, 3rd ed., Joel Makower, editor; Vintage Books, 1992

Some heavy-duty books about mapmaking and GPS:

Map Use: Reading, Analysis, and Interpretation, Phillip C. Muehrcke, JP Publications, 1986

Global Positioning System: Theory and Practice, 2nd ed., B. Hofmann-Wellenhof et al., Springer-Verlag, 1997

The Navstar Global Positioning System, Tom Logsdon, Van Nostrand Reinhold, 1992

Understanding the Navstar: GPS, GIS and IVHS, Tom Logsdon, Van Nostrand Reinhold, 1995

A fine book about Amerigo Vespucci. It is short, but interesting. *Forgotten Voyager: The Story of Amerigo Vespucci*, Ann Fitzpatrick Alper, Carolrhoda Books, 1991.

At the time of publication, the following Internet address was a good source of GPS information:

http://www.utexas.edu/depts/grg/gcraft/notes/gps/gps.html

GPS Receiver Information

Reception	Antenna	The type of antenna.
	External Antenna	✓ means an external antenna can be attached to the receiver.
	Channels	The number of parallel channels.
	Satellites Tracked	The number of satellites tracked regardless of the number of channels.
Accuracy	Horizontal (m)	Best case horizontal accuracy ignoring Selective Availability.
	Averaging	✓ means the receiver does perform averaging. Some receivers average the signal without user intervention. They start averaging when the receiver moves slower than a preset threshold.
	DOP	✓ means the receiver displays the calculated DOP value.
Weight (oz.)		Weight including batteries.
Batteries	Duration (hrs)	Best case battery life during continuous operation.
	#(AA)	Number of AA batteries required.
	Lithium Backup	Internal battery used to protect stored data when the AA batteries are dead.
External Power		✓ means the receiver can be connected to an external power source.
Coordinate Systems	Latitude/Longitude	✓ means the receiver provides the latitude/longitude grid.
	UTM	✓ means the receiver provides the Universal Transverse Mercator grid.
	OSGB	✓ means the receiver provides the Ordnance Survey Great Britain grid.
	UPS	✓ means the receiver provides the Universal Polar Stereographic grid.
	MGRS	✓ means the receiver provides the Military Grid Reference System.
	Maidenhead	✓ means the receiver provides the Maidenhead grid.
	Thomas Bros.	✓ means the receiver provides the Thomas Brothers Page and Grid grid.
	Over & Up	✓ means the receiver provides the Trimble Over & Up grid.
Navigation Features	Map Datum	The number of map datum stored in the receiver.
	Nearest Waypoint	✓ means the receiver provides a list of the nearest waypoints.
	Proximity List	✓ means the receiver can warn you when you come too close to selected locations.
	Automatic Tracking	✓ means the receiver periodically records your position.
Steering Screens	Highway	✓ means the receiver has a navigation screen that looks like a road.
	Compass	✓ means the receiver has a navigation screen that looks similar to a compass.
	Moving Map	✓ means the receiver graphically shows your position in relation to nearby waypoints.
	Maps in Memory	✓ means the receiver has road information stored in its memory that it displays on the screen along with your position.
Display	User Custom Fields	✓ means the user can select what data is displayed on a screen or which screens are displayed.
	Color	✓ means the display shows colors.
	Gray Scale	✓ means the display shows black, white and several shades of gray.
	Flip Screen	✓ means the writing on the display can be shown either horizontally or vertically.
	Backlight	✓ means the display has a backlight for use in the dark.
Units	Statute	✓ means the receiver provides distances in statute units of miles and miles per hour.
	Metric	✓ means the receiver provides distances in metric units of meters and kilometers per hour.
	Nautical	✓ means the receiver provides distances in nautical units of nautical miles and knots.
	Altitude	✓ means the units for altitude can be selected independent of the units for horizontal position or speed.
	Area	✓ means the receiver can calculate the area enclosed by a set of waypoints.

Waypoints and Routes	Waypoints	Number of waypoints the receiver can store in memory.
	Routes	Number of routes the receiver can store in memory.
	Waypoints/Route	Number of waypoints in a route.
	Reverse Route	✓ means the receiver can automatically reverse the waypoints in a route.
	Goto	✓ means the receiver can steer you to a waypoint.
	User Icons	✓ means the user can select a symbol for each waypoint in addition to a name.
	Coordinate by Reference	✓ means the receiver can calculate the coordinate of a new waypoint that is a certain distance and bearing from your present position or any other waypoint.
I/O Interface	Input Capable	✓ means the receiver can receive data from another GPS unit, a computer or a DGPS beacon.
	Output Capable	✓ means the receiver can send data to another GPS unit or a computer.
Input Format	Proprietary	✓ means the receiver accepts data in a format that is specified by the manufacturer.
	NMEA	✓ means the receiver accepts data in the NMEA standard format.
	RTCM	✓ means the receiver accepts DGPS correction data in the RTCM standard format.
Output Format	Proprietary	✓ means the receiver supplies data in a format that is specified by the manufacturer.
	NMEA	✓ means the receiver supplies data in the NMEA standard format.
Simulation Mode		✓ means the receiver can act like it is navigating without receiving satellite signals.
Navigational Statistics	Ground Speed	✓ means the receiver reports ground speed.
	Average Speed	✓ means the receiver reports average speed as measured over a period of time.
	Maximum Speed	✓ means the receiver records the maximum speed reached.
	Velocity Made Good	✓ means the receiver reports VMG.
	Track	✓ means the receiver provides the bearing of your current course of travel.
	Desired Track	✓ means the receiver provides the bearing you should be going to get to your destination.
	Odometer	✓ means the receiver measures the distance you have gone.
	CDI	✓ means the receiver provides a measure of your deviation from course.
	ETA	✓ means the receiver reports estimated time of arrival.
	ETE	✓ means the receiver reports estimated time en route.
	EPE	✓ means the receiver provides position error as an indication of the satellite geometry.
Speed	Max (k/h)	Maximum operating speed in kilometers per hour.
	Max (m/h)	Maximum operating speed in miles per hour.
Rise & Set	Sun	✓ means the receiver calculates the time of sunrise and sunset at a given location for a given time of year.
	Moon	✓ means the receiver calculates the phase of the moon at a given location for a given time of year.
Norths	True	✓ means the bearing provided by the receiver can be referenced to true north.
	Auto Magnetic	✓ means the bearing provided by the receiver can be referenced magnetic north and the receiver automatically calculates the declination.
	User	✓ means the user can specify the bearing reference.
Temp. Range	Celsius	Minimum/maximum operating temperatures in degrees Celsius.
	Fahrenheit	Minimum/maximum operating temperatures in degrees Fahrenheit.
Water	Resistant	✓ means the receiver can be used in a damp environment or possibly even be submerged for a short period of time without damage.
	Proof	✓ means the receiver can be submerged without damage.
DGPS Ready		✓ means the receiver is capable or receiving and using RTCM correction data.
Audible Alarms		✓ means the receiver can make an audible noise when you reach a waypoint.
Cost (US$)		Street cost of a specific receiver model.

		Brunton XL1000	Brunton XL1000 Forest	Eagle Explorer	Trimble Scoutmaster	Garmin GPS 12	Garmin GPS 12XL	Garmin GPS 48	Garmin GPS III	Magellan Pioneer	Magellan 2000 XL	Magellan 4000 XL	Magellan Color Trak
Reception	Antenna	patch	patch	patch	patch	patch	patch	quad	quad	quad	patch	patch	quad
	External Antenna	✗	✓	✗	✓	✗	✓	✓	✓	✗	✗	✓	✓
	Channels	5	5	12	3	12	12	12	12	2	12	2	12
	Satellites Tracked	9	9	12	8	12	12	12	12	12	12	12	12
Accuracy	Horizontal (m)	15	15	15	15	15	15	15	15	15	15	15	❹15
❹ see note 4	Averaging	✗	✓	✓	✓	✓	✓	✓	✓	✗	✓	✓	✓
	DOP	✓	✓	✓	✓	✗	✗	✗	✓	✗	✗	✗	✗
Weight (oz.)		15	15	12	14	9.5	9.5	9.5	9	7	10	10	12
Batteries	Duration (hrs)	12	12	10	6	12	12	12	8	12	12	10	6
	#(AA)	6	6	4	4	4	4	4	4	24	24	24	30
	Lithium Backup	✓	✓	✓	✗	✓	✓	✓	✓	✗	✗	✗	✗
External Power		✓	✓	✓	✓	✓	✓	✓	✓	✓	✓	✓	✓
Coordinate Systems	Latitude/Longitude	✓	✓	✓	✓	✓	✓	✓	✓	✓	✓	✓	✓
	UTM	✓	✓	✓	✓	✓	✓	✓	✓	✓	✓	✓	✓
	OSGB	✗	✗	✗	✓	✓	✓	✓	✓	✗	✓	✓	✓
	UPS	✗	✗	✗	✗	✓	✓	✓	✓	✗	✗	✗	✗
	MGRS	✗	✗	✓	✓	✗	✓	✓	✓	✗	✗	✗	✓
	Maidenhead	✗	✗	✗	✓	✓	✓	✓	✓	✗	✗	✗	✗
	Thomas Bros.	✗	✗	✗	✓	✗	✗	✗	✗	✗	✗	✗	✗
	Over & Up	✗	✗	✗	✓	✗	✗	✗	✗	✗	✗	✗	✗
Navigation Features	Map Datum	102	102	123	100	108	108	108	103	11	73	73	73
	Nearest Waypoint	✓	✓	✗	✗	✓	✓	✓	✓	✗	✓	✓	✓
	Proximity List	✗	✗	✗	✗	✓	✓	✓	✗	✗	✗	✗	✗
	Automatic Tracking	✓	✓	✗	✗	✓	✓	✓	✓	✗	✓	✓	✓
Steering Screens	Highway	✗	✗	✓	✗	✓	✓	✓	✓	✗	✓	✓	✓
	Compass	✗	✗	✓	✗	✓	✓	✓	✓	✓	✓	✓	✓
❶ see note 1	Moving Map	✗	✗	✓	✗	✓	✓	✓	✓	✗	✓	✓	✓
❸ see note 3	Maps in Memory	❶✗	❶✗	✗	✗	✗	✗	✗	❸✓	✗	✗	✗	✗
Display	User Custom Fields	✗	✗	✗	✗	✓	✓	✓	✓	✗	✓	✓	✓
	Color	✗	✗	✗	✗	✗	✗	✗	✗	✗	✗	✗	✓
	Gray Scale	✗	✗	✗	✗	✗	✗	✗	✓	✗	✗	✗	✗
	Flip Screen	✗	✗	✗	✗	✗	✗	✗	✓	✗	✗	✗	✗
	Backlight	✓	✓	✓	✗	✓	✓	✓	✓	✓	✓	✓	✓
Units	Statute	✓	✓	✓	✓	✓	✓	✓	✓	✓	✓	✓	✓
	Metric	✓	✓	✓	✓	✓	✓	✓	✓	✓	✓	✓	✓
	Nautical	✓	✓	✓	✓	✓	✓	✓	✓	✓	✓	✓	✓
	Altitude	✓	✓	✗	✓	✗	✗	✗	✓	✗	✓	✓	✓
	Area	✗	✓	✗	✗	✗	✗	✗	✗	✗	✗	✗	✗

1. Attaches to the Brunton Navimap, which correlates current position to any map.
2. Requires the Navimap to provide distance and bearing measurements.
3. The maps in memory cover either the continental U.S. or international. The U.S. version includes all interstate and state highways, many major surface streets, railroad tracks and bodies of water.
4. The Color Trak uses an internal electronic barometer to reduce fluctuations in the altitude measurement. The unit also has an internal electronic thermometer.

		Brunton XL1000	Brunton XL1000 Forest	Eagle Explorer	Trimble Scoutmaster	Garmin GPS 12	Garmin GPS 12XL	Garmin GPS 48	Garmin GPS III	Magellan Pioneer	Magellan 2000 XL	Magellan 4000 XL	Magellan Color Trak
Waypoints and Routes	Waypoints	1000	1000	200	250	500	500	500	500	100	200	200	500
	Routes	1	1	20	26	20	20	20	20	1	5	5	10
	Waypoints/Route	1000	1000	40	20	30	30	30	30	10	20	20	20
	Reverse Route	✘	✘	✓	✓	✓	✓	✓	✓	✘	✓	✓	✓
	Goto	✓	✓	✓	✓	✓	✓	✓	✓	✓	✓	✓	✓
	User Icons	✘	✘	✓	✘	✓	✓	✓	✓	✘	✘	✘	✓
❷ see note 2	Coordinate by Reference	❷✓	❷✓	✘	✘	✓	✓	✓	✓	✘	✓	✓	✓
I/O Interface	Input Capable	✓	✓	✓	✓	✓	✓	✓	✓	✘	✓	✓	✓
	Output Capable	✓	✓	✓	✓	✓	✓	✓	✓	✘	✓	✓	✓
Input Format	Proprietary	✓	✓	✘	✘	✓	✓	✓	✓	✓	✓	✘	✘
	NMEA	✘	✘	✓	✘	✓	✓	✓	✓	✘	✘	✘	✘
	RTCM	✓	✓	✓	✓	✓	✓	✓	✓	✘	✓	✓	✓
Output Format	Proprietary	✓	✓	✘	✘	✓	✓	✓	✓	✘	✘	✘	✘
	NMEA	✘	✘	✓	✓	✓	✓	✓	✓	✘	✓	✓	✓
Simulation Mode		✘	✘	✓	✘	✓	✓	✓	✓	✘	✓	✓	✓
Navigational Statistics	Ground Speed	✓	✓	✓	✓	✓	✓	✓	✓	✓	✓	✓	✓
	Average Speed	✘	✘	✘	✘	✓	✓	✓	✓	✘	✘	✘	✓
	Maximum Speed	✘	✘	✘	✘	✓	✓	✓	✓	✘	✘	✘	✓
	Velocity Made Good	✘	✘	✓	✘	✓	✓	✓	✓	✓	✓	✓	✓
	Track	✓	✓	✓	✓	✓	✓	✓	✓	✓	✓	✓	✓
	Desired Track	✓	✓	✓	✓	✓	✓	✓	✓	✓	✓	✓	✓
	Odometer	✓	✓	✘	✓	✓	✓	✓	✓	✘	✓	✓	✓
	CDI	✓	✓	✓	✘	✓	✓	✓	✓	✓	✓	✓	✓
	ETA	✓	✓	✓	✓	✓	✓	✓	✓	✘	✓	✓	✓
	ETE	✘	✘	✓	✘	✓	✓	✓	✓	✓	✓	✓	✓
	EPE	✘	✘	✘	✘	✓	✓	✓	✓	✘	✓	✓	✓
Speed	Max (k/h)	1847	1847	1202	1608	1850	1850	1850	2130	1530	1530	1530	1448
	Max (m/h)	1148	1148	747	999	1150	1150	1150	1323	951	951	951	900
Rise & Set	Sun	✘	✘	✘	✓	✓	✓	✓	✓	✘	✓	✓	✓
	Moon	✘	✘	✘	✓	✘	✘	✘	✘	✘	✓	✓	✓
Norths	True	✓	✓	✓	✓	✓	✓	✓	✓	✓	✓	✓	✓
	Auto Magnetic	✓	✓	✓	✓	✓	✓	✓	✓	✓	✓	✓	✓
	User	✘	✘	✘	✘	✓	✓	✓	✓	✘	✘	✘	✘
Temp. Range	Celsius	-30/70°	-30/70°	-20/66°	-10/60°	-15/70°	-15/70°	-15/70°	-15/70°	0/50°	-10/60°	-10/60°	-10/60°
	Fahrenheit	-22/158°	-22/158°	-4/150°	24/140°	5/158°	5/158°	5/158°	5/158°	32/140°	14/140°	14/140°	14/140°
Water	Resistant	✓	✓	✓	✓	✓	✓	✓	✓	❺✓	✓	✓	✓
❺ see note 5	Proof	✘	✘	✘	✘	✘	✘	✘	✘	✘	✘	✘	✘
DGPS Ready		✓	✓	✓	✓	✓	✓	✓	✓	✓	✓	✓	✓
Audible Alarms		✘	✘	✓	✘	✘	✓	✘	✓	✘	✓	✓	✓
Cost (US$)		920	1111	190	500	155	250	250	370	100	150	246	265

5. The Pioneer is highly water resistant and floats.

Index